This War Called Peace

THIS WAR
CALLED PEACE

Brian Crozier
Drew Middleton
Jeremy Murray-Brown

UNIVERSE BOOKS
NEW YORK

Published in the United States of America in 1985
by Universe Books
381 Park Avenue South, New York, N.Y. 10016

© 1984, 1985 by Brian Crozier, Drew Middleton
and Jeremy Murray-Brown

85 86 87 88 89 / 10 9 8 7 6 5 4 3 2 1

Printed in Great Britain

Library of Congress Cataloging in Publication Data

Crozier, Brian
This war called peace.

Includes index.
1. World politics—1945–   I. Middleton, Drew,
1913–   II. Murray-Brown, Jeremy, 1932–
III. Title.
D843.C742   1985   909.82   84-24137
ISBN 0-87663-463-3

Contents

Introduction

The idea of this book came from Jeremy Murray-Brown, who talked it over, first with Drew Middleton in New York, then with myself, Brian Crozier, in London. One day in the spring of 1980, the three of us met in a New York hotel and discussed it.

We all agreed that an objective history of the cold war was badly needed. We all felt that existing accounts, however sound academically, were in some respects flawed or unsatisfactory. On one vital point, for instance, the conventional wisdom in the West was, and still is, that the cold war—that undeclared state of hostilities, largely though not entirely, falling short of military conflict between the Soviet Union and the Western powers—ended at some undefined date in the early 1960s.

All three of us were aware that, on the Soviet side at least, the cold war continued, and is still continuing. The Soviets, however, define the cold war as the sum of hostile words and deeds from the West against the Soviet bloc. If that narrow 'ideological' definition is accepted, then indeed the cold war is over. Soviet spokesmen, however, use a different expression to describe the permanent war waged by the Soviet bloc, largely by non-military means, against the West, and indeed against all countries that have not adopted the Soviet system. They call it 'peaceful co-existence'.

We thought it important to put the record straight, especially for the post-war generation of readers who either did not live through the immediate post-war years when it all started with the permanent Soviet occupation of Eastern Europe, or were too young at the time to be aware of what was happening.

Having agreed on the need, and on the audience, we discussed the best division of labour, and again reached agreement. Brian Crozier would deal with the Soviet side, with what happened under Stalin, Khrushchev and Brezhnev (the advent of Andropov was still in the future). Drew Middleton would deal with the reaction to Soviet pressures from the United States, under a succession of Presidents:

Truman, Eisenhower, Kennedy, Johnson, Nixon, Ford and Carter (again, the advent of Ronald Reagan lay in the future).

To Jeremy Murray-Brown would fall the tricky but vital role of placing the narrative in the context of the times, in other words to provide the essential background, such as the McCarthy period in the United States, and the effect of the Vietnam war on American public opinion. His was also to be a co-ordinating editorial role, reconciling any contradictions that might arise, eliminating repetitions and overlapping coverage in the work of his two co-authors.

In the event, there was a remarkable harmony between the authors, working in three different places and separated in one case by the width of the Atlantic. Apart from minor points, there was broad agreement both on the selection of relevant facts and on their interpretation.

A quick look at the authors' credentials is perhaps in order. All three of us are journalists. The two older men, Brian Crozier and Drew Middleton, in particular, reported or commented on lengthy phases of the cold war in many home or foreign assignments, the former for a number of organisations, including Reuters and *The Economist*, the latter for the *New York Times*, of which for many years he has been the Defense Correspondent. Jeremy Murray-Brown has had extensive experience in radio and television and is the author of a biography of Kenyatta. Brian Crozier has written biographies of Franco, de Gaulle and Chiang Kai-shek and numerous political works, of which the most relevant are *The Future of Communist Power* (US title: *Since Stalin*) and *Strategy of Survival*. He was a co-founder of the Institute for the Study of Conflict, London, and its first Director, until 1979. Drew Middleton has received numerous awards for his work, including the US Medal of Freedom and the Order of the British Empire. His many works include *The Struggle for Germany*, *The Atlantic Community* and *Can America Win the Next War?*

Brian Crozier

PART 1
THE STALIN YEARS:
THE COLD WAR BEGINS

1 Yalta: Image and Reality

On 11 February 1945, at the Black Sea resort of Yalta, in the Crimea, three warlords of an alliance which was on the point of breaking Hitler's Germany put their signatures to a document summarising the results of seven days of deliberations. Two of them hoped this document would provide a blueprint for the future peace of the world; the third hoped so too, but he put a different interpretation on the wording of the document. For him, peace meant a continuation of war, but war of a different kind and directed as much against his two allies as against Hitler's Germany.

It was, on any account, a rather odd alliance which brought together a wheeler-dealing republic, a constitutional monarchy and a communist police state. Representing the United States of America was Franklin Delano Roosevelt, who had entered the White House in 1933 at the height of the Depression and was now in his fourth term as President. Crippled by poliomyelitis from the waist down, he had spent his last reserves of energy on his recent election campaign and was now gaunt and frail. Friends had never known him look so ill; he had, in fact, only a few more weeks to live. For Great Britain and her Empire, there was Winston Churchill, brought in as Prime Minister in 1940 when Britain stood alone against Hitler. At seventy, he was the oldest of the three, but his mental energies were prodigious, if erratic, sometimes taking him back to the First World War, when he had been the political head of the most powerful navy in the world. Britain's role now, Churchill realised, was to play second fiddle to America, her own resources expended in the long struggle against Nazi Germany. But the man of the hour, on that heady occasion in February 1945, was undoubtedly Joseph Vissarionovich Stalin, for twenty years the ruler of Soviet Russia. 'How many divisions has the Pope?' was Stalin's way of addressing himself to international problems. His crimes were as great, if not greater, than Hitler's, but despite all the evidence to the contrary Roosevelt and Churchill believed Stalin was a man they could handle.

It was Roosevelt and Churchill who had asked for this meeting. The three had met together once before, at Teheran in the autumn of 1943, but this time Stalin was unwilling to leave Soviet territory and Yalta in the Crimea had finally been agreed upon, despite Churchill's grumbling. You could not, he complained, have found a worse place if you had looked for ten years. The buildings were infested with bugs and everywhere there was evidence of the destruction of war. But Stalin had done his best to make his guests comfortable. Three palaces had been hurriedly restored with opulent furnishings sent down from Moscow. The grandest of these, the Livadia Palace, a fine Italianate building with a splendid view of the sea, was placed at the disposal of the Americans and to save Roosevelt's energies the plenary sessions were all held in a large banqueting hall downstairs, where the Tsar had once entertained his guests. Until recently, the palace had been the headquarters of the German High Command. The British delegation was housed twenty minutes away along the corniche, the Russians further inland. Their palace, it was noted, was the most heavily guarded. Although living conditions were cramped, there were beautiful gardens and fine views to be enjoyed, and the dry, warm weather enabled the visitors to detach themselves momentarily from the hurly-burly of war. In such surroundings it was easy to believe you could shape the destinies of mankind.

There comes a moment in all wars when the actual fighting no longer has any point in military terms. One side is clearly beaten and what remains are political considerations. In the old European order diplomacy then took over to bring about a settlement in the interests of civilisation as a whole. In the war against Nazi Germany this moment was reached in the final weeks of 1944 with the failure of Hitler's last military gamble in the Ardennes, better known as the Battle of the Bulge. But the Allies had pledged themselves to obtaining Germany's unconditional surrender and the rival propaganda machines of the warring sides made it hard, if not impossible, to arrive at alternative solutions—although neither the Soviets nor the Anglo-Americans were ever absolutely certain that the other party might not make a separate peace with Germany. Hitler had survived an assassination attempt in July 1944. Although mentally and physically he was a wreck, his will still prevailed, his hold over the German people was still absolute. In his underground bunker in Berlin, he was encouraged by his propaganda minister, Goebbels, to read about Frederick the Great. Propaganda could not now win them the war, but it could prolong it and possibly affect its political outcome. Some miracle, they believed, would save them at the last minute. Their opponents might fall out with each other; a secret weapon might suddenly give Germany the upper hand again; some unknown factor might transform the situation, as Hitler's horoscope indicated. If not, they had the power to bring Germany down in a final hurricane of destruction and meet their own deaths in the holocaust. Such was the logic of nihilism; it would be their legacy to the world. In this, at least, they were realistic; it was, in effect, their contribution to the conference at Yalta.

With Germany's end in sight, the victorious warlords had different preoccupations from those which had first united them. The Americans were now less concerned with Europe than with the Pacific and Far East, where the bitter war against Japan looked as if it could last another eighteen months. Roosevelt nurtured a personal vendetta against empires which were not American or Russian, and he turned a deaf ear to men who warned him about the danger of communism in the post-war world, putting his trust in a new international organisation, the United Nations. For Churchill, the maintenance of the British Empire was a prime objective, while he looked for some device whereby Soviet power in continental Europe might be held in check—perhaps by the United Nations Organisation, perhaps by a rejuvenated France. However, the man who could have inspired this new France, Charles de Gaulle, was not invited to Yalta.

Stalin, it seemed, held all the aces. His help was needed against Japan, as the Japanese were thought to have their most powerful army in Manchuria, numbering some two million fanatical troops, with the industrial power to support them there. Although Stalin had been glad to sign a neutrality pact with Japan in 1941, and Japanese military attachés still attended his parades in Red Square, he was ready to change sides if the price was right. Name your own price, was Roosevelt's answer at Yalta, and Stalin quickly obliged. He would like to be given Southern Sakhalin and the Kurile Islands (Japanese); he would like Dairen and Port Arthur to be placed at his disposal and Soviet control to be asserted over certain Chinese railways passing through Manchuria (all Chinese); Outer Mongolia, of course, he would keep and no questions asked. Then, Stalin's armies would remain intact after the Americans had withdrawn from

Europe, which Roosevelt announced would have to be within two years. After all, Stalin had no electorate to bother him, no public opinion to exhort him to bring the boys back home. Soviet Russia had already made up by conquest the appalling losses in men and material she had suffered when Hitler's whirlwind attack had almost annihilated her. With Germany and Japan destroyed, she would be the dominating power in the Euro–Asian land mass.

During the conference, Stalin had caught every nuance in the personal jealousies between Roosevelt and Churchill and had cunningly played upon them to conceal his own troubles. Each one had sought him out privately and made catty remarks about the other. Stalin had many problems of his own, but the other two did not seem to be aware of them, so wrapped up were they in their ideas for the future of the world. Wartime propaganda had turned them into figures of legend; but, after all, they were human beings, trapped by the intoxication of power and each one envious of the other's position, abilities and rating in the media. Had the general public in America and Britain known all that went on in the topmost councils of the alliance, there would probably have been no alliance.

So the conference had run its course, the fate of millions depending on a diplomatic turn of phrase which the experts had argued over for hours. There had been ups and downs, but never a likelihood that it would end without agreement. Had de Gaulle been present, things would have been different, which is why all three agreed not to invite him. Nor were the Chinese represented, although they, too, were theoretically a great power and an ally. It was better, from Stalin's point of view, to let Roosevelt handle the Chinese for him.

On that final day, then, the atmosphere was cheerful, almost festive. The staffs had laboured all night to prepare a concluding draft and what remained were a few last touches and the formal agreement of the three leaders. They went through the clauses one by one and signified their agreement at each proposal or amendment, Stalin using the popular vernacular 'Okay!', Roosevelt and Churchill replying with the Russian equivalent, 'Horosho!' Everything was agreed at last; the three immortals could sign (a blank page, actually, the text would be typed up later); photographs could be taken. The previous evening Churchill had devised a formula which enabled Stalin to raise his glass to the King–Emperor of Great Britain. Next day, Roosevelt had appointments with three kings in the Middle

East, Churchill discovered he had urgent business in those parts too, and Stalin prepared to withdraw, as was his wont, into the recesses of the Kremlin.

In the official text released to the press on Monday, 12 February 1945, the world was able to read that the upholders of democracy, America and Britain, were in complete accord with the Soviet Union, guardian of communist orthodoxy. The three powers were united both in their war aims and in their peace aims. Germany was doomed; Nazism and militarism would be extirpated for ever; the liberated peoples of Europe would be helped to settle their own destiny through free elections. The allies were agreed, apparently, even upon Poland, the subject of the hardest talk at the conference, with Stalin promoting his own nominees and Churchill speaking up for the exiled Poles in London. 'We came to the Crimea Conference resolved to settle our differences about Poland . . . We reaffirm our common desire to see established a strong, free, independent and democratic Poland.' The new United Nations Organisation, to which this wartime alliance would give way, would maintain peace and security for all and for ever. 'Our meeting here in the Crimea has reaffirmed our common determination to maintain and strengthen in the peace to come that unity of purpose and of action which has made victory possible.'

The conference had been given the code-name Argonaut—not a happy legend—but it is as Yalta that it goes down in history. The public image was one of unity and smiles, preserved in print as a handout to the press, in celluloid as a pose for the photographers with the three principals seated side by side in the dry Crimean sun on the steps of the former Tsar's palace. This public image was, at the time, the most important thing about Yalta, as was emphasised in the speeches Roosevelt and Churchill made before their respective assemblies. Roosevelt's words were poignant, being the last he made before Congress. At least he did not live to see the clouding of his dream. In the House of Commons Churchill, as usual, was robust. Stalin and the Soviet leaders, he felt, wished to live in 'honourable friendship and equality' with the West. (Cheers.) 'I feel also that their word is their bond.' (Renewed cheers.) 'I decline absolutely to embark here on a discussion about Russian good faith'. (Cheers.)

There seems little doubt that both men genuinely believed they had achieved great things. American and British officials certainly came away from Yalta in a mood of euphoria, while the final communiqué received wide support in America and Britain. 'Highly satisfactory' was the British War Cabinet's view.

Today, with nearly four decades of cold war separating us from Yalta, it seems incredible that Roosevelt and Churchill should have allowed themselves to be so bamboozled by Stalin and in turn to have so bamboozled their own electorates. But we shall not understand the history of the cold war unless we face the facts squarely, both facts about Yalta itself and what Yalta symbolises. For what went on at Yalta was only partly the result of the conditions of war; at a deeper level, it signified a profoundly disturbing trend in human affairs, one that is still with us.

One of the supreme paradoxes of the twentieth century is that the more available and widespread the means of communication, the more blinded people have become to the reality of what is being communicated. The more information about the state of the world is disseminated, the less does the truth about it strike home. The greater the liberty of the press—that is, the media in general—the less is liberty prized.

In no area of contemporary affairs is this paradox more striking than in that which concerns the defence of Western civilisation, from which all our freedoms derive. And in particular, in recognising the nature of the struggle which is actually raging in the world today. Each time communism swallows up a nation or a people, it shocks free people to realise that it has happened before. The Russian people themselves were the first to suffer, then the various nations now trapped within the Soviet Union; the Spanish Civil War, the Nazi–Soviet Pact, Yalta itself, these were all further stages in the same process. Then came the rape of Czechoslovakia in 1948, the invasion of Hungary in 1956, the invasion of Czechoslovakia again in 1968, together with Korea, Cuba, Vietnam, Afghanistan and so on; the list is endless, and each name stands for more than the event itself; they are signposts, all pointing in the same direction.

This book, then, is an attempt to put all these events into their right context and to provide readers with the necessary points of reference whereby they can judge for themselves the course the struggle which we call cold war is likely to take in the future. But first, one thing must be made clear.

From the very moment of Lenin's seizure of power in Russia in 1917 there has been ample evidence that no outrage, no cruelty, no falsehood is beyond contemplation by the powers that be in Moscow.

But the West has consistently turned its back on this truth, either from complacency or from ignorance, and anyone who has the temerity to point it out runs the risk of being accused of bias, if not bigotry. The fact that Leninist textbooks themselves spell out the desirability for such conduct appears to be no defence against the charge of bias. 'We must at least maintain a dialogue,' say some. 'Things are not as bad as they seem,' say others. Yet it is plain that no totalitarian system such as communism can permit a meaningful dialogue with those outside the system. In totalitarian terms, the only dialogue possible is one between an executioner and his victim. And if things are not as bad as they seem, it can only be because they are worse. For totalitarianism has never voluntarily relinquished its hold on power nor found a way to reform itself. All this was clearly demonstrated in the brief experiments with totalitarianism which took place in Hitler's Germany and Mussolini's Italy and which led to the upheaval of the Second World War. Why, then, with these experiences behind them do Western democracies continue to deceive themselves over the totalitarian regime established by Lenin in Moscow?

There seems to be no satisfactory answer to this question, except the one found by Gibbon for the decline of the Roman Empire: namely, a spiritual sickness at the heart of civilisation; a collapse within and not on the frontiers. Until the nineteenth century, it was hardly thought necessary to produce an intellectual defence of civilisation. Its enemies were all too obvious and menacing— barbarians, Arabs, Mongols, Turks. But as their threat receded, so new enemies appeared in civilisation's own midst, and against these the West has yet to find an adequate defence.

This brings us up against something which forms the backdrop, as it were, to the drama which this book tells. And this is the problem posed by a certain habit of mind, widespread in the West, which describes itself as liberal. Born in the Enlightenment, Western liberalism is committed to taking an optimistic view of human nature and human affairs. It is a habit of mind which is easily taken in by utopian dreams and is therefore singularly ill-equipped to comprehend the workings of a political system whose only principle is a lack of principle, which is not swayed by any moral scruple or consideration of ordinary humanity, and which openly announces its intention of destroying liberalism and all that liberalism stands for.

Indeed, communism's success in appealing to the liberal mind is one of its most striking characteristics. The very terminology of political debate in the West supports this appeal. Words like 'liberal' and 'left'—even 'revolution'—have acquired for themselves a kind of moral virtue, although we should remind ourselves that those who sat on the left of the Chamber during the French Revolution, from whom we have borrowed the term, were the Jacobins, the ones for whom no price in terror or anarchy or blood was too high to pay for power. It was these original men on the left who thus first introduced totalitarian ideas—that is, fascism—into Western political life. Despite this, despite all the known excesses of communism, it is still the case that liberalism gives the left the benefit of the doubt. So that this fascism of the left, since 1917 disguised by Marxist idealism, can always be made to appear attractive to youthful and generous spirits. In communism's baggage-train there have always been found liberal enthusiasts, the traditional fellow-travellers of the left, in addition to embittered individuals, who are its shock troops, and lost souls seeking a cause to which they can submit themselves. For communist purposes, each makes as good a fifth column as the other.

A necessary corollary to the liberal way of thinking is that the opposite view of history is damned as 'reactionary': namely, one which holds that man's nature is essentially wicked and that social life is tolerable only if this wickedness is held in check by moral law and authoritarian power. Each generation, it seems, has to find out for itself that a revolution takes you back to your starting point, only much suffering will have taken place in the process and things will generally be worse than they were before.

In the 1930s, the only Western writer of note to draw attention to this failing of liberalism was Malcolm Muggeridge, whose book *Winter in Moscow*, published in 1934, has been described by the Oxford historian, A.J.P. Taylor, as 'probably the best' contemporary account of what communism really meant for the Russian people in Stalin's day. After Muggeridge had quit Moscow in disgust, the great organ of liberal opinion in Britain, the *Manchester Guardian*, under whose auspices he had gone there in the first place, tried to suppress his views. Even the conservative *Morning Post*, which accepted his articles about the Soviet Union, declined to print the last one, on Red Imperialism, judging it to be too extreme. Free speech then, as now, meant freedom to attack fascism of the right, not fascism of the left.

Subsequently Malcolm Muggeridge elaborated his theme into what he called 'The Great Liberal Death Wish', the title of one of his most important essays, which he published in 1970. To this acute observer of affairs the decline of the West has been a steady process, and the war only accelerated it. As he sums it up in his masterpiece of autobiography, *Chronicles of Wasted Time*: 'People, after all, believe lies, not because they are plausibly presented, but because they want to believe them.'

In 1956, as a tactic in the cold war which is narrated in detail in this book, the communist leaders chose to rewrite part of Soviet history in order to make Stalin the scapegoat for evils which are inherent in the communist system itself. They charged Stalin with fearful crimes, but they were all crimes against communism, not against humanity, and this allowed a new generation of Western intellectuals to invent new self-deceptions to carry them through the next phase of the cold war. Meanwhile more and more evidence accumulated that no value whatever could be placed on communist words or declarations, or on communist facts or figures, or on anything else the communists might say or purport to have said. Inside the Soviet Union, the communist lie had been exposed by too many men and women who had suffered personally from it. Indeed, the communists themselves had long since stopped believing in their own ideology. But at the same time it also became clearer than ever that the intelligentsia of the West had invested too much in their own self-deceptions for these eye-witness accounts, or for any other words or deeds, to make any fundamental difference. In *The Great Terror*, a scrupulously careful account both of the enormity of communist crimes in the Stalin era and the enormity of the West's cover-up of them, published in 1968, the author Robert Conquest writes with feeling: 'What has become plain is that not even high intelligence and a sensitive spirit are of any help once the facts of a situation are deduced from a political theory, rather than vice-versa.' In other words, slogans triumph over reason.

We cannot here go into the deeper question of why Western intellectuals in the twentieth century should have felt impelled to become political activists. Anyone interested in this subject should turn again to Benda's famous essay, *La Trahison des Clercs*, and to the novelists of the period, notably Malraux, Koestler and Silone. But in the final chapter of this book we shall attempt to explore the relationship between public opinion in the West and the growth of its communications industry; that is, to look at the role of the media in the cold war.

In any case, the task of at once exposing the falsehoods of communism along with the failings of liberalism has now been accomplished by Alexander Solzhenitsyn, whose colossal achievement has been to cut away the entire intellectual framework within which Western historians have hitherto approached the Soviet Union. Solzhenitsyn apart, there have, of course, been notable contributions by experts such as Conquest which have shed light on different aspects of communism's theory and practice, but these have not made any serious impact on the basic posture of the West's liberal establishment. Solzhenitsyn's achievement, however, is on a different level. What he has given us, quite simply, is the truth. Not just factual or scientific accuracy, which might suffice a handful of specialists in history schools, but the essence, the reality, as it affects every man and woman in the world today. All Solzhenitsyn's writings, fiction or otherwise, reveal the clarity of this vision, but his monument will forever be *The Gulag Archipelago*, three volumes which tell the terrible story of the oppression and suffering inflicted by communism upon the inhabitants of the Soviet Union. Solzhenitsyn has forced his readers to choose: either recognise the truth, which means revolutionising liberal attitudes, or ignore it, which means suicide. But there is no middle ground, no neutral position, no muddling through with some vague idea of a balance that can be struck between communism's supporters and opponents. As a Russian, a victim of communism and the victor over it, Solzhenitsyn's right to be heard comes from personal experiences which authenticate his words in a manner no academic or political expertise can hope to rival. In the words of Milton:

> He all their ammunition
> And feats of war defeats
> With plain heroic magnitude of mind
> And celestial vigour armed.

At the heart of its self-deception, the West generally holds that the events which took place in Russia in 1917, and which are normally described as the Russian Revolution, must be 'a good thing', if only because of the enormity of their consequences. According to this view of history, such events ultimately justify themselves. They are irreversible and therefore necessary to the working-out of history;

and because of his belief in the perfectibility of society, the liberal-minded man in the West has to place himself on the side of whatever happens in history.

Solzhenitsyn's writings, however, present a totally different perspective on these earth-shattering events, especially the series of volumes which begins with *August 1914* and from which his *Lenin in Zurich* is a key extract. It is interesting to note that since his arrival in the West Solzhenitsyn has increasingly come under fire from academic circles in the United States, since his view of Russia and her history offers such a radical challenge to that normally purveyed in schools and campuses in the West. But until his works are more accessible at a popular level, some account has to be given of the steps by which the system of power which Stalin represented at Yalta came into being, and was accepted by Roosevelt and Churchill as an equal partner in the war against the Nazi form of totalitarianism.

One of the most successful myths spread abroad by communist propaganda is that the Bolshevik seizure of power in November 1917 (October, by the old Russian calendar) was a great popular revolution which overthrew the tyranny of the Russian Tsars. Almost the reverse was the case. There was, indeed, a popular uprising in which the Romanov dynasty collapsed, but it took place in March (or February, Russian-style). The men who then came to power, led by Alexander Kerensky, believed in liberal democracy along American or British lines. But they were weak and inefficient and no match for the small group of revolutionaries calling themselves Bolsheviks who were implacably opposed to parliamentary democracy. In November, the Bolsheviks succeeded in carrying out a *coup d'état* against Kerensky's government and abruptly terminated Russia's brief experiment in Western-style democracy. The tyranny that followed was worse than anything the Russians had known under the Tsars.

It is one of the great ironies of history that the Bolshevik's seizure of power was made possible by the German High Command. The Provisional Government in Petrograd (St Petersburg) which took over from the Tsar disturbed the Kaiser's generals because it continued to stand by the Western allies even though the Russian army had been utterly defeated in battle. Meanwhile in neutral Switzerland a number of socialist extremists were in despair. A major war was in progress and the capitalist powers had not disintegrated as their theories had led them to believe they would. What was worse, a revolution had taken place in Russia, the one country they had dismissed as being unworthy of any historical role. Now it seemed, all their calculations were wrong and history would leave them high and dry in bourgeois Switzerland.

The leader of the group was a short, stocky man, with a balding, dome-like forehead and a pointed beard, whose eyes and high cheekbones betrayed his Asiatic origins. His real name was Vladimir Ilyich Ulyanov, but he called himself Lenin. With his in his Swiss exile were Gregory Zinoviev, Karl Radek and Anatoli Lunacharsky. Radek and Zinoviev were to die by execution in Stalin's great purges; Lunacharsky was luckier and died in France of natural causes, an exception to the rule that the profession of revolutionary is a high-risk occupation.

Lenin was a supreme opportunist with a single goal: power. His every word and deed was calculated with this end in view. No touch of idealism, no moral scruple came between Lenin and his will to power. All was improvisation and propaganda, first to acquire power, and then to hold on to it. In Solzhenitsyn's words: 'The creation of slogans for present needs was the ultimate purpose of his thinking. That, and the translation of his arguments into the Marxist vernacular: his supporters and followers would not understand him in any other language.'

Caught unawares by the revolution in Russia, Lenin was at a loss to know how he could profit by it. He tried unsuccessfully to persuade the British and French governments to let him return to Russia, and then the idea that the Germans might help came increasingly to the fore. It had originally been fostered by one of Lenin's associates, but discounted by Lenin himself. The German High Command finally agreed to transport the group from Switzerland to Sweden in the compartment of a train which would be sealed against contact with anyone in Germany. In return they could be counted upon to produce chaos in Russia and so eliminate her from the war.

From Sweden Lenin and his party made their way in sleds across the frontier of Finland, then occupied by Russia, where they were able to board another train crowded with Russian troops returning to the capital, Petrograd. They arrived in Petrograd on 16 April 1917 and immediately began to plot the overthrow of the government. Against the liberal idea of parliamentary democracy, they opposed the totalitarian one of the 'dictatorship of the proletariat'. In the name of 'the people', an indefinite concept which could be made to mean anything, the Bolshevik party became the sole repository of power, of decision-making and of ideological orthodoxy.

A month or so after Lenin's return, another leading figure also arrived in Petrograd. His real name was Lev Davidovich Bronstein, but in revolutionary fashion, he called himself Trotsky. Like Lenin, he was short and broad-shouldered, with dark glowing eyes. Together, these two men would make the Bolshevik Revolution, Lenin as planner, Trotsky as organiser.

As for Stalin (Joseph Vissarionovich Dzhugashvili), he had returned on 25 March from five years' exile in Siberia, and taken over the editorship of *Pravda* ('Truth') from the man who later served him faithfully as foreign minister, whose revolutionary name was Molotov (Vyacheslav Scriabin, a relative of the composer). Stalin at this time was a grey shadow whose revolutionary past included organising bank raids to finance his friends in the Georgian underground.

As it happened, Lenin's first attempt to seize power, in July 1917, failed and he took refuge in Finland. What took place next is of supreme importance in understanding the predicament of liberalism. Alexander Kerensky, the leader of the Provisional Government, believed that normal democratic processes would naturally frustrate a few men bent on seizing power for themselves. But he failed to see that these few men were not playing the game by the same rules as the liberals themselves were. In the name of 'free speech' Kerensky allowed Lenin's Bolsheviks to keep up a stream of hostile propaganda which sapped the morale of the Provisional Government perhaps even more than its own inadequacy to cope with unrest and inflation. The Bolsheviks, or communists as they now styled themselves, were able to plan another *coup d'état*—that is, to seize power by force—under cover of the troubles encountered by the infant parliamentary democracy.

On 6 November, the Bolshevik military committee, the troops of the Petrograd garrison, the sailors from Kronstadt and the workers' Red Guards stormed the Winter Palace, captured most government offices and arrested the members of the Provisional Government. Alexander Kerensky escaped and went into exile. Next day the Second All-Russian Congress of Soviets—Lenin's nominees—formally approved the *coup* and handed over power to the Bolsheviks. It is important to understand that the communist regime in the Soviet Union has no other legitimacy than this 'approval' by a hand-picked chamber from which even the socialists had been excluded. When Lenin returned from exile, his gang—it was no more than that—numbered about 5,000. It was never a popular movement; ordinary people remained passive, the masses were neutral. Although the party built up its membership during the civil war, it was at the outset and has remained ever since a small clique of men and women determined to seek power by any means and hold on to it at any cost. Lenin's own interpretation of Karl Marx's theory of history, now known as Marxism–Leninism, was the ideology propagated to justify this seizure of power. He, Lenin, would be history's instrument, even if it meant destroying Russia, or for that matter destroying the world, in the process.

Western attempts to reach an understanding with the present leaders in the Kremlin on terms truly acceptable to both are doomed to failure since there is no way of getting around the fact that the communists are Lenin's actual and ideological heirs. They came to power by force and force has kept them in power ever since. If they abandoned the theoretical basis on which the Soviet state rests, that is, the fiction that the Communist Party is the only section of society entitled to speak for 'the people', they would be throwing away the only justification for their present monopoly of power. The same inexorable logic binds communists the world over to the Kremlin. It was the party—Lenin and his associates—who made the 'revolution' first in Russia. Therefore the Communist Party of the Soviet Union is the trustee of the 'revolution' everywhere in the world. Chinese communists and Yugoslav communists have likewise no justification for their power other than actually possessing it. But once you possess power in this way, you can rewrite history to prove you are entitled to possess it and redefine words to clothe your possession of it in a manner that looks respectable enough to outsiders. You can even say, as the Kremlin bosses sometimes say, that you are speaking for the Russian people as distinct from 'the people', or for the Chinese people or the Yugoslav people as distinct from 'the people'. But the small group of men who hold power know very well that if it were left to the Russian people or the Chinese or the Yugoslav people, they would repudiate their communist masters in no time at all. So the Communist Party has to have its police to maintain itself in power. The party *is* the state, and the state *is* a police state.

Lenin recognised this from the very beginning. It was he who set up the totalitarian police state that we know, and in its essentials it has remained unchanged from the form he gave it. The Tsars had a secret police of their own, the Okhrana, at whose hands the Bolsheviks themselves had suffered until their seizure of power gave them control of the Okhrana. But the apparatus of repression under the Tsars was as nothing compared with what it became under the Soviet regime, as readers of Solzhenitsyn's *Gulag Archipelago* will know.

As early as 19 December 1917, only a few weeks after the Bolsheviks' *coup d'état*, Lenin appointed Feliks Dzerhinsky, at that time the commandant of Smolny, to organise what he termed the 'struggle against counter-revolution and sabotage'. Next day, the Soviet cabinet—then known as the Council of People's Commissars—approved a decree setting up the 'All-Russian Extraordinary Commission for the Struggle against Counter-Revolution and Sabotage'. Soon known as the Cheka, from two of the initial letters of its cumbersome title, it immediately launched a reign of terror in which thousands were executed.

Today, after many changes of name and many sinister sets of initials, Lenin's Cheka has become Andropov's KGB.

Other early decisions of Lenin's are perhaps of even more direct concern to this book. The Provisional Government that took power after the *real* Russian Revolution immediately relaxed the Tsarist grip on the imperial dominions. Finland was recognised as independent within a Russian federation. Poland's complete independence was conceded and Estonia was granted autonomy.

In other ways, too, the Tsarist empire was breaking up. In the confusion that followed the defeat of the Tsarist armies in 1917, independent governments had been set up in Khiva and Bokhara, and to the west in Azerbaidjan and Georgia. The nationalists who set up these governments thought they were responding to communist revolutionary propaganda. For as soon as Lenin and Trotsky had overthrown Kerensky's democratic government, they appealed to the 'Moslem toilers of Russia and the East' to throw in their lot with the Bolsheviks. In return they were to be guaranteed freedom from imperialist exploitation, and protection for their 'beliefs and usages', their 'national and cultural institutions'. The local nationalists interpreted this as an offer of independence, but they had not yet been educated in Leninist ideology. Lenin set out to teach them, as always, by force.

The Leninist label for the nationalists who had staged anti-Russian uprisings was 'bourgeois democratic national movements'. In his mind, this implied that there was to be a further stage of 'proletarian' (that is, communist-led) revolution. In quick order, the Red Army suppressed the nationalists in Khiva, Bokhara, Azerbaidjan and Georgia. By 1921, the local governments had been supplanted by communist administrations controlled from Moscow. Anti-Russian uprisings in Armenia and Georgia were suppressed.

In Outer Mongolia, also in 1921, the communists were able to turn anti-Chinese feelings to their advantage by setting up a satellite government. Thus within four years of the anti-imperialist revolution, Lenin was well on the way towards restoring the empire of the Tsars, and even extending it. From the outset, the world's first 'workers' state' was imperialist.

But from the first there was another dimension to communist imperialism. Even now it is not widely understood that we are at the receiving-end of a war while under the illusion that we are at peace. Lenin regarded it as his historic mission not only to bring communism to Russia, but also to extend it to all other countries in the world. Not because he believed in all the propaganda he produced, but because he realised better than anyone that those who seize power on such flimsy pretexts and with such thinly veiled motives are themselves vulnerable unless they can maintain the momentum of constantly expanding their power. Were the reverse process to set in, the whole edifice might speedily disintegrate—which is exactly what happened when Hitler attacked the Soviet Union in 1941. If we want to understand the expansionist policy of the Soviet government in the 1970s and 1980s, we have to grasp Lenin's predicament in the 1920s. For nothing has changed: the Soviet leaders still maintain, as Lenin did, that their party is entitled, in the name of History, to perpetuate its own power and extend it to the rest of the world in order to 'prove' its claim that it is the voice of 'the people'.

Lenin, therefore, reformulated this situation in Marxist–Leninist terminology. War, he said, was inevitable between communism and capitalism, that is, between governments controlled by Moscow and governments which resisted communist pressures. To fight this war, and to retain Moscow as their power base, communists had to learn techniques to extend their power elsewhere without it looking like an obvious attempt at world military conquest. But it was, nevertheless, total war; therefore all questions of personal morality, of loyalty, honour and decency, of truth and dogma, of life and death—these were all held at the absolute disposal of the party in Moscow. The end justified every conceivable means the party in its absolute wisdom might decide.

The essence of Lenin's idea was the creation of small, underground cells who would be wholly responsive to Moscow's orders and who had to undermine the existing order wherever they were, penetrating parliaments and trade unions and other organisations, and gradually creating the 'revolutionary situation', that is, society's breakdown, which would enable them to seize power and overthrow existing governments. They would be the vanguard of the communist police state in their designated areas of operation, just as the Communist Party in Moscow was the vanguard of the world police state.

To translate his ideas from theory into practice, Lenin set up the Comintern (Communist International) in 1919. Comintern agents were sent all over the world to set up communist parties. In France and India, in China and South Africa, and in many other countries, these instruments of Soviet policy sprang into action in this period.

After a series of strokes which left him paralysed and without the power of speech, Lenin died in 1924. That year, the Comintern approved a draft programme, which was adopted in its final form four years later. The Comintern Programme remains the most explicit expression of communist plans and ambitions and, in all essentials, it is still in force today, more than half a century later.

Three passages from this fundamental document may be quoted here:

1. 'The ultimate aim of the Communist International is to replace the world capitalist economy by a world system of Communism.'
2. 'The successful struggle of the Communist International for the dictatorship of the proletariat presupposes the existence in every country of a compact Communist Party, hardened in the struggle, disciplined, centralised and closely linked up with the masses.'
3. '. . . it is most important to have the strictest international discipline in the Communist ranks. This international Communist discipline must find expression in the subordination of the partial and local interests of the movement to its general and lasting interests and in direct fulfilment, by all members, of the decisions passed by the leading bodies of the Communist International.'

In Lenin's own works, especially *Left-wing Communism—an Infantile Disorder*, he called for patient and systematic propaganda within
mass organisations, such as trade unions, and laid down the principle
that good revolutionaries must be prepared to carry out illegal, as
well as legal, forms of struggle. Another precept of his was that the
communists must be prepared to change course at any time, even
appearing to retreat, so long as they kept the final objective of
overthrowing the 'bourgeoisie' well in mind. What he meant by such
terms as 'bourgeoisie' and 'capitalism' was essentially the system of
free enterprise and liberal democracy familiar to the British, the
Americans and others in the Western tradition.

One of the toughest obstacles in grasping what Leninism means,
and what it implies, is a phrase that plays an important part in this
book: 'peaceful co-existence.' This, too, must be interpreted. It has,
in fact, undergone subtle changes of meaning, even in the communist
world, as we shall see in a later chapter. The meaning that is relevant
to this chapter is its original meaning in Lenin's day, although it was
not Lenin himself, but his foreign commissar, G.V. Chicherin, who
coined it.

Lenin honestly believed that world revolution was imminent. The
Comintern Programme said: 'The capitalist system as a whole is
approaching its final collapse.' There is no way of interpreting this
confident prophecy as meaning that 'capitalism' would still be alive
and kicking more than half a century later. In the last two or three
years of his life, Lenin observed the failure of communist attempts at
revolution in Germany, Hungary and elsewhere. It became clear that
world revolution was *not* imminent. For some years, perhaps for a
lengthy period, the world's first workers' state was going to have to
live with the 'capitalist' states. Trade deals might be necessary, and
relations would have to be maintained. Chicherin's phrase for this
twilight period of indefinite duration was 'peaceful co-existence'. It
is important to remember that it was never, in communist eyes, a permanent condition. The final aim was still the same: to overthrow
other regimes and put communist ones in their place.

Lenin even saw some advantages in this situation. Russia was poor
and backward, and devastated by war, revolution and civil war. It
needed the skills, money and technology of the West. At the end of
1920, Lenin wrote a memorandum to Chicherin in which he
declared that the capitalists of the world would provide credit for the
Soviet state, along with materials and technology. 'In other words,'

he wrote, 'they will work hard in order to prepare their own suicide.'
Many years later, when launching his 'détente' policy, Brezhnev
showed himself an apt pupil of Lenin's.

Even before Lenin died, a struggle for power had started among
his followers. The protagonists were Stalin and Trotsky. Stalin, the
pockmarked Georgian, with his cunning eyes and large moustache,
had played a relatively minor part in the October Revolution. But he
had managed to get himself appointed secretary-general to the Communist Party, and with patient efficiency he set about bringing all
party organisations under his personal control.

Trotsky had played a far more important part in the revolution,
and later, as War Commissar, he defeated the White armies that
were challenging the victorious Bolsheviks. Reluctant to come forward as Lenin's successor while the stricken leader was still alive, he
was outmanoeuvred by the bureaucratic Stalin. Denounced on all
sides, he was driven from the Politburo (the supreme policy-making
body of the party), then exiled to Siberia, and finally deported from
the USSR in 1929. In 1940, he was murdered in Mexico on
Stalin's orders.

The clash between Stalin and Trotsky has often been presented in
ideological terms, but it was simply a struggle for power. Trotsky
was presented as the advocate of 'world revolution', in contrast to
Stalin, the upholder of 'socialism in one country', but the differences
were of degree rather than of kind. Both men hated the West and
Stalin especially hated Western intellectuals. It is true that Trotsky
thought the revolution would not survive in Russia unless there were
revolutions elsewhere but this did not mean that Stalin had dropped
the idea of world revolution. It suited him that people should think
so, as the notion that world revolution had been abandoned contributed to disarm the many countries in which Stalin's agents conducted their unceasing agitation and propaganda.

For Stalin, however, world revolution, at least in the 1920s, was
pie-in-the-sky. For the here-and-now, he opted for 'socialism in one
country'. Playing upon tactical divisions in the party, he first outmanoeuvred one group of rivals, then another, and he consolidated
his own absolute power in the fearful purges of the 1930s, when
nearly all the old Bolshevik leaders were eliminated.

From the start the Communist Party's foreign policy was based on
a similar realism. Lenin was closer to Trotsky than to Stalin in expecting
revolutions in other countries, and one of his first concerns was to

take Russia out of the world war, so that he could concentrate on the revolution and incipient civil war at home. In this respect, he lived up to the expectations of the German High Command when they provided him with the sealed compartment which carried him through Europe from his exile.

Lenin believed that by conceding everything the Germans demanded on their Eastern front, the war would lead to a mutual destruction of the capitalist powers still in the war. On 3 December 1917, therefore, he sent Trotsky to Brest-Litovsk to negotiate a separate peace with the Germans. But the German terms were even worse than the Communists expected, and Trotsky was unwilling to accept them. He returned to Petrograd to argue his case. To describe the state of affairs as he saw it, he coined a phrase that accurately describes the whole course of Soviet relations with the outside world. It was, he said, 'neither war nor peace'.

The Germans, losing patience, renewed their offensive in mid-February, and the Bolshevik Central Committee could delay a decision no longer. Trotsky and his followers abstained from the vote, and Lenin's view narrowly prevailed. On 3 March 1918 the Communists signed the treaty of Brest-Litovsk. In it Russia agreed to relinquish her hold over Poland, Lithuania, the Ukraine, the Baltic provinces of Latvia and Estonia, Finland and Transcaucasia.

In the summer of 1918, while the civil war was raging in Russia, the British, French and Americans sent expeditionary forces to intervene in the struggle on the side of the anti-Bolshevik armies. Winston Churchill, then Britain's Secretary for War, was the most passionate advocate of continuing intervention, but in the end he was over-ruled, and in September and October 1918 the Allies evacuated Archangel and Murmansk. A month later the defeat of Imperial Germany reduced Central Europe and the Balkans to chaos. The Austro–Hungarian and Turkish empires disintegrated. Along with the Romanovs, the Hapsburgs, the Hohenzollerns and the Sultan of Turkey disappeared from history.

Once the Allies had withdrawn from Russian territory, anarchy broke out. From the works of Isaac Babel (*Red Cavalry, Tales of Odessa* and other stories), Bulgakov (*The White Guard*), Paustovsky (*Story of a Life*) and Pasternak (*Dr Zhivago*), to name no others, the outside world has been able to catch a glimpse of this terrible period in which it was as if the four horsemen of the apocalypse veritably swept across the Russian countryside destroying everything in their path. In due course, the Bolsheviks defeated the White Russian forces, and by the end of 1920 the Bolshevik victory was complete. It was not until 30 December that year that the Ukraine and the other Soviet republics joined Russia in setting up the Union of Soviet Socialist Republics.

From the first, Lenin's contemptuous assumption that the 'capitalists' would provide the Soviets with the credits and technology they needed proved true. As early as 1918, the US War Trade Board had decided that American aid in improving the Bolshevik economy would help 'bring about the establishment of moderate and stable social order'. This belief, for which there was no evidence, then or later, has continued to underlie American policy towards the Soviet Union. After more than a decade of research, Professor Antony C. Sutton, a British-born American scholar, concluded in the mid-1970s that more than 90 per cent of all Soviet technology was of Western origin. Among imports from the West must be included the painful drugs which KGB officers disguised as doctors use against dissidents in Soviet psychiatric prisons.

The Soviet policy of attracting Western help was greatly facilitated by Lenin's decision in 1921 to allow a temporary return to private enterprise under the so-called New Economic Policy (NEP), to inject a little prosperity into the prevailing communist misery. An important emissary of Lenin's at this time was Dr Julius Hammer, who went to the United States, helped to set up the American Communist Party, yet also made a fortune in trade with revolutionary Russia. His son, Armand, was to continue in the same tradition half a century later.

Lenin's associate, Bukharin (later executed by Stalin), summed up the Bolshevik attitude with typical cynicism: 'On the one hand, we admit the capitalist elements, we condescend to collaborate with them, but on the other hand our final goal is to eliminate them radically.'

As part of this policy of 'peaceful co-existence' Russia took part in the economic conference at Genoa in April 1922, and that month concluded the Treaty of Rapallo with its erstwhile enemy, Germany. At that time, Germany and Soviet Russia shared the distinction of being outcast nations in the eyes of the world. The treaty forged close political and economic relations between them, which went on until the Nazi attack in 1941.

During the 1920s, under secret agreements, the Soviets helped the

Germans to manufacture arms in defiance of the Treaty of Versailles. Later collaboration between Nazi and communist thugs successfully destroyed the Weimar Republic in Germany and brought Hitler to supreme power.

While Stalin was consolidating 'socialism in one country', his agents never ceased to be active abroad. The most striking instance of this Comintern activity between the two world wars was Moscow's role in the Spanish Civil War (1936–9). At the outset, Spain's Communist Party was of little importance in Republican Spain. By the end of this bitter struggle, the Comintern and the Spanish Communists, between them, dominated the Republican side of the civil war. An important Soviet defector, General Krivitsky, Stalin's Intelligence chief for Western Europe who fled to the West in 1937, disclosed in his memoirs that an agent of his had picked the moderate Socialist Dr Juan Negrín as the Republican Premier because 'he would frighten nobody by revolutionary remarks'.

Dr Negrín, however, was 'ready to go along with Stalin in everything, sacrificing all other considerations to secure this aid'. It soon became evident that, in areas controlled by the Republican government of Spain, Stalin's henchmen were more concerned to gain complete control over the anti-Franco forces than to win the war. Executions of non-communists and deviants from the line advanced by Moscow reproduced inside the diminishing frontiers of the Republican camp all the horrors of the purges then taking place inside the Soviet Union. Facing defeat at the hands of General Franco's Nationalists Dr Negrín rewarded the Russians by shipping all the Republic's gold reserves to the Soviet Union.

The Republican defeat in the Spanish Civil War was a major international reverse for Soviet foreign policy, a major triumph for the Nazis and the fascists who had used Spain as a testing ground for their forces. In 1938, while the war still raged in Spain, Hitler seized first Austria, then Czechoslovakia. There was little the Western Powers could do to prevent the union (or *Anschluss*) of Germany and Austria, which was confirmed by a 99.97 per cent majority in a plebiscite. As for Czechoslovakia, the Western prime ministers, Neville Chamberlain of Britain and Edouard Daladier of France, condoned Hitler's actions at the Munich conference in September that year.

Although Chamberlain declared that the Munich settlement meant 'peace in our time', it did not look that way to Stalin. A peace in Western Europe could only be an anti-Bolshevik peace, with Hitler free to indulge his dream of seizing the Ukraine and even Siberia as 'living room' for the German people. But from the vantage point of the Kremlin, it was possible to envisage another kind of peace—one between Stalin and Hitler himself. The Soviet propaganda machine was accordingly set in motion to prepare the ground for such an undertaking, which to non-Russian communists was utterly unthinkable. In March 1939 Stalin led the way in a speech to the party in Moscow: 'There are between Germany and the Soviet Union no unsurmountable differences and only dark forces who would like to fish in troubled waters have an interest in aggravating them.' Existing trade links between Germany and the Soviet Union were extended while the possibility of a more far-reaching deal was explored. In the United States, Soviet and Nazi agents compared notes and began working together. As a result, on 23 August 1939, Hitler's Foreign Minister, the one-time champagne salesman Joachim von Ribbentrop, arrived in Moscow to greet his opposite number, Vyacheslav Molotov, the Soviet Premier who had also taken on Foreign Affairs in May 1939. In the early hours of the 24 August, in the presence of a beaming Stalin, the pact was signed. Fifteen months later, Molotov returned the compliment by visiting Hitler in Berlin. Their dinner together, however, was interrupted by a British air-raid.

Let us pause to consider this pact which, whatever else may be said about it, made the Second World War inevitable.

There could scarcely be a more cynical act in all diplomatic history. As Stalin and Molotov raised their glasses in a toast to Hitler, Ribbentrop told them that Berliners, who were noted for their cabaret witticisms, had a new joke: Stalin's next move, they were saying, would be to join the anti-Comintern Pact between Germany and Japan, made in 1936. Stalin would have enjoyed the joke. It was his kind of humour and it was just about true, too. In the early part of 1941, the Japanese did indeed come to Moscow and sign a pact. And when it was time for the envoys to leave, Stalin was seen to do something he had never done before. Emerging for once from the Kremlin, he accompanied the Japanese to the railway station and embraced them.

By then Hitler had Europe at his feet. But in August 1939, when Stalin first welcomed Ribbentrop to the Kremlin, the full power of Hitler's armies was not realised. The Nazi–Soviet Pact was a carve-up of Eastern Europe. Hitler gained freedom to attack Poland, which he did on 1 September 1939, without declaring war and in disregard of the Franco–British guarantee to come to Poland's aid. Stalin gained, or thought he had, immunity from German aggression, hoping all the while that Hitler and the Western democracies would destroy themselves. With later modifications and extensions, the arrangement gave Stalin a free hand in eastern Poland, in Finland and in the Baltic Republics of Latvia, Estonia and Lithuania. In return, the Soviet Union provided Hitler's war-machine with vital raw materials – oil and wheat, principally, but also platinum, phosphates and manganese. In addition to passing on to the Germans information give him by the French mission to Moscow about the military preparedness of the democracies, Stalin also made certain military facilities available to Hitler, such as the use of the naval base at Murmansk by German submarines.

To both sides, therefore, it seemed a good bargain. On 17 September 1939, prompted by Hitler, Stalin crossed the eastern frontier of Poland to take his portion of that unhappy nation. He was intervening, he said, in the interests of peace and he blamed the misfortunes of the Polish people on their leaders.

Although they were taken completely by surprise by the Nazi–Soviet Pact and its consequences, communist parties throughout the world, like Tito's in Yugoslavia, slavishly toed the new Moscow line as they had every other change of front since Lenin's *coup d'état*. Hitler's Germany was now defended against the machinations of capitalist Britain and France; British espionage activity was alleged in justification for the suppression of the Finns—a war which gave the Red Army greater trouble than Stalin anticipated, although he had no right to be surprised considering the decimation of the Red Army leadership carried out in his purges. The Baltic Republics were occupied to protect these small states from war. Tito himself, as it happened, was in Moscow at the time of the Pact, having mysteriously survived Stalin's purges of foreign communist leaders. He was able to spend four months seeing a Yugoslav translation of Stalin's *History of the Bolshevik Party* through the press while the Red Army went about its business in the interests of peace. As European nations went down one after the other before Hitler's war-machine, communists everywhere remained passive and silent. Nowhere more so than in Yugoslavia, where on his return Tito continued to take his orders directly from Moscow, silently acquiescing in German occupation of his country in the short interval that elapsed before Hitler turned on the Soviet Union itself.

The announcement of the Nazi–Soviet Pact shocked non-communists as much as communists. But the event, like the case of Lenin's sealed train and the Rapallo Pact, was true to type. The Nazi and Soviet regimes were mirror images of each other; everything that is now associated in the public mind with Nazi Germany had already been perfected in communist Russia by 1933, the year Hitler came to power and Roosevelt gave diplomatic recognition to the Soviet Union. That is: the systematic use of illegal arrest, torture and killings; of terrorising individuals through their families; of concentration camps; of enforcing the registration of certain classes of people and then liquidating them; of exterminating all opposition parties; of genocide; and, through internal passports, of forced labour which was nothing less than modern slavery. Hitler always said, with truth, that he learned a lot from Lenin.

The Pact brought other dividends to the two dictators whose regimes had so much in common. Their partition of Poland had given them a common frontier so that, in proof of their friendship, Hitler's Gestapo and Stalin's equivalent, the forerunners of the KGB, were able to conclude a business which has no parallel in the history of perfidy. Stalin's concentration camps were filled with many international communists, men and women who for one reason or another found themselves on the wrong side in the topsy-turvy world of Moscow's politics. Among them were numerous Jewish communists who had fled from Germany and found themselves in the Gulag Archipelago as a reward for their party loyalty. One day in September 1940, a group of these men and women were told that their sentences were being commuted and they were to be expelled from the Soviet Union. They were brought to Brest-Litovsk, scene of the imposed peace of 1918, where the bridge over the River Bug now joined the two totalitarian systems, and there their KGB guards saw them safely into the hands of the Gestapo waiting on the far side of the bridge. The Jews among them immediately came in for the roughest treatment. But one of the group, Margarete Neumann, the wife of a prominent communist liquidated by Stalin somehow survived. After suffering terrible ordeals in Ravensbruck, part of Hitler's Gulag Archipelago, her story was to become a sensation when it was told in court during a famous libel action in the early days of the cold war (see Chapter 13).

Small wonder that on his sixtieth birthday, in December 1939, Stalin could reply to a birthday greeting from Hitler: 'The friendship of the peoples of Germany and the Soviet Union, cemented by blood, has every reason to be lasting and firm.'

But a yet more horrible tragedy resulted from the Nazi–Soviet Pact. All but annihilated by Germany's assault from the west—the signal for the start of the Second World War—Poland was unable to resist when Stalin ordered the Red Army to cross her eastern frontier. Thereupon some 250,000 officers and men of the Polish army fell into Soviet hands. Many of them would later be reformed into Polish regiments to fight alongside the Allies. But 15,000 of the Poles captured by the Soviets were never seen alive again. The missing included 800 doctors, 12 university professors and over 8000 officers. The actual fate of two-thirds of these 15,000 men is unknown to this day. A persistent rumour was that they were placed in battened barges which the KGB sank in the White Sea.

What happened to the remaining third, however, is known with reasonable certainty. In the course of April and May 1940, when the Nazi–Soviet Pact was being strengthened and while it still provided vital war materials for Hitler's campaigns in the west, rather more than 4000 of these Polish officers were transported in special prison convoys from their camp at Kosielsk to the forest of Katyn, near Smolensk. There spring was returning to the earth, the days were brilliant, fresh scents were in the air and small pockets of snow still lay on the ground. From a small railway siding screened by trees and shrubs and heavily guarded by units of the KGB with fixed bayonets, the men were taken in groups in a bus with whitewashed windows to a site a few minutes' drive away. Here their arms were tied behind their backs with identical lengths of rope and one by one they were systematically shot in the back of the neck. Anyone who tried to resist had his jaw smashed or his skull beaten in; to stifle cries of defiance, some had their greatcoat thrown over their heads and others had straw stuffed into their mouths. When all the executions were over the killers planted a small grove of conifers over the spot and went on their way.

Roosevelt and Churchill did not think it proper to raise the subject of Katyn at Yalta. The discovery of the mass grave by the Germans in April 1943, during their occupation of western Russia, had been highly embarrassing to the leaders of the Western democracies. Soviet attempts to explain away the murders were clumsy, although the Western press generally preferred to believe the Soviet version. In America, Roosevelt ordered a departmental clamp-down on evidence supplied by American officials which implicated Stalin, a cover-up which lasted until 1952. In Britain, where the Polish government-in-exile was located, suppression was not so easy. The best the British government could do was to describe the story as a propaganda stunt of the Germans, who certainly made the most of it. Churchill's attitude was summed up in the remark he made to the Soviet ambassador: 'This is no time for quarrels and charges.'

A little later, another mass grave was discovered, this time at Vinnitsa in the Ukraine. As at Katyn, the victims' hands were tied with rope and nearly all had been shot in the back of the neck, their bodies being laid alternately head first and feet first. A few had been clubbed to death. In all, 9000 bodies were uncovered in a town of 70,000. The victims were Ukrainians and their executions dated from 1938, the climax of Stalin's great purge. But the exposure of this new evidence of communist atrocities aroused little interest, and the Soviets made no attempt to play it down.

The year 1943 was a difficult one for the anti-German alliance and there were times when it seemed Stalin might be contemplating a new deal with Hitler. The Katyn affair gave him an excuse to break off relations with the London Poles and so prepare the way for his own nominees. Thus he inflicted a double knife-wound on the Polish people and in 1944 he twisted the knife further. When the Red Army was within striking distance of Warsaw, Poland's capital, the Polish underground responded heroically to Soviet radio broadcasts urging them to rise against the Germans. But instead of coming to their aid, as his propaganda led them to believe he would, Stalin halted his armies and allowed the Germans to annihilate them. Then he continued his advance. The Warsaw uprising, Stalin declared, had been the work of criminals out to seize power for themselves. Privately, Roosevelt and Churchill may have been shocked, but in public they felt obliged to condone another crime.

The necessities of war, it is said, dictated this approach. But as the British expert closest to the Katyn tragedy pointed out in a brilliant résumé of the case: 'We have in fact perforce used the good name of England like the murderers used the little conifers to cover up a massacre.' Suppressing the truth in this way, he warned, could only 'darken our vision and take the edge off our moral responsibility.'

Unhappily, this sombre judgement was to prove all too true. At

Yalta, Roosevelt and Churchill approved of something of even graver moral significance than their acceptance of Katyn.

Along with the official communiqué signed by the three warlords at Yalta, a brief announcement was made of a separate agreement covering the repatriation of Allied soldiers released from German prisoner-of-war camps by the Soviet or Anglo–American armies. Naturally, the Americans and British wanted their nationals home as soon as possible and the text announcing the agreement looked unexceptional. But behind it lay a history of secret negotiations whose consequences were tragic.

Ever since the Normandy landings in June 1944 the Americans and British found an increasing number of Russians falling into their hands. Most wore German uniform, some were engaged in civilian work and there were women and children among them. Their plight, as it turned out, stemmed in part from Stalin's refusal to sign the Hague Convention on prisoners-of-war or to pay contributions to the International Red Cross on behalf of the Soviet Union. Thanks to Stalin's incompetence, hundreds of thousands of Russian soldiers had been captured in the first German attack on the Soviet Union. Having been totally abandoned by their own Soviet state, they found that they were subjected to the most wretched conditions imaginable in German camps. Many of them accordingly chose to work for the Germans rather than perish of starvation. In any case, in repudiating responsibility for them, Stalin discharged them from any loyalty to his regime. Thousands more Russians were deported by the Germans for forced labour. Then there were others—again their numbers ran to hundreds of thousands—who saw in a German victory over the Soviet Union an opportunity to liberate Russia from the communist dictatorship which Lenin had fastened onto the necks of the Russian people. Among these were men who had never been Soviet citizens, like the respected White Russian General Krasnov, who had fought against the Bolsheviks in 1918 and lived in exile ever since. In that earlier war he had also received German assistance and been supported by Churchill, then British Secretary for War, and he knew several British officers who were now senior allied commanders, like Field-Marshal Alexander.

The extent of this anti-communist movement was not fully realised by the Western democracies until after Germany's defeat, when it was discovered that in their withdrawal from Russian territory the German armies had been accompanied by whole divisions of anti-Soviet Russian forces, including colourful regiments of Cossacks. Nor was the potential of this movement fully appreciated by the Germans. Being Slavs, they were long treated as unworthy to bear arms alongside the master-race. Too late to affect the course of the war, Hitler had at last given permission' for a Russian National Army of Liberation to be formed under the command of General Vlasov, one of Stalin's most able commanders who had fallen into German hands during the seige of Leningrad. These anti-communist Russians were winning battles against the Red Army as late as the last Christmas of the war. Indeed, the numbers of Russians deserting the Red Army to join this anti-Soviet army of liberation were apparently growing as Germany's collapse drew near.

What was to happen to these Russian nationals? In all, some six million of them were stranded in Germany and a little over half this number were in the hands of the Western democracies. Stalin wanted them all back, including the White Russians who had never been Soviet citizens, and Poles, Ukrainians, Latvians—anyone, in fact, he could get his hands on. Returning them meant condemning them to Stalin's terrible labour camps in the Arctic circle, and condemning their leaders to torture and execution. Everyone involved knew this. Nevertheless, in Moscow in 1944 Churchill and Eden, Britain's Foreign Secretary, agreed secretly that the Russians would be re-patriated. At Yalta, this policy was confirmed, again secretly. It was put into effect at once. Numbers were sent by sea to the Crimea, ironically in the same ship used by the British leaders at Yalta. Within weeks of Germany's surrender vast numbers more had been handed over to the Soviets, including the White Russians, and almost all, it is safe to say, against their will.

For many years information about their fate was restricted to a few score officials in government who were obliged to keep silent, to a smaller number of journalists who, perhaps not realising the scale of what was happening, did not feel called on to protest, and to the officers and men of the armed forces who had to carry out their orders, however repugnant.

Now, however, this grim episode has been brought out into the open. The best account is by Count Nikolai Tolstoy. His book, *Victims of Yalta*, describes in painful detail how the Russians had to be forced, often with extreme brutality, into vehicles, ships and trains for handing over to Soviet authorities; how many of them committed suicide rather than fall into Stalin's hands; how many others were marched

straight from their place of disembarkation in the Crimea to execution yards, the sound of shots being drowned by the sudden
manoeuvring of low-flying Soviet aircraft; how individuals who
might have slipped through the net were rooted out by zealous
administrators in a hideous effort to placate Stalin's demands. The
betrayal of the Cossacks makes particularly shameful reading. But
the record throughout is black. It reveals a moral cowardice by
leaders, treachery by Allied officers in the field, deception and even
downright lying by officials at home, and the argument so often
heard at the Nuremberg trial of the Nazi leaders that orders from on
high have to be obeyed, however morally objectionable they
may be.

But the strangest aspect of this terrible affair is that it apparently
did not occur to any of the Anglo–American policy-makers to ask the
obvious question: why did so many Russians take up arms against the
Soviet state? Even now, the enormity of the betrayal has not penetrated to the mass conscience of the West. But it has to be accounted
as a crime on a par with the Nazi attempt to exterminate Jews and the
Soviet murder of tens of millions of men and women whom communist 'law' condemned as 'enemies of the people'.

The existence of so many anti-communist Russians raises an
important aspect of the pre-history of the cold war. When Hitler
attacked the Soviet Union on 22 June 1941, Stalin was a very
frightened man—and frightened, we may be sure, for his own skin.
Despite all warnings of the impending invasion passed on to him
from his own intelligence agents, like Richard Sorge in Tokyo, and
from Churchill, who knew of it from intercepted German messages,
Stalin refused absolutely to believe that Hitler would turn against
him. The speed and ferocity of the German attack overwhelmed the
Red Army, despite the latter's technical and numerical superiority,
and produced consternation in Moscow. What went on then in the
Kremlin may never be properly known. Stalin is believed to have
gone into hiding for a few days and then a voice, said to be Stalin's,
came on the radio appealing to the Russian people as 'brothers and
sisters'—a form of address not heard in Russia since the Leninist
take-over. In the Soviet newsreel of what purports to be this broadcast, the figure of Stalin is clearly an actor.

Meanwhile, as the Wehrmacht advanced ever deeper into Soviet
territory, the population turned out in large numbers to welcome the
Germans as liberators from the regime which Lenin had foisted on

them in 1917. Hitler and his generals had actually underestimated the strength of the Red Army, but their staggering victories in the first months of the war were as much political as military. The Baltic States and the Ukraine saw their independence being restored to them. In every Russian city, as soon as the Germans arrived, churches were flung open and worshippers streamed in, KGB prisons were ransacked, the guards lynched and the corpses of Stalin's victims brought out for weeping relatives to carry away for proper burial.

There can be little doubt that Stalin could have been unseated and the entire Leninist system demolished had Hitler acted with a modicum of good sense in exploiting this mood. Instead, the Nazis behaved with such crass brutality in pursuit of their fanatical racial policies that they soon lost the support of the local populations and with it the political advantage which their early successes gave them. Stalin somehow regained his authority, and he thereupon executed one of those propaganda somersaults to which the Russian people had grown accustomed. Only this time it was of a much more radical nature than ever before. The heavy-handed Marxist–Leninist jargon was abandoned and the Russian people were appealed to in the name of Russian nationalism. The most momentous turnabout, as far as Russia's long-term future is concerned, was the restoration of certain privileges to the Russian Church, which had been almost extinguished in Stalin's pre-war terror.

The admission that communism had failed, that atheism was a creed no-one actually believed in, and the open appeal to Russian nationalism, were matters which presented the Western democracies—and especially to the United States—with certain openings, to say the least. But Roosevelt and Churchill never pressed them home. Had the principles of the Atlantic Charter, for example, been applied to Russia with the same rigour as they were to Germany, it would have meant the disintegration of the Soviet State. But we find that, far from contemplating this, Roosevelt and Churchill agreed that these principles should be suspended when it came to dealing with Stalin's empire. They preferred to trust in Stalin's good faith.

This astonishing fact is so difficult to accept that some consideration has to be given to the personality of Stalin himself and to the relationships which developed between the three warlords of Yalta.

To most Westerners Stalin was an enigma. The American

diplomat, George Kennan, who was to play an important role in formulating American policy during the cold war, returned to Moscow in 1944 after an absence of seven years. In September of that year, in a powerfully written essay, Kennan drew a picture of the Soviet Union under its communist masters which offered no comfort to the State Department. Stalin's suspicious Georgian nature, his ignorance of the outside world and his secluded manner of living combined, in Kennan's view, to make him dependent on the small group of men who were his Kremlin cronies; and they, Kennan pointed out, were the same men who had directed the vitriolic attacks on Western democracy before the war and negotiated the Nazi–Soviet Pact. 'It is not our lack of knowledge which causes us to be puzzled by Russia. It is that we are incapable of understanding the truth about Russia when we see it.' No real meeting of minds was therefore possible between Americans and Russians; their two societies had evolved in such different ways and held out such different expectations to their people, the one being naturally inclined towards openness and simplification, the other towards paradox and closed doors. To Kennan, the future was dark: 'Forces beyond our vision will be guiding our footsteps and shaping our relations with Russia.'

The one thing upon which all observers were agreed was that Stalin was obviously the man in charge. Nothing could be done inside the Soviet Union without his sanction. But his methods were so devious you could not discern his ultimate purpose from his words or deeds. You could not tell whether he had arrived at any decision himself or whether he was biding his time. Somehow a decision would be made and he would let someone else make the running if it suited for the moment so as to be able to trip him up later if circumstances required a different line. You could not tell whether his cruelty, which knew no bounds but which was capricious, was cold-blooded calculation or pure sadism; whether the loyalty he demanded and received was based on fear or respect. You could not tell on what basis he estimated the ultimate profit and loss, although it was certain that the Russian people were the losers. Did he have some idea of a Greater Russia, perhaps? It was what many Westerners thought at the time, and continue to believe of Stalin's heirs.

By the end of the 1930s there was nobody left alive in Russia who dared stand up to him; all were bound to his devious methods, to his secretive nature. But the contrasts which he presented to outsiders were so glaring: the blatant luxury of his entertainments in the middle of a ravaged continent; his apparent shrewdness in sizing up men and situations, and his folly in trusting Hitler; the murder of almost all his military commanders on the eve of war. Seeing Stalin conducting affairs, a visitor found it hard to believe he represented the doctrines broadcast by communist propaganda. He appeared to be a man who used communism as a convenient tool to maintain himself in power. Indeed, he was a living contradiction of Marxist dogma. Instead of being the product of social and economic forces, he and the small clique around him had moulded Russian society to suit their own lust for power. Had he not himself once declared that the idea of equality was 'a repulsive survival of petit-bourgeois ideology'?

Stalin was not an embittered intellectual like Lenin, nor a wild destructive force like Trotsky, nor a tightlipped party professional like Molotov. He seemed to be a man you could enjoy a joke with; his eyes filled with real humour and when pleased his smile was truly disarming. He had a human side, too, like a fondness for tobacco and a rebellious tummy whose rumbles he tried to drown by talking louder or knocking his pipe noisily against the ash-tray. When you first met him you expected to find a big, burly fellow, like a bear, so successful had his image-creating apparatus been. Instead, there was this short, grey-haired and slightly stooping old man, who wore special shoes to give him some extra height. His face was pockmarked and white, with unnaturally red cheeks which came from spending so much time behind the Kremlin's doors, his teeth were uneven, and one of his arms had stiffened at the elbow. Other people said you had to look Stalin straight in the eye, but strangely you found he looked almost furtively at your shoulder and not at your face.

There was, said de Gaulle, 'a sort of shadowy charm' about Stalin, but his endless doodling, his sinister silences and his unexpected comments were disconcerting. How could a man be such fun one minute and so insulting the next? As Arthur Koestler put it in his famous novel, *Darkness at Noon*, 'What went on in Number One's brain?' Stalin's toasts especially, could set your hair on end. There was that dinner party, for instance, when Stalin toasted the British intelligence service and reminded them how dangerous their work was and how horrible were the penalties of failure. Or that other evening, when Stalin and his guests were discussing the best way to handle a tommy-gun and suddenly one appeared at the table— unloaded, it is true—and the Generalissimo (a title he invented for himself) demonstrated how he would use it by raking all his senior generals present. De Gaulle was at another dinner party when Stalin went round the table and toasted each of his generals in turn, but in such a manner as to make them quake in their boots.

This was the man, then, whom Roosevelt and Churchill began courting from the moment his friend, Hitler, turned against him on that devastating June day in 1941. Western propaganda quickly transformed Stalin into the image of an avuncular, warm-hearted, big-muscled friend. He was 'Uncle Joe', a title to which Stalin once took offence until it was explained to him that in bourgeois circles it was a term of affectionate respect. It would have been hard in the middle of the war to persuade public opinion in America and Britain that the reality was different. Indeed, wartime polls taken in Britain indicate that public opinion began to show marked favour towards communism, so much so that Churchill at one point became seriously worried.

And what, we may wonder, did Stalin make of his two comrades-in-arms at Yalta? Western records show us a Roosevelt who was more jealous of Churchill than concerned about Stalin or communism. Greek communists only had to shout 'Long live Roosevelt!' and the President was on their side and accusing Churchill of illiberal tendencies. This was Roosevelt the cripple, whose courageous overcoming of his malady was the mark of an extreme egoism, who compensated for his physical immobility by keeping policy fluid and who played with other men's loyalties with no thought for their feelings. A Roosevelt who understood so little of the British constitution that he imagined a letter from him to King George VI would force Churchill to hand over Hong Kong. At Yalta, Roosevelt told Stalin how, when he first entered the White House, he decided to recognise the Soviet Union because his wife thought American schoolchildren should know more about it. After the war, the same Mrs Roosevelt, bearing a torch for American liberals, visited the Soviet Union for herself and there she was so completely gulled by the KGB as to make the United States the laughing-stock of the Gulag population. Roosevelt enjoyed swapping anti-semitic jokes with Stalin (these, at least, were deleted from the American published record) and when Stalin once proposed a toast to the execution of fifty thousand German officers, Roosevelt was delighted. Churchill, however, growled back: 'I will not drink to such a monstrous toast!' But it was Roosevelt who had put Stalin up to making the toast and when, later on, Churchill came to see the

President alone to warn him against Stalin's blood-lust, Roosevelt just laughed. Other men had warned him about communism, and he had laughed them off, too. Even when he was told that one of his senior advisors in attendance at Yalta was suspected of being a communist agent, Roosevelt had laughed. His attitude towards Stalin and Soviet power could be summed up in a note passed to him one day during the Yalta conference by his friend, Harry Hopkins: 'The Russians have given in so much at this conference that I don't think we should let them down.' To Stalin, Roosevelt was the appeaser-in-chief.

As for Churchill, he responded to Roosevelt's jibes and Stalin's insults with schoolboy outbursts, but always, in the end, came back for more. After his first meeting with Stalin in 1942 he turned to the British Ambassador in Moscow and said 'I want that man to like me'. While in office, his whole policy towards the Soviet Union was seemingly built upon this premise. At first, Churchill's boiler-suit outfit utterly confounded Stalin's entourage in their prim bourgeois clothes. The visit began well, but then hit a low point when Stalin levelled a string of insults at Churchill and the British, so much so that Churchill contemplated leaving Moscow with nothing accomplished. Instead, he was persuaded to have dinner in the Kremlin in a man-to-man session in Stalin's private apartment. Stalin's red-haired daughter was ordered to attend and Churchill patted her on the head saying that he, too, had been red-haired in his youth. From her we learn that Stalin clearly did like Churchill. The evening was a success. Churchill returned saying 'What a pleasure it is to work with that great man'. On a later visit to Moscow—the occasion when Churchill and Eden first agreed to the repatriation of Russian nationals—Churchill produced a piece of paper which he called 'a naughty document'. On it he scribbled a series of figures opposite the countries of the Balkans to indicate different spheres of interest between Britain and the Soviet Union. In Rumania, 90 per cent to Russia, 10 per cent to Britain; in Greece, 90 per cent to Britain, 10 per cent to Russia; in Yugoslavia, 50 per cent each. Stalin thought highly of that document, and he kept to his side of the bargain, much to the chagrin of Greek and Yugoslav communists. Perhaps this was one reason why Churchill felt that Stalin could be trusted, and why, in the House of Commons, he was at pains to call Greek communists 'Trotskyists', since 'Trotskyists', he explained, were 'equally hated in Russia'. Perhaps, too, this is why he felt the lives of the Russian nationals would have to be sacrificed.

But Stalin put no faith in Churchill. Hitler had been the only man Stalin ever trusted. As for Churchill, he told Tito's emissary, Milovan Djilas: 'Churchill is the kind of man who will pick your pocket of a kopeck if you don't watch him. Yes, pick your pocket of a kopeck! By God, pick your pocket of a kopeck! And Roosevelt? Roosevelt is not like that. He dips in his hand only for bigger coins. But Churchill? Churchill will do it for a kopeck.'

In his pre-war speeches and writings Churchill had been a foremost critic of communism. His essay on Trotsky in *Great Contemporaries*, for instance, was very much to the point: 'No faith need be, indeed may be, kept with non-Communists. Every act of goodwill, of tolerance, of conciliation, of mercy, of magnanimity on the part of Governments or Statesmen is to be utilised for their ruin . . . Democracy is but a tool to be used and afterwards broken; Liberty but a sentimental folly unworthy of a logician.' Yet at Yalta he could drink a toast to Trotsky's one-time associate in terms which make one wonder if he was sober: 'It is no exaggeration or compliment of a florid kind when I say that we regard Marshal Stalin's life as most precious to the hopes and hearts of us all . . . I earnestly hope that the Marshal may be spared to give to the people of the Soviet Union and to help us all to move forward to a less unhappy time than that through which we have recently come. I walk through this world with greater courage and hope when I find myself in a relation of friendship and intimacy with this great man whose fame has gone out not only over all Russia, but the world.'

Was this gullibility on Churchill's part, or premeditated? Was it an attempt to outplay Stalin in statecraft and cynicism? You could not win that kind of game with Stalin. Once when Churchill felt they were getting on well at dinner—it was during his first visit to Moscow—he put on his baby-face smile and turned to Stalin, saying 'I hope that Stalin has forgiven me for my past', meaning, of course, Western intervention against the Bolsheviks in 1918. And Stalin replied: 'Who am I to forgive? Only God can forgive.' Churchill's smile and dimples disappeared, and the other guests looked at each other in silence.

Why, it may be asked, should we dwell on these events, now, almost forty years past, and which arose out of the unusual circumstances of a savage world war?

Because it is only by seeing this past clearly that we are able to see the present clearly. Through their leaders, Roosevelt and Churchill, the Western democracies were made accomplices in Stalin's crimes. Their readiness to strike bargains with him in the shadow of his torture chambers and execution yards conferred a form of legitimacy on his rule. Stalin surely saw this for himself. It is, after all, the technique of the blackmailer, and it was one he had used to good effect in his own rise to power. If it is the case that the Soviet Union is saddled with the lies by which Lenin justified his seizure of power, and which saw their logical fulfilment in Stalin and his heirs, it is equally the case that the West is saddled with the intellectual and moral consequences of those wartime dealings. Only complete honesty in both respects can settle the account.

So the Yalta Conference, in the end, has become a symbol of the West's tacit acceptance of Stalin's version of history. The fate of the Baltic Republics, for example, was never raised at the conference. It was not just a question of appeasing Stalin in the matter of two million Russians who had to be forcibly repatriated: active support in the form of Allied money and weapons was given to Stalin's henchmen, to Tito in Yugoslavia, Togliatti in Italy and Thorez in France. When Tito turned out to be the winner in the cruel civil war between rival partisan groups in Yugoslavia, no protests were raised in the West at the fate of the losers, men like Draza Mihailovic, whom Britain originally supported but who, after a show trial, was summarily executed. Not the least of de Gaulle's services to France was his refusal in 1944 to become implicated in this sordid game. In asserting his own authority on his native soil over the objections of Roosevelt and Eisenhower, de Gaulle forestalled the armed groups of communists who, under the guise of resistance, were preparing to seize power in the confusion left by the departure of the Germans and at the end of the Vichy regime. Their resistance had been directed as much against non-communist rivals as against German occupation.

After Yalta, events moved irresistibly to the collapse of Nazi Germany. Already Soviet forces had installed themselves in Poland, Bulgaria, Rumania and Hungary. Tito had emerged in overall control in Yugoslavia. In the West, American British and French forces crossed the Rhine, encircled a large body of German troops in the Ruhr, and under General Eisenhower's cautious command moved forward on a broad front across Germany. Both America's General Patton and Britain's Field-Marshal Montgomery pleaded for a bolder strategy, but Eisenhower's view prevailed. In American textbooks, wars were fought for military, not political, objectives. When

it seemed that the Germans on the Italian front might surrender
under their local commanders, Stalin at once accused the West of
treachery. An attempt by Himmler, head of the German SS, to
negotiate a separate peace with the Western democracies also came
to nothing.

Meanwhile, on 12 April 1945, the world was stunned to learn of
Roosevelt's death. With victory so near it seemed too cruel of fate to
strike down one of the architects of the grand alliance in this way.
Propaganda identifies individuals with causes, and Roosevelt per-
sonified America's commitment to the sentiments expressed at Yalta.
His last message was an avowal of faith in Stalin. The news of his
death brought a momentary gleam of hope to Hitler and Goebbels.
This must surely be the miracle they had waited for. But Roosevelt's
departure changed nothing; it would take time for the new president,
Harry Truman, to find his feet in international affairs. Roosevelt had
not kept him informed about government policy and Truman's only
knowledge of Europe was as an artillery officer in the First
World War.

From west, east and south, Allied armies continued their remorse-
less advance. On 13 April, the Red Army entered Vienna, capital of
Austria. On 25 April, American units reached the Elbe to meet up at
last with Soviet units advancing from the east. Berlin was now encircled by Soviet forces, Eisenhower taking the view that the capital
of Germany was of no military value. On 30 April, Hitler committed
suicide in his underground bunker; the next day, Goebbels followed
suit. Orderlies doused their bodies with petrol and then set fire to
them, leaving their charred remains to the victors. A week later, on 7
May 1945 in a schoolroom at Rheims where Eisenhower had his
headquarters, the German generals surrendered. Their kind of war
was over; but it had already taken second place to that other war, the
cold one, which was being waged from Moscow ever since Lenin's
coup d'état.

Soon after the Yalta conference broke up, Goebbels, the most
intelligent of the Nazi leaders, published an article in a German
magazine, parts of which were quoted in *The Times*. In it Goebbels
wrote: 'If the Germans lay down their arms, the whole of eastern and
south-eastern Europe, together with the Reich, would come under
Russian occupation. Behind an iron screen [or curtain, the word
could be translated either way], mass butcheries of people would
begin, and all that would remain would be a crude automaton, a dull

fermenting mass of millions of proletarians and despairing slave animals knowing nothing of the outside world.' This seems to be the first use of a phrase which, better than anything, describes the nature of Soviet imperialism. How well the Nazis knew their communist counterparts! Soon enough, Russia's allies discovered for themselves the reality of this iron curtain. They were unable to find out what was going on in territories liberated by the Red Army. A sinister wall of silence descended on people who, according to the Yalta declaration, should be organising free elections and installing democratic governments. The Soviets were interpreting these terms differently from other people. To Stalin a 'friendly' government meant a government which was not free and democratic as the rest of the world understood these words. What kind of liberation was it when the Red Army marched in?

On 10 May 1945, just after Germany's surrender, the Red Army entered Prague, capital of Czechoslovakia. At Stalin's request, Eisenhower had ordered Patton to halt to enable the Soviets to get there first. In the twilight of the collapsing German order, the city had been saved from a last-ditch German resistance by Russians— but by those Russians who were fighting against Stalin and not for him, and whom America and Britain had already agreed to betray. Three years had to pass before Americans realized what Eisenhower's decision meant for the Czech people.

Two days later, on 12 May, Truman received a lengthy telegram from Churchill. In it, the British leader spoke of the bad faith of the Soviets, of the trouble in the Balkans made by Tito and of the looming threat to Western Europe. Churchill went on: 'An iron curtain is drawn down upon their front. We do not know what is going on behind. There seems little doubt that the whole of the regions east of the line Lubeck–Trieste–Corfu will soon be completely in their hands.' He pleaded for Truman to keep the American armies in their most advanced position as a bargaining counter against Stalin's promises made at Yalta.

This famous telegram gives cause for reflection. Only three months had elapsed since Yalta. What had happened in those three months to cause Churchill's change of attitude? As we have seen, there had been plenty of evidence of the same bad faith *before* Yalta; in the intervening three months further evidence of the same bad faith was certainly forthcoming, but not to a more significant degree. Did Churchill think that he should return to the House of Commons and confess that he now felt that Stalin's word was no longer his bond?

The question is a difficult one, and perhaps it can never be properly answered. In his memoirs, Churchill wrote of this 'iron curtain' telegram: 'Of all the public documents I have written on this issue I would rather be judged by this.' Most commentators writing of this period have taken Churchill at his word. They have, in general, contrasted his appreciation of the reality of events in Europe with the naivety of the Americans. But at the time it was sent, the telegram, of course, was *not* a public document. Public opinion in Britain and America was still being fed the wartime propaganda line about the Russians as 'our glorious Allies'. The return of the Cossacks and other Russian prisoners-of-war was about to get into its stride. No-one, least of all Roosevelt and Churchill, had educated the public in the essential difference between the Russian people and their communist rulers. Western leaders, Churchill included, were themselves hardly aware of the difference, and they ignored the few experts who explained it to them.

We must also remember that the final volume of Churchill's memoirs was not published until 1954. By then, nine years had passed since Yalta and the world had long since settled down to accept the cold war as a permanent fact of life. By then, too, Churchill had established a new reputation for himself as a leading propagandist against international communism. It was in a speech at Fulton, Missouri, in March 1946, that his use of the phrase 'iron curtain' first attracted wide publicity, when the media immediately turned it into a catchword of the cold war. But it is one of the many ironies of this history—fortunately for Churchill's reputation, unnoticed at the time—that this catchword, the 'iron curtain' image, should have come originally from Goebbels, the German's most skilful manipulator of public opinion and Churchill's bitterest opponent in the recent world war. With Goebbels dead, Churchill evidently felt free to take up the German argument. But why, one wonders, had he not made his own position clear *in public* those few months earlier, at Yalta?

But the Fulton speech itself needs careful study. At the time it appeared to be, and it has ever since generally been taken to be, a tough 'cold war' statement. Some even regard it as the real starting-point of the cold war. In making it, Churchill was indeed taking a public stand against Soviet aggression. He seemed to be warning the

Western world, and America in particular, against giving in to communist pressures. 'Our problems', said Churchill, 'will not be relieved by a policy of appeasement'. 'What is needed is a settlement', he kept repeating, 'We must reach a good understanding . . . and persevere through many differences and rebuffs in establishing lasting friendships'.

But Churchill never spelled out what he meant by this 'settlement' or these 'friendships'. It was the same in his telegram of 12 May 1945: 'Surely it is vital now to come to an understanding with Russia, or see where we are with her, before we weaken our armies mortally or retire to the zones of occupation. This can only be done by a personal meeting.' Likewise the calls he made from time to time after the war for 'a parley at the summit' left vague the exact purpose of such meetings. What, after all, had been achieved at Yalta? Both then and later he and Roosevelt had used strong words to counter Stalin's insults and false accusations, but where in the end had it got them? Did he still wish to count Stalin among his friends? To us, it is difficult to see any great difference between Churchill's idea of a 'settlement' and the actual policy of appeasement which he and Roosevelt pursued at Yalta.

In this context, one further curious incident deserves a mention. Soon after the publication of his last volume of war memoirs, when he was once again Prime Minister, Churchill claimed that when the Germans surrendered in 1945 he had instructed Field-Marshal Montgomery to keep hold of their weapons, as Britain might need German help against the Russians. His statement created a stir, especially among left-wingers, and Churchill then remarked that circumstances had found him allied with communists against Nazis; but, he added, it could have been the other way about. A search of the archives, however, failed to turn up the order and the controversy blew over.

Is the truth of the matter that Churchill knew in his heart that he had compromised with Stalin? That he was trying, at this late stage, in his memoirs and elsewhere, to rewrite history for the sake of his reputation? That he dared not look the past in the eye for fear the shades of all those Russians he had returned to Stalin would rise up and accuse him of betraying them? In writing his war memoirs, Churchill was actually breaking British civil service rules for the publication of state documents, though his prestige was such that no-one could gainsay him. By contrast, the papers dealing with the returned Russian prisoners-of-war were guarded with the utmost secrecy. Perhaps at some future date it will be possible to look with greater detachment at Churchill's strangely disturbing personality.

Despite Churchill's plea, Truman was not yet ready to break with Roosevelt's policy of appeasement. More straightforward than his predecessor, Truman was shocked at Soviet methods, especially when it looked as if Stalin intended to wreck the United Nations from the start. A special mission to Moscow by Roosevelt's old friend, Harry Hopkins, helped to paper over the cracks, which were becoming increasingly apparent to American public opinion. To demonstrate America's good faith, the new President ordered all American forces in Europe to withdraw to their designated zones of occupation, which they began to do on 1 July. Stalin agreed to meet the President once again—and, of course, Churchill had to be invited, too—and the site chosen was Potsdam, just outside Berlin, or as American columnists described it, 'what the Bronx is to New York City'. The conference, code-named *Terminal*, began on 17 July 1945.

The Potsdam Conference was the last attempt to preserve the image of unity to which so much had been sacrificed already in the struggle against Hitler. With Germany in ruins, the pretence that America and Britain shared the same interests, let alone ideals, as the Soviet Union was wearing thin. True, Japan was still undefeated, but the need for Russia's participation in the war against Japan had disappeared. For it was at Potsdam that Truman received details of the successful test of the first atomic bomb and authorised its use against Japanese cities, stipulating only that the first one should not be released until 2 August or after, the date by which he expected to have left Potsdam. On 6 August 1945, Hiroshima was destroyed; on 9 August, Nagasaki. The following evening, in an unprecedented scene, the Emperor Hirohito intervened in the Japanese War Cabinet to accept the surrender terms of the Great Powers which had been broadcast from Potsdam. These powers, as it happened, did not include the Soviet Union, since at the time Stalin had still not committed himself in the Far East. It was not until 8 August, when the end was imminent, that Stalin declared war on Japan to give the Soviet Union the right to claim what he had been promised by Roosevelt at Yalta. In the few days of hostilities that remained, the Soviets gained a position which gave the communists a decisive advantage in the approaching Chinese civil war.

Hostilities ended officially on 15 August, when the stunned Japanese heard the Emperor's voice on the radio as he read the Imperial Rescript of surrender which included the words, so much in keeping with Japanese circumlocution, 'the war situation has developed not necessarily to Japan's advantage'.

The Potsdam Conference confirmed the realities which the war-time alliance had brought about. Stalin remained in control of Eastern Europe and had his way over Poland. The West, perforce, had to accept his definition of the terms 'friendly' and 'democratic'. Short of an immediate threat of war, there was no way America and Britain could force his hand in places where the Red Army had troops on the ground. But the Western democracies held the line elsewhere. The Soviets were prevented from encroaching on Italy and Austria and from plundering the Western sectors of Germany; Franco's Spain was not totally ostracised as Stalin wished; in Trieste and Greece, Stalin seemed ready to abide by the arrangement he had made with Churchill over spheres of interest; and Stalin's attempts to gain footholds in Tangier, Libya, Turkey, Syria, Persia and Suez were everywhere frustrated.

President Truman was unaccustomed to the way these conferences were conducted. He felt ill at ease and at times was caught out in Stalin's verbal traps. In his inexperience, the new President leaned heavily on his military advisers. He and Churchill had warmed to each other from the moment they met, but their political association proved to be short-lived, and Truman, who had so recently been thrust into the leadership of the wartime alliance, was to find himself suddenly deprived of the support of the West's most prestigious statesman.

On 25 July 1945, half-way through the Potsdam Conference, Churchill and Eden were obliged to return to London for a general election, the first in ten years. Voting had taken place on 5 July and the results were to be announced on 26 July, which allowed time for the votes of the armed services to come in. After a morning spent haggling with Stalin over German reparations, Churchill went to bed in Downing Street on the night of the twenty-fifth assured by party managers that his Conservative government would be returned. Just before dawn he awoke, as he later described it, 'with a sharp stab of almost physical pain. A hitherto subconscious conviction that we were beaten broke forth and dominated my mind. All the pressures of great events, on and against which I had so long maintained my "flying speed", would cease and I should fall. The power to shape the future would be denied me.'

The results as they came in on 26 July confirmed Churchill's dark presentiment. Despite his personal popularity as a war leader, the British people had voted overwhelmingly against his party. To console her husband, Mrs Churchill called the verdict 'a blessing in disguise'. Whether it was a blessing for Great Britain or for the Western world is one of the imponderables of history. Roosevelt used to tease Churchill by saying that he was more useful out of office than in it, and Churchill certainly regained a freedom to speak his mind on world topics without having the responsibility of actually deciding policy. His amazing dominance over the House of Commons during the war years masked the fact that Parliament had become a most unrepresentative body. Had Churchill remained in power, he would probably have led Britain into some kind of European federation, which would have been of great benefit to all concerned. All great men suffer from excessive praise in their lifetime and excessive denigration afterwards. In the case of Churchill, his great contribution to history had been to keep Britain in the war when there were many senior figures ready to make terms with Hitler. But the price was that he became a prisoner of the image which wartime propaganda created of him, a matter which may be studied in greater depth in Michael Balfour's fascinating *Propaganda in War*.

The task of taking Great Britain into the opening rounds of the cold war thus fell to the Labour Party, whose leader, Clement Attlee, was a methodical but colourless personality, and who, largely for appearances' sake, had been Churchill's deputy Prime Minister in the wartime coalition government.

Back at Potsdam, Stalin was now confronted with two new faces. The appearance of British socialists in the international arena was not at all to the Soviet dictator's liking. He had been able to do business with Churchill, but these representatives of Western social democratic parties were better versed in communist techniques. Ernest Bevin, Britain's new Foreign Secretary, was the leader of Britain's largest trade union. A bulky, warm-hearted man, with an earthy common sense, he never hesitated to use his trade union block vote to crush communist initiatives in Britain's labour movement.

It could be held against British socialists that they had been mostly pacifists before the war, but Bevin now proved to be as pugnacious as Churchill, and he had none of Eden's prima donna characteristics. At meetings with his Soviet opposite number, Molotov, he would sometimes shuffle his papers about on the table and pull out from them the photograph recording Stalin's genial reception of Ribbentrop at the time of the Nazi–Soviet Pact. As the cold war settled over the world, the solidity of Britain's Labour government, typified by Bevin, helped steady the forces of democracy in those countries of Western Europe where men were still free to express their opinions. Within its ranks the Labour Party boasted a number of fellow-travellers and high-minded idealists who believed that British social democracy could provide a bridge between America and the Soviet Union. Fortunately for the West, they had little influence over Britain's cold war policies which, in all essentials, supported the initiatives taken by President Truman's administration. The great majority of British workers were united in opposing communists and disallowed them any sort of affiliation to the Labour Party, while it was Prime Minister Attlee who personally authorised the research and development of Britain's own atomic weapons.

But Britain was in difficulties at home and overseas. Her reserves were used up long ago, she needed American credit more than ever. The terms on which this credit was provided, however, ensured Britain's final eclipse as a world power. On the American side, the chief negotiator was Harry Dexter White, a man later accused of being, if not an active Soviet agent, at least a communist sympathiser and intriguer. Prompted by White, the American government insisted that all controls should be lifted from sterling in the international market. The resulting collapse of Britain's sterling balances left the pound at the mercy of foreign exchange markets, a weakness which could only impair the effectiveness of the West as a whole.

Britain's new Labour government was committed to a wide-ranging programme of social and economic change. Nationalisation of major industries like coal and railways and of the Bank of England, and the introduction of a National Health Service, rapidly transformed the institutional life of the country. While overseas, the pretence that she was still a great power could not be maintained for long. The sinking of the *Prince of Wales* and the *Repulse* by Japanese bombers on 10 December 1941, and the loss of Singapore to a Japanese army advancing overland on 15 February 1942, had indicated clearly enough that Britain no longer ruled the waves. Economic necessity now hastened her decline. In Greece and Turkey, in Iran, in Palestine and Egypt, throughout the Far East, above all in India, Britain's imperial role was fast drawing to a close. More than anyone could see at the time, the power vacuum thus created set the scene for the Stalin era of the cold war.

2 The Iron Curtain Falls

In the months following the Potsdam Conference Stalin had to move warily. His experience with Roosevelt and Churchill indicated that America and Britain were not interested in intervening directly in Soviet internal affairs, although in their position he would certainly have felt free to exploit any situation created by war—had not Lenin, indeed, made this the springboard of his actions? On the contrary, the Western powers appeared to be going out of their way to facilitate Stalin's job of restoring Communist Party control over Russia.

First of all, active opponents of the regime had to be disposed of, and their large numbers proved how necessary it was to act severely to preserve the Soviet system. Thanks to the co-operation he had received from the West, the two million or so Russians who had taken up arms against communism were quickly eliminated, the 'Vlasovites', as they were termed, being treated particularly harshly. General Krasnov and other leaders were the KGB's most highly sought-after victims and all were duly executed, their uniforms for some reason being preserved in the KGB's private museum.

Then Stalin had to ensure that Red Army generals, like Marshal Zhukov, who had rallied the Russian armies when Stalin himself collapsed in 1941, should not take it into their heads to believe all that had been said in the propaganda somersault about it being a war for the freedom of the Russian people. Political commissars, among whom Nikita Khrushchev was prominent, were given the task of asserting party control over the army. Alexander Solzhenitsyn has vividly described his own arrest in the early part of 1945, when he was serving at the front as a twice-decorated artillery officer, and charged with insulting Stalin, for which crime he spent eight years in labour camps.

Finally, Stalin could not be absolutely sure what his erstwhile allies would do once the fight against Germany and Japan was over.

Despite its appearance of strength, the Red Army had been extended to the utmost in its bid to capture Berlin. It was certainly in no position to fight a new war against the United States, whose military and economic strength was enormous and which now possessed this new, terrifying weapon which put the Soviet Union at such a disadvantage.

One of Stalin's first moves in the cold war, therefore, was to mobilise his formidable espionage network for an all-out attack on Western intelligence. Among American agencies which had been thoroughly penetrated before the war by communist cells were all those concerned with the conduct of the war, as well as the State Department and the Treasury. In September 1945, a Soviet cypher clerk, Igor Gouzenko, defected to the Canadian police, bringing with him evidence which showed that from the early part of the year a British atomic scientist, Allan Nunn May, had been supplying the Soviets with information about work on the atomic bomb. Later, another atomic physicist, Klaus Fuchs, was also identified as a Soviet spy. Much later still, it became clear that the head of the Soviet desk in British intelligence, Kim Philby, was also a Soviet agent, and among the men he controlled was a senior British diplomat, Donald Maclean. In Washington, Maclean's job gave him access to top-secret American thinking on atomic warfare. From these and many other sources, Stalin was able to obtain reasonably accurate information about Western political moves. Just how much he obtained in the way of military know-how is uncertain; between them, the Soviets and the Americans had carried off as many German scientists as they could respectively lay their hands on, and among these were presumably men with advanced knowledge of atomic science. At all events, it took until September 1949 before the Soviet Union was able successfully to explode an atomic device. In November 1952, the United States announced the successful detonation of a hydrogen bomb at Eniwetok Atoll in the Pacific; less than a year later, in August 1953, the Soviet Union announced that it, too, possessed a hydrogen bomb.

However, it would be entirely fanciful to suppose that any military threat to the Russian nation existed once Hitler's Germany was defeated. It was subsequently shown that both Finland and Austria could remain neutral in a military sense without constituting a danger to Russian security. In the immediate post-war years what Stalin saw threatened was the survival of Soviet party dictatorship. As we have seen, the party had been badly hit by the war. Marxist dogma had had to be abandoned and the failure of communism admitted. But, like cancer, communist power can only survive by reproducing itself. Once the growth is arrested, a recession is likely to set in. Goebbels' image of an iron curtain was apt. Stalin was able to use the advancing Red Army as just such a screen behind which he could impose, or reimpose, Soviet party dictatorship. To us, four decades later, this device seems obvious, but at the time it could be presented to the outside world as the re-establishing of the legitimate interests of the Russian state. In one form or another, this argument had come up at all the meetings of the 'Big Three', and it never failed to impress Churchill, whose mind all too easily could be turned back to the beginning of the century, when Tsarist Russia belonged to the old order of power in the world. It was a difficult argument to gainsay unless the distinction was clearly made between the interests of the Russian nation and those of world communism based on the Soviet Union.

All these concerns dictated caution. Soviet power was to be extended piecemeal. As the Red Army moved westwards, therefore, Stalin's political commissars re-established his rule in the portions of Finland, Poland and Rumania which had been annexed in 1939 and 1940 during the period of the Hitler–Stalin Pact. The Baltic States were re-incorporated into the USSR. The Soviets also grabbed Transcarpathian Ruthenia, which had been part of Hungary from the Middle Ages until 1918 and had come back under Hungarian rule in 1939 after twenty-one years under the authority of Czechoslovakia. It had been the one province of Ukrainian population which had remained outside Soviet control. The Soviets also annexed half of East Prussia, and its ancient German capital, Kønigsberg, was renamed Kaliningrad—after the then-nominal president of the USSR, Kalinin.

In the Far East, the Soviets annexed the southern half of the island of Sakhalin, which the Tsarist Empire had been forced to cede to Japan in 1905, and the Kurile Islands, which Imperial Russia had recognised as Japanese in 1875. The People's Republic of Tannu Tuva on the Mongolian border, was incorporated into the USSR in 1944.

In February 1946 Stalin announced that the doctrine of world revolution was still valid. Just one year after Yalta, the pretence that the Russian people needed a protective screen of 'friendly' states could be abandoned. This statement came as a shock to Western observers and apologists for the Soviet regime, to those who thought that Stalin himself had settled for 'revolution in one country' when he rid himself of Trotsky. It was equally shocking to those who accepted at face-value the Soviet announcement of 15 May 1943, officially dissolving the Comintern. At that time, Stalin had declared that this decision 'exposed the lie of the Hitlerites to the effect that Moscow allegedly intends to intervene in the life of other nations and to Bolshevise them . . . It exposes the calumny . . . that Communist Parties in various countries are allegedly acting not in the interests of their people but on orders from outside.'

We now know that, at the time of Stalin's 1946 announcement, the apparatus of the Comintern was being rebuilt and its functions transferred to the International Department of the Soviet Communist Party's Central Committee. It is instructive to note that the head of the International Department, Boris Ponomarev, was formerly a member of the Executive Committee of Lenin's original Comintern. Officially, the International Department is simply charged with relations with non-ruling communist parties. But, in fact, its functions are infinitely more wide-ranging. The ID has an important, perhaps decisive, voice in Soviet foreign policy, transmits the Politburo's directives to the communist parties in the satellite countries of Eastern Europe (and Cuba), formulates Soviet subversive strategy on a world scale, and closely co-ordinates its activities with those of the Soviet secret police and espionage system—known today as the KGB (Committee of State Security), but continuing unchanged through a whole series of sinister initials, of which the best known are Lenin's CHEKA and Stalin's NKVD and MVD.

The full facts of the secret revival of the Comintern did not become known in the West until the early 1970s. It was at one time supposed that the successor to the Comintern was the Communist Information Bureau (Cominform), set up by Stalin on 5 October 1947. But the functions of the Cominform were far more limited than those of the Comintern. The founder-members of the Cominform were the communist parties of the Soviet Union, Yugoslavia, Bulgaria, Rumania, Hungary, Poland, France, Italy and Czechoslovakia. Its primary function was to counter the effects of the Truman Doctrine and the Marshall Plan, two major initiatives by the United States in the cold war which are described in the next chapter.

The Cominform was a limited, although for a time fairly potent, instrument of Soviet propaganda. But the real work of subversion was entrusted to the Soviet International Department.

During this immediate post-war period the Soviets developed new techniques of subversion and new methods for the secret financing of communist parties and auxiliary bodies. A major device for subversion throughout the world was the creation of 'International Front Organisations'. In communist terms, a 'front' is an organisation which may appear to be under non-communist control, but in which all the real decisions are taken by communists within it. Lenin thought of such organisations as 'transmission belts to the masses'.

Most of the International Front Organisations were set up under Stalin's orders immediately after the war. Nearly all of them are still in existence and still active. The major ones were the World Federation of Trade Unions or WFTU, created in February 1945; the World Federation of Democratic Youth or WFDY (November 1945); the International Union of Students or IUS (August 1946); the Women's International Democratic Federation or WIDF (December 1945); the International Organisation of Journalists or IOJ (June 1946); the World Federation of Scientific Workers or WFS (1946); the International Association of Democratic Lawyers or IADL (October 1946); the International Radio and Television Organisation or OIRT (1946); the International Federation of Former Political Prisoners of Fascism or FIAPP (1947), which later became the International Federation of Resistance Movements or FIR; and not least, the World Peace Council or WPC, initially termed the International Liaison Committee of Intellectuals, itself an offshoot of the World Congress of Intellectuals for Peace; held in Wroclaw, Poland,—formerly the German city of Breslau—in August 1948.

To finance these organisations and communist parties and their auxiliary bodies in different countries, ingenious methods of syphoning off funds from commercial transactions were devised. There were, of course, direct cash grants but the other methods worked out during the period when the world believed the Comintern to be dead and buried included:

Payment of inflated commissions or prices to firms controlled by non-ruling communist parties;
The provision of goods free or at low cost for sale by communist parties;

Direct gifts of various goods, including capital equipment, for use by the West European parties. These included cars and lorries, printing plant and newsprint, propaganda material, Marxist–Leninist training manuals, books and articles for distribution.

With such methods and organisations at his disposal, Stalin set out to do what Lenin had dreamt of doing; extending the Soviet system to all countries of the world.

Stalin could dissimulate over his long-term intentions, but his imposition of communist regimes in Eastern Europe could not be concealed, although the process by which it took place was obscured by a smokescreen of false words, bogus declarations and lies—in communist jargon, by 'disinformation'. It was during a congressional debate in 1947 that the American financier and presidential adviser, Bernard Baruch, coined the term 'cold war' to describe what was happening.

Although this form of warfare was implicit in Lenin's actions in 1917 and after, it was only with the demise of other forms of dictatorship, like Hitler's and Mussolini's, that democratic parties and governments inclined towards the Western way of life realised that they were the next targets. The first indication that this was so took place during the latter phase of the Second World War with a communist-led mutiny in the Greek Navy in Alexandria harbour in April 1944. The previous year, Greek communist guerrillas had attacked other resistance groups fighting the German–Italian occupation. A similar war within a war was taking place in Yugoslavia, but it does seem as though the Greek communists were the first of the foreign parties to go into action on Stalin's direct orders.

In the atrocious civil war that followed, the communists murdered thousands of men, women and children and took large numbers of hostages, driving them along the roads and leaving many to die. Only Churchill's personal intervention at Christmas 1944 and the deployment of British troops which were needed in the Italian campaign saved Greece from a communist take-over. Churchill came in for much abuse for his action, especially in America, and in the House of Commons debate on Greece he spoke of his anxiety for the future at this turn of events. At the time, Stalin appeared to accept the situation since, according to the agreement he had made with Churchill in Moscow, Greece fell within the British sphere of interest.

In 1946, however, the communists in Greece made another attempt to seize power by force and they were now directly supported by the communist regimes of Albania, Bulgaria and Yugoslavia. This further civil war dragged on until 1949, when the communists were finally defeated by American initiatives in the cold war and the abrupt termination of Yugoslav aid following. the break between Tito and Stalin.

In Turkey and Iran, Stalin's expansionist plans were also foiled. He had advanced claims in both countries at Yalta and again at Potsdam without success. The Turks, neutral for most of the war and now backed by the United States and Britain, stood firm against Soviet demands for joint defence arrangements in the Dardanelles and for a military base on Turkish soil.

In Iran, the situation was more complicated. Britain and the Soviet Union had occupied Iranian territory in a preventive action against the Germans and made it one of the principal supply routes by which American aid reached the Red Army. Both powers agreed to withdraw their forces within six months of the end of hostilities. The British complied, but the Soviets stayed on. On Stalin's orders, the Iranian communists (whose party was named Tudeh, or 'Masses') set up two separatist police states on the Soviet model: the 'Autonomous Republic of Azerbaidjan' and the 'Kurdish People's Republic'.

The Iranians appealed to the United Nations Security Council in January 1946, the first open clash between the Soviets and the West before that body. In the wake of unpleasant publicity and Truman's insistence, the Soviets suddenly withdrew their forces, leaving the Iranian communists to their own devices. Neither of the separatist republics survived their departure by more than a few months.

To this day, the real reasons for Stalin's decision to quit Iran remain obscure. The Soviets are not given to withdrawing once they have occupied other people's territory. In retrospect, the Soviet dictator may have thought his plans further afield—in the Arab world—would be ill-served by too blatant an attempt to bully the Turks and subjugate the Iranians. Alternatively, it may have been a hidden reply to Churchill's speeches in America, in which the former British war leader cited the case of Iran as being a testing-ground of Soviet intentions. Or was it much more simple—Stalin's fear that Truman would carry out his threat and move American forces into the area?

For the peoples of Eastern Europe, however, there was no escape.

Bulgaria, Albania and Rumania were occupied as a matter of course as the Red Army moved westwards. Hungary and Poland likewise had to be traversed before the tide of war brought Soviet forces to the frontiers of Hitler's Reich. Yugoslavia, Austria, Czechoslovakia and Germany—each country in turn had its own tale to tell of Communist 'liberation'. But the technique that established local communist parties in power in these countries only partly depended on the presence of Red Army bayonets. It was known as 'the united front'. The communists are willing, initially, to share power with other parties, such as the Christian Democrats, the Liberals or the Peasants, as some democratic parties in Eastern Europe were called. The communists' first concern, however, is to gain control of a key ministry, usually the Ministry of the Interior, which controls the police. The next phase may take months or years, depending on the degree of resistance offered by other parties in the governing coalition.

The communist seizure of power in Hungary was a classic example of this procedure. Matyas Rakosi, the Hungarian party boss, describe the technique as 'salami' tactics: small groups in coalition parties were to be 'cut off in slices' one at a time. Individuals or groups within these parties that are known to oppose communist control are singled out for pressure tactics, including slander campaigns. The pressure mounts until the parties concerned yield and expel those who resist or disapprove of communism. Purges, mergers and absorptions follow until the single party–police state is firmly in control. Conditions were not, of course, exactly the same in all the Eastern European satellites, but in each of them the united front and salami tactics proved effective.

The Soviet take-over of Czechoslovakia in February 1948 provided the most notorious case of all, finally removing all doubts in America as to the reality of Stalin's intentions. In March 1945, the widely respected President of the Czech government-in-exile, Dr Benes, went from London to Moscow to form a government acceptable to the Soviets and their Czech protégés. The outcome, a month later, was the creation of a National Front which included the Czech and Slovak communists and other parties. In May 1945, as we have seen, the Red Army entered Prague, although the city had been liberated by anti-Soviet Russians and the Americans could easily have got there first. Had General Patton been allowed to do so, the future of Czechoslovakia might have been very different. As it was, three years of political struggle followed, in which the non-communist Czech parties strove desperately to preserve their identity and independence. Czech democracy had been let down once before, by Britain and France at Munich in 1938. Now the Czechs found themselves on their own again against another tyrant, while the Western powers looked the other way.

In 1946, at a time of fear and uncertainty, elections gave the communists 38 per cent of the votes, and their leader, Klement Gottwald, became Prime Minister. The following year, 1947, he attacked his colleagues in the coalition government in a speech entitled 'Reactionary forces within the Front'. Pressure against non-communists was stepped up.

In May 1948 further elections were due to be held. In view of the bad name the Soviets had already acquired, the communists in Czechoslovakia were likely to be heavily defeated. Stalin decided to move first. On 19 February, Valerian Zorin, formerly Soviet ambassador to Czechoslovakia and later Deputy Foreign Minister, arrived in Prague, almost unheralded. He was, said an official statement, to supervise Russian wheat deliveries. Simultaneously, the Soviet Army was ordered to conduct manoeuvres along the Czech border. On the 27th, under cover of a massive display of police power and a stage-managed workers' demonstration, the Czechoslovak communists ousted the other parties and seized power. True, two non-party men—Jan Masaryk and General Svoboda*—were in the cabinet, as Foreign Minister and Defence Minister, respectively. But there could be no doubt about the reality of the communist takeover. In America Stalin was openly equated with Hitler. Two weeks later, Masaryk jumped, or was pushed, to his death from a third-floor window in the Foreign Ministry. Other non-communist leaders were arrested or fled the country. In June, President Benes resigned, and soon after, died. Gottwald took his place. The long Stalinist terror settled over Czechoslovakia.

Poland and Germany

The cases of Poland and Germany call for separate treatment. They were inextricably bound together, for the frontiers of both countries

*Svoboda means 'freedom' in Czech. Twenty years later, this same General Svoboda stood up to Russian attempts—partially successful—to bully Dubchek's government into submission to the Soviet will.

were drastically altered by the war. The Soviets had seized eastern Poland under the Hitler–Stalin Pact; and this frontier, which approximated to the old Curzon Line drawn up in the days of Tsarist Russia, was accepted by Roosevelt and Churchill. To compensate for Poland's loss of territory in the east, America and Britain agreed that her western frontier should be extended westwards, at Germany's expense, to what was loosely described as the Oder–Neisse line, even though this meant uprooting millions of people. Roosevelt and Churchill liked to think Stalin meant by this the eastern Neisse. But at Potsdam, it was clear he meant the western Neisse, and by then it was too late for the Western powers to do anything. So a new slice of territory, which included the ancient German university city of Breslau, changed hands and eventually was incorporated within Stalin's empire.

There is a tragic irony in the fact that Britain and France had declared war on Germany in September 1939 because of the Nazi invasion of Poland, yet they were in no position to prevent the colonisation of that country by Stalin at the end of the war. As soon as the Red Army had marched into eastern Poland in 1939, Stalin simply annexed the territory as part of the USSR. Polish nationals were forced to take Soviet citizenship. About one and a half million Poles were deported to Russia and some 250,000 Polish officers and troops were interned. The conditions in which they were held were appalling and the fate of some of them, notably those massacred at Katyn, has already been described.

Matters changed when the Germans invaded Russia in June 1941. On 30 July the Polish government-in-exile in London concluded agreements with the Soviet government establishing diplomatic relations, abrogating the partition of Poland under the Hitler–Stalin Pact, restoring freedom to Polish citizens in Russia and allowing the Polish government to form an army on Soviet soil. The army was indeed formed and in 1942, its commander, General Anders, was allowed to leave Russia with 114,000 officers and men, and some 10,000 children. They fought with great distinction in Italy and Polish airmen flew alongside the RAF, playing an honourable part in the overall war effort.

Stalin, however, sabotaged the other parts of the agreement. The Poles in Soviet captivity were kept behind bars or barbed wire. Polish citizens of Jewish, Byelorussian or Ukrainian descent were treated as Soviet citizens.

As we have noted, Stalin turned the revelation of the Katyn atrocity to good purpose by making it the excuse for breaking off relations with the Polish government-in-exile in London in April 1943. His own plans for the future of Poland became clear when he betrayed the Polish underground forces in Warsaw in August 1944, allowing the Germans to annihilate them.

Having thus seen to the elimination of possible opponents, Stalin went on to set up a Polish National Liberation Committee in Lublin. On the last day of 1944, the Lublin Committee, in which Polish communists predominated, was allowed to proclaim a provisional government, which the Soviets immediately recognised. At Yalta, Churchill, lacking support from Roosevelt, failed to make much impression on Stalin when it came to discussing Poland, with the result that the published communiqué was at once denounced by Poles who were still free to express an opinion. As had happened to Czechoslovakia, at Munich before the war, so now at Yalta, Poland was sacrificed by Roosevelt and Churchill in the interests of a peace that was no peace. Although clearly without any kind of popular mandate from the Polish people, the provisional government concluded a treaty of alliance with Moscow on 21 April 1945, and under a further treaty on 16 August 'legalised' the annexation of nearly half of the territory of pre-war Poland by the Soviet Union.

Under continuing pressure from Prime Minister Churchill and President Truman, Stalin agreed to negotiations between the two rival Polish governments. On 28 June 1945, after prolonged bargaining, a government of national unity was set up under Eduard Osubka-Morawski of the Lublin administration. The new Polish premier was nominally a socialist, not a communist, but in practice this made no difference. The new government was in fact dominated by the communists (and therefore by the Soviets). His deputy, Stanislaw Mikolajczyk, had led the government-in-exile in London.

Back in Warsaw, the Polish government moved swiftly in a pro-Soviet direction. All industries employing more than 50 workers were nationalised in January 1946. Mikolajczyk and his Peasant Party were harassed and his political activities restricted. On 19 January 1947, the Peasants won only 28 seats to the government bloc's 394. The Allies protested that the Yalta provisions for free elections had been flouted, but Stalin took no notice. In the autumn, Mikolajczyk was forced to flee Poland and his followers were purged.

As elsewhere in Eastern Europe, the creation of a Soviet-model state went ahead. In 1948, the Socialist Party was fused with the Communists and the Peasant Party was compelled to join the government bloc. A compulsory youth organisation was set up and the judiciary was reorganised on communist lines.

Germany was, of course, a special case, being the defeated military and economic giant of central Europe. Various ideas had been canvassed by the Allies for the dismemberment of Germany, the most radical being the so-called Morgenthau Plan, after Roosevelt's Treasury Secretary, Henry Morgenthau, which proposed putting the clock back in Germany by more than a hundred years and reducing the country to something like a series of small pastoral states. This idea seems to have been the work once again of Harry Dexter White, who was one of Morgenthau's senior departmental heads and was later identified as being a likely communist supporter, if not agent. But it came to nothing. At one time, Stalin hoped to bring all of Germany into the Soviet orbit, and therefore favoured a central government for the whole country, in which communists would hold important portfolios. He called for an international administration for the Ruhr and demanded high reparations for the USSR out of current German production. His ambitious plans, however, foundered on the realities of the post-war situation, not least the partition of Germany into four occupation zones (Soviet, American, British and French). As Foreign Secretary Ernest Bevin and Secretary of State George C. Marshall pointed out, any reparations, in practice, would be paid for by British and American taxpayers who were putting more into the German economy than they were taking out. As Marshall put it: 'We put in, and the Russians take out.'

In November 1946 the four powers began to negotiate on Germany's future. The negotiations dragged on in fruitless acrimony until a year later, on 6 November 1947, in a speech during the celebrations for the thirtieth anniversary of the Bolshevik Revolution, Stalin's foreign minister, Vyacheslav Molotov, accused the USA and Britain of departing from the democratic principles of Yalta and Potsdam. The two concepts of 'democracy' were incompatible. A month later, a conference of foreign ministers in London broke down.

Already in the Soviet zone of Germany, the elimination of unwanted political partners had been carried out under the protection of Red Army bayonets, the Social Democrats being absorbed by the

Communist Party under the name of 'Socialist Unity Party' (usually known as SED from its German name, the *Sozialistische Einheitspartei.*)

As elsewhere, the establishment of a communist state came by degrees. On 16 May 1948, the Soviets staged elections for a people's congress in their zone of Germany. Despite all pressures, only 66 per cent of the voters came out in favour of the single list of communist-approved candidates. On 30 May, the congress approved a draft constitution for a Democratic Republic, and on 7 October 1949, the German Democratic Republic was duly proclaimed, with Wilhelm Pieck as President and Otto Grotewohl as Minister-President. These moves were in answer to developments in West Germany.

But in Berlin, the former capital of a unified German state, Stalin's East Germany contained an Achilles' heel. The city was under four-power control, as had been agreed at the conferences. For administrative convenience it had been divided into four zones. Now American, British and French zones increasingly displayed the benefits of the Western way of life and Western political freedom in constant refutation of the claims Soviet propaganda made for the communist world, as exemplified in the Soviet sector. With this permanent advertisement of communist failure in its midst, East Germany was the most vulnerable of Stalin's East European satellites, and required the stationing of over 300,000 Soviet troops within its frontiers. Against such forces, the West had only token troops in Berlin, numbering some 6,500, but these were enough to deter a direct military attack by the Soviets which might trigger nuclear retaliation against the Soviet Union itself.

But Stalin calculated that such military action was unnecessary, since Berlin was surrounded by East German territory and could therefore be put under siege until such time as a new arrangement was worked out, leaving the city at his mercy. What this new arrangement would be was indicated when, on 30 November 1948, German communists ousted the democratic majority of the Berlin municipal assembly and set up a new administration, ostensibly for the whole city, including the Western sectors.

What came to be called the Berlin Blockade began in June 1948 and lasted for a little under a year. The Western powers this time were in no mood to give way. After the *coup d'état* in Czechoslovakia in February, American opinion wholeheartedly supported Truman's counter-measures, which included a massive air-lift of supplies through the West's air corridors. Taken by surprise, Stalin had to admit failure, and he left it to his successors to devise other means for shoring up this weakness in his European empire.

Yugoslavia

Yugoslavia is another case that calls for separate treatment. Unlike other communist leaders in Eastern Europe, Tito had played a leading part in anti-German resistance as soon as the rules governing communist action changed with the German attack on the Soviet Union. Born Josip Broz, his training in communist underground work had been tough and varied; at one time he was responsible for organising volunteers for the communist brigades in the Spanish Civil War. As a leader of the communist partisans in Yugoslavia he showed qualities which earned him the respect of both the Germans and the Allied officers who were parachuted in to assist him. Thus he was probably justified in elevating himself to the rank of Marshal in view of the part he played in liberating his country from German occupation. His liking for fine uniforms and his expensive personal tastes, however, showed he was no doctrinaire people's politician.

This, at least, is how Westerners have liked to think of Tito. But there are major gaps in our knowledge of his activities both before, during and after the war, and no-one can say whether future revelations will not make it necessary to rewrite his biography.

At all events, geography and historical circumstances put Tito in a stronger position than other communist leaders. As events turned out, the agreement between Stalin and Churchill over spheres of interest—that 'naughty document' which Churchill had produced in Moscow in October 1944—worked to Tito's advantage. At the time, however, Tito was dismayed to find he was not supported by the man all communists revered, either in small things, like the red star his partisans wore in their caps, which Stalin disliked because it identified them too obviously as communists, or in bigger things, like Tito's ambitions in Trieste, which angered Stalin as they conflicted with his overall strategy in Europe. 'What is Tito trying to be, the Stalin of the Balkans?' the Soviet dictator is supposed to have said.

Nevertheless, throughout the war Tito remained in close touch with Moscow through radio transmitters, despite the sudden moves he had to make and rugged terrain he had to cross to evade the Germans. For much of the time he was fighting a savage civil war against other partisan groups who supported the royal government-in-exile or one or other of the local nationalities. Tito emerged victorious, more than ever the devoted supporter of Stalin. As Stalin had to dispose of anti-Soviet Russians, so Tito ruthlessly eliminated all opponents of a communist Yugoslavia, many of them being handed over to him by the Allies in confusion over what the secret Yalta agreement actually required. His National Liberation Movement easily won the elections of 11 November 1945, and the new Constituent Assembly proclaimed a Federal People's Republic of Yugoslavia. The new constitution was closely modelled on that of the Soviet Union. Under Stalin's directives, Yugoslavia concluded political and economic agreements with the other East European regimes, and became a founder-member of the Cominform. There was talk even of Yugoslavia becoming a constituent member of the USSR.

Behind the scenes, however, Tito was becoming more and more exasperated by the attitude of the Soviet ambassador and of Soviet personnel in Yugoslavia, who were behaving as a colonial occupying force, especially in the matter of joint-stock companies and other economic devices whereby Stalin exploited his dependent states. Soviet military advisers were paid four times as much as generals commanding Yugoslav armies and three times as much as Yugoslav ministers. The Soviet NKVD vigorously recruited Yugoslavs as agents, without consulting Tito's government. In a confidential talk with the Soviet Ambassador, Tito complained of looting and raping by the Red Army in north-eastern Yugoslavia in 1944. Finally, he had the audacity to complain to Stalin about the high-handed behaviour of his ambassador. He had gone too far. On 18 March 1948, Stalin recalled all his military and technical advisors from Yugoslavia. A tense exchange of letters followed in which Stalin heaped abuse on Tito and his partisans, and on 28 June, the Yugoslavs were formally expelled from the Cominform, for doctrinal errors and hostility towards the Soviet Union. 'Titoism' became a new heresy in Soviet vocabulary, on a par with 'Trotskyism'. To the general astonishment, Tito held his ground. The Red Army did not invade Yugoslavia, and Tito's regime survived.

'I will raise my little finger, and there will be no more Tito,' Stalin boasted. But the Yugoslav dictator outlived his mentor by more than a quarter of a century. Yugoslavia became another symbol of the cold war. As the British Foreign Office put it in a confidential note soon after the break with Stalin: 'Although we have no illusions about Tito we consider it to our advantage to provide him—in such measure as we may consider desirable—with enough economic assistance to keep him afloat.'

The absoluteness of Stalin's power, and the extent of the activities under his control beyond the boundaries of the Soviet Union, strain the imagination. The ultimate power of tyrants lies in their ability to decide whether a subject shall live or die. That Stalin had that power within the Soviet Union is today widely known. What is perhaps not so readily understood, even today, is that this life and death power extended to the Soviet satellite empire in Eastern Europe.

The list of communist party officials gaoled or executed between 1949 and 1953, the year of Stalin's death, makes chilling reading. Bear in mind that these were not, in the normal sense of the word, 'reactionaries', saboteurs or enemies of the people; though this is what they were charged with being at the time of their trial or removal. They were communists, fellow-believers in Marxism–Leninism, anxious, no doubt, to please the dictator and carry out his policies to the best of their abilities, including a willingness to purge, shoot or persecute those who resisted the communist imposition of a resented way of life. But this was not enough to save them. A whim of the Georgian tyrant, a change of mood as well as a deliberate change of policy—these things were enough to deprive them of even their own circumscribed liberty, of their privileges and, if necessary, of their life, often after terrible tortures.

Most were charged with 'Titoism', the fashionable crime in Stalin's eyes. Kostov in Bulgaria, Slansky in Czechoslovakia and Rajk in Hungary were all victims. They were powerful figures in their respective communist organisations, but after show trials each was executed.

For a time, Western leaders were reluctant to accept the cruel reality of Stalinism, which seemed incompatible with the image of a 'glorious ally'. But the show trials, by definition, were public knowledge, and with the start of the cold war the truth had in the end to be faced.

3 Where the Buck Stopped

The cold war came as a shock to the American government and people. Their response was compounded, at the outset at least, by surprise and disillusionment. Fear, a natural enough ingredient for Europeans living next to the Red Army, did not touch the Americans. The victories over Hitler's Germany and Imperial Japan and what was considered a monopoly of atomic weapons created a military euphoria not to be dissipated by Russian troop movements or threats of aggression in the three years immediately after the Second World War.

But Americans were surprised. At the climax of the wartime alliance strenuous efforts had been made by the administration, working through newspapers, magazines and motion pictures, to present a pleasant and almost entirely inaccurate picture of Russia. Magazines of the right as well as the left carried thoughtful articles about the flourishing state of religion in the Soviet Union. A film called *North Star* gave an idyllic picture of life in a Russian village. Editorialists who should have known better professed to see the germs of democracy in the Soviet system. The Red army, the air force and the navy were praised in terms that might have been considered extreme at the court of an Arab prince.

All this, of course, was good strong drink for resident American communists and party sympathisers.

There were those Americans with a reasonable knowledge of Russia who understood the high nonsense content of this propaganda. Only a few spoke out. Others, because they were in government service or could sublimate their misgivings to the higher cause of winning the war and establishing a new international order, kept quiet.

But to the great mass of Americans, who had swallowed the propaganda along with their old forebodings about the purges and the famines, surprise was the obvious response. As the flickering lamps of liberty were extinguished in the Baltic states and Eastern Europe, as the Red Army settled briefly into Iranian Azerbaidjan, as Soviet agents promoted insurgency in Greece, Indo-China and elsewhere, a fundamental psychological change came over the Americans. It was the loss of their innocence in world affairs. They realised they had been taken for a ride. Surprise gave way to disillusion with Soviet Russia, generating a tide of overwhelming support from Republicans and Democrats alike for the measures Truman's government found itself forced to take against Soviet ambitions.

In this respect, 5 March 1946, the date of Winston Churchill's 'Iron Curtain' speech at Westminster College, Fulton, Missouri, may be taken as a watershed. There was, as we have seen, nothing new in what Churchill said, as far as governments were concerned. But coming from him, a statement of this kind could not fail to make an enormous impression on American public opinion, especially as the President of the United States accompanied Churchill to the College and personally introduced him from the podium. In Winston Churchill Truman knew he had a powerful propaganda weapon in this early and crucial round in the cold war, which is why thousands of communists and communist sympathisers turned out to protest against Churchill's presence in the United States.

Although few realised it at the time, the Republic was fortunate in the quality of its political, diplomatic and intellectual leadership.

Recurrent crises brought out the best in President Harry Truman. Largely unversed in international affairs when he took office at the death of Franklin Roosevelt, he displayed both an inner toughness and a capacity for choosing the right men for the key jobs. But he accepted that the awesome responsibilities of being President were his alone. *The Buck Stops Here* was the motto displayed on his desk in the White House.

Dean Acheson, perhaps the most gifted Secretary of State of this century, wrote of Truman: 'Free of the greatest vice in a leader, his ego never came between him and his job . . . Among the thirty-five men who have held the Presidential office, Mr Truman will stand with the few who in the midst of great difficulties managed their offices with eminent benefit to the public interest.'

Acheson and Truman, working together in harmonious accord, were the driving force behind the great initiatives that marked the free world's answer to the communist bid for world power. They were seconded by a galaxy of public servants from both parties of outstanding ability: John J. MacCloy, Robert Lovett, General George C. Marshall, John Foster Dulles, Allen Dulles, General Walter Bedell Smith, Admiral Alan Kirk, David Bruce, General Lucius D. Clay, Robert Murphy and many others. Seldom in American history since the days of the founding fathers have so much talent and wisdom been concentrated in government.

Two rising stars of the diplomatic corps contributed significantly to the government's, and the people's, understanding of the implications of Soviet policy. They were Charles E. Bohlen and George F. Kennan, comparatively young veterans of the opening skirmishes of the cold war.

Kennan's first major impact on policy-making came in February 1946, after the brutal announcement by Stalin that world revolution was still the ultimate goal of Soviet policy. The Soviet leader argued that no peaceful international order was possible because a capitalist – imperialist group still controlled the outside world. Russia, consequently, must treble production of the basic resources for national defence, iron and steel, and the output of coal and oil must be doubled. The Russian people, suffering from 20,000,000 casualties and the devastation of some of the richest industrial and agricultural regions, must do without the rewards of victory. Rearmament was the be-all and end-all.

This was one of the early surprises for the Truman administration and the American people. For the benefit of the administration, Kennan, then Chargé d'Affaires in Moscow, cabled a remarkable dispatch which powerfully affected thinking within the government. Later large sections of the dispatch were published in the periodical *Foreign Affairs* under the pseudonym 'X', and this article, which first proposed a strategy of 'containment', had a comparable impact upon those leaders of the intellectual and academic communities whose disillusionment with the Soviet Union was stirring.

Kennan believed that the base of the Kremlin's 'neurotic' view of the outside world reflected a people's fear of physical insecurity, understandable among a nation that had endured two invasions in thirty years, and a tyrannical regime's almost paranoiac concern over political insecurity. Pentration by the West was a continuing danger to Russian governments, Bolshevik or Tsarist.

Marxism, Kennan continued, provided the Soviets with a justification for their hostility towards the West. 'In the name of Marxism,' he continued, 'they sacrificed every single ethical value in their methods and tactics. Today, they cannot dispense with it. It is the fig leaf of their moral and intellectual respectability.'

The diplomat's predictions were chilling and were proven accurate. Soviet policy would be to infiltrate, divide and weaken the West, using foreign communist parties, international organisations, conventional diplomacy. Soviet policy would seek to block movements and measures the Kremlin saw as inimical to Soviet objectives, would try to divert Western governments from such policies and would probe the outside world for weak spots to be exploited. Any attempt to maintain a *modus vivendi* with the Soviets would be folly leading to an exacerbation of political warfare.

'In these circumstances,' wrote Kennan, 'it is clear that the main element of any United States policy toward the Soviet Union must be that of a long-term, patient but firm and vigilant containment of Russian expansive tendencies . . . with unalterable counter-force at every point where they show signs of encroaching upon the interests of a peaceful and stable world.'

It was often said in the Truman years that American policy consisted largely of reactions to Soviet initiatives. This is acceptable only if we remember that the responses often were of such magnitude that the original Soviet moves were dwarfed in comparison. Had Stalin been less blatant in his lust for power, things might have been different.

The first significant example of a powerful American initiative was the proclamation of the Truman Doctrine. By early 1947 the situation in Greece was deteriorating rapidly. Communist guerrillas were growing in strength and there were signs that they might attempt to take over the government. Turkey, too, was at risk and in no position to repel Soviet aggression. The Turkish army was out of date and the economy was at a standstill. At that time responsibility for both countries fell upon the British. But Britain did not have the resources to meet the communist challenge, her own economy having been severely weakened, partly because of American economic aggression. Drawing attention to the sad state of the Greek economy and the worsening military situation, the British government suddenly informed the United States that British aid to Greece would have to end in six weeks.

The President and General Marshall, who was then the Secretary of State, together with the commanders of the fighting services, were all convinced that it was vital to the security of the United States that

Greece and Turkey should receive material aid to bolster their non-communist governments. This was a far-reaching proposition. How could American security be threatened on such distant shores? For Truman, the problem was to sell the programme to a Congress largely unaware of the stakes in the game. In other words, to win the backing of public opinion by sounding the alarm. Acheson, then Marshall's assistant, spelt out the danger. Backed by a wealth of detail he told Congress that Russian pressure on the Dardanelles, on Iran and on northern Greece had reached the point where a Soviet breakthrough could open three continents to communist penetration.

'Like apples in a barrel,' he wrote later, 'infected by one rotten one, the corruption of Greece would infect Iran and all to the east. It would also carry infection to Africa through Asia Minor and Egypt and to Europe through Italy and France, already threatened by the strongest domestic Communist parties in western Europe.'

Truman's successor, President Eisenhower, would apply the same argument to South-east Asia, inventing the phrase 'falling dominoes' to describe the danger.

Acheson's summary of the dangers impressed the Congressmen. A major turning-point in American history was in the offing: the expansion of American economic and military power thousands of miles across the seas in peacetime. On 12 March 1947, Truman addressed a joint session of Congress and this speech enshrined the Truman Doctrine. His biographer, Robert J. Donovan, has described the speech as 'the most controversial of his presidency and [it] remains probably the most enduringly controversial speech that has been made by a president in the twentieth century'.

'Should we fail to aid Greece and Turkey in this fateful hour,' Truman said, 'the effect will be far-reaching to the West as well as to the East. We must take immediate and resolute action.'

The action was a request to Congress for authority for massive and speedy assistance to the two countries as well as for the establishment of American military and civilian personnel to assist in reconstruction. By implication, the Truman Doctrine committed America to help free peoples everywhere who found themselves threatened by communism.

Two months of Congressional debate ensued. It was not until 22 May 1947, that the Greek–Turkish Aid Act was signed by the president. But in Greece and Turkey, at least, communism was held at bay.

One little-remembered spin-off from the aid act was the establishment of an American presence in the Eastern Mediterranean. This was largely naval and began in a small way. But with the entry of Greece and Turkey into the North Atlantic Treaty Organisation, the American squadron was augmented, becoming the Sixth Fleet. Thus early in the East–West duel, the Sixth Fleet with its aircraft carriers was established as an outpost of United States' power in an area which, otherwise, might have been open to Soviet naval penetration. Not until the mid 1960s were the Soviets able to mount a naval presence of any importance in the area.

The second great politico-economic initiative of those years, the Marshall Plan, was intended to meet Europe's widespread economic malaise, brought about by the war. Hunger, unemployment, economic stagnation, political frustration, all created a situation which the communists were exploiting. Britain, after the brutal winter of 1946-7, was close to economic disaster. France and Italy were bedevilled by economic and political unrest and industrial stagnation. West Germany, occupied by the Americans, British and French, was numb with physical and psychological shock.

To American leaders, and to those in other Western countries, the implications were clear. Unless there was an economic revival of Western Europe, including West Germany, and, coincidentally, some movement toward economic co-operation, there was little to halt the steady expansion of communism throughout the continent. This was, incidentally, a crisis that was little understood in the United States outside of Washington and the major banking powers of New York because the mass of Americans knew little about post-war Europe.

General Marshall, on his return to the capital, enlightened his countrymen in a notable radio address. 'In Europe,' he said, 'the United States was faced with immediate issues. The recovery of Europe has been far slower than had been expected. Disintegrating forces are becoming evident. The patient is sinking while the doctors deliberate.'

Acheson took up the burden. In a speech in the south he noted that both Europe and Asia had been shattered by 'planned, scientific destruction . . . carried out by both sides during the war', that Germany and Japan, 'two of the greatest workshops' of the industrialised world, had not yet begun the reconstruction process, and that two murderous winters had been 'unprecedented natural disasters'.

The United States goal, Acheson said, was not relief but the revival of industry, agriculture and trade to the point where the economic victims of the war became self-supporting. Moreover, he pointed out that the non-communist states of Europe and Asia would not recover unless the Germans and Japanese recovered as well.

Acheson's speech and the subsequent planning in Washington signified more than an American effort to restore the economies of Europe and Asia. They also wrote *finis* to the programmes for penalising Germany and Japan for their roles in the Second World War.

The band of able men around Harry Truman recognised the magnitude of the task facing them. Vast new funds would be needed from Congress, probably through methods outside existing Congressional procedurers. A system for allocating commodities around the world would have to be drawn up and implemented. Ships would have to be found.

The sums required were enormous for the time. In a memorandum Will Clayton estimated that Europe needed $2.5 billion annually for coal, bread, grains and shipping services. In addition Europe must receive a grant of $6 or $7 billions' worth of goods for three years for coal, food, cotton, tobacco and services. The use of this grant was to be based on a plan drawn up by the European powers themselves, led by Britain, France and Italy.

The concept of the plan was disclosed by Marshall in his speech at the Harvard Commencement of 1947. And so, as befitted the nation with the most powerful economy in the world, the United States launched its greatest offensive of the cold war. It was directed not at communism but at the conditions that bred and fostered communism. Because of the emphasis placed on a European initiative it could not be dismissed by Soviet propaganda as a purely American plan, although *Pravda* tried this line, while it soon became apparent that the Soviet Union was in no position to match the plan either in the enormous sums involved or in its unselfish character. By 1950, thanks to Marshall Aid, economic conditions in Western Europe had improved immeasurably, and nowhere more so than in West Germany, which received slightly more than $4 billion in aid. So the Marshall Plan can be accounted as a major victory for the West in the first cold war period, and potentially the decisive one. It was capitalism's most convincing answer to the theories of Marx and Lenin.

The Marshall Plan was open to all Europe, including the Soviet

Union. But Stalin's refusal to participate in it inevitably led to the permanent division of Europe into two economic blocs, something which was bound to happen anyway, given the political facts of life in Stalin's empire. What Marshall Aid effectively achieved was to hold the line on further communist encroachments in Europe. Unable to compete in this form of economic warfare, Stalin embarked on two steps in the centre of Europe which, coming together, raised for the first time the possibility, even the probability, that the United States and the Soviet Union were set on a collision course that would lead to war.

The first move was the communist *coup d'état* in Czechoslovakia, a pre-emptive strike which sealed off that nation from Western aid and liberal ideas. Here, the communists got away with it; they were too well organised, they had moved too quickly and the West was too weak.

But the very ruthlessness of their action produced one of those American responses which in the end far outweighed the Soviet gain in Czechoslovakia. The *coup* demonstrated both the military weakness and the consequent political instability of most of Europe in the post-war years when the first steps toward the Marshall Plan as yet had little effect. To meet this insecurity the United States Senate, on 11 June 1948, in the Vandenberg Resolution, advised Truman that in the sense of the Senate the government should pursue:

> Progressive development of regional and other collective arrangements for individual and collective self-defence in accordance with the purposes, principles and provisions of the Charter of the United Nations; Association of the United States, by constitutional process, with such regional and other collective arrangements as are based on continuous and effective self-help and mutual aid and as affect its national security.

It is unlikely that Stalin and his henchmen paid much attention to this American legislative initiative. In Berlin the Soviets had embarked on their second move, the most daring they had yet made. But they would have done well to study the resolution. For it contained the genesis of the North Atlantic Treaty Organisation and the United States military involvement in the defence of Europe, which endures to this day.

The Berlin blockade was a direct challenge to the United States,

Britain and France, the three Western occupation powers in Germany, and the three most powerful democracies, although French military power, and resolution, ran a bad third to the Americans and the British.

The provocation, as the Soviets saw it, was the report of a six-nation group, the three occupation powers and Belgium, the Netherlands and Luxembourg, on means of strengthening Western Germany against Soviet political and economic pressure. The report recommended the economic co-ordination of the three Western zones of occupation for association with the European Recovery Programme, the official name for the Marshall Plan. The report also announced broad agreement that a federal government was best suited to planning for the eventual attainment of German unity, then the aim of the Western powers.

The final recommendation, announced on 7 June 1948, in London, covered political institutions for the West Germans with 'the minimum requirements of occupation and control'. To placate the French, provision was made for the control of the great industrial area of the Ruhr and for the continuation of supreme Allied authority. To these recommendations was appended a plan for currency reform in West Germany, although not in Berlin, which was regarded as being under four-power control.

Seventeen days after the recommendations had been made public, the Soviets imposed a full blockade on Berlin. this, itself, was the culmination of a series of steps taken with cold calculation and sheathed in deceit against the city's communications with West Germany. All rail traffic between Berlin and the West was halted for two days on 11 June. Road traffic on a bridge on the highway leading from West Germany to the capital was halted on 12 June for 'repairs' of the bridge.

On 16 June the Soviet representative walked out of the *Kommandatura*, the four-power military group that exercised control over Berlin. Two days later the West announced currency reform in West Germany. On 23 June the Russians ordered the imposition of their own currency for East Germany and *all* Berlin. the allies responded by extending the currency reform in West Germany to West Berlin.

This jockeying for position ended on 24 June when the Russians imposed a full blockade on Berlin and the Western powers retaliated by halting freight shipments from the Western zones to the Soviet zone.

Blockade is a military action, and the Americans and their allies met it by military means; the establishment of the Berlin airlift. From all over the world American and British transports flew into West Germany to take their place in an unending stream of aircraft flying into Tempelhof in the United States sector of Berlin, and Gatow in the British sector. In June the combined lift was 70,000 tons. In May 1949 it stood at 250,000 tons. The aircraft carried coal, medicinal supplies, food and hundreds of other items needed by the Berliners.

The Russians were startled and impressed by what was to them a novel use of air power. The air bridge between West Germany and Berlin went far beyond their own capabilities and, consequently, beyond their imaginations.

The imposition of the blockade was a daring Soviet initiative, the boldest step Stalin had yet taken against the West. But the Soviets also displayed a certain prudence. Once the airlift got into its stride, they could have reduced its effectiveness and increased the hazards for the Allied airmen by raising barrage balloons on the approaches to Tempelhof and Gatow, as these approaches were over Soviet-occupied territory. Both the American and British air commanders knew this, and they were deeply worried at the prospect.

Why did not the Russians use the balloons? The most likely answer lies in the transfer early in the crisis of two squadrons of American bombers, designated as atom bombers, to British airfields. Atom bombers of the RAF were on adjacent airfields. There is no doubt that the Soviets knew the bombers were there. This may explain their prudence about the barrage balloons.

But, given their superiority in strategic power, why did not the Americans and British attempt to push a force up the highway to Berlin? General Lucius D. Clay, the United States Commander-in-Chief in Germany, and his political adviser, Ambassador Robert D. Murphy, suggested this move.

They counselled Washington that the Russians should be advised that on a specific date an armed convoy would move up the autobahn to Berlin equipped with engineering material to deal with the 'technical difficulties' which the Soviets confessed themselves unable to solve. Clay believed that the chances of the convoy being met by force, with the prospect of escalation to war, were small. He was confident that the convoy would get through to Berlin and the blockade broken.

President Truman replied that if the Joint Chiefs of Staff approved the measure, in writing, he would give his approval. In the meantime, the president asked what risks would be involved. Clay's answer was hardly reassuring to a government facing the prospect of war. He thought that the initial Soviet reaction would be to establish road-blocks along the highway—there were about six Soviet divisions deployed between Berlin and the frontier at the time—but that American engineers could clear these obstacles. But Clay also thought that the next Soviet step would be to attempt to turn back the convoy with armed force.

This assumption was not acceptable to the Administration. The convoy strategy could be based on a miscalculation of Soviet intentions. Clay and Murphy might think that the Soviets were bluffing and that America should call their bluff. But if the Russians were not bluffing, then the strategy could lead, at least, to a battle on the autobahn or, at worst, to the start of another war. The unknown element was how far Soviet policy would be influenced by the presence of atom bombers in Britain. At that time, the United States had a monopoly of the atom bomb, although the Soviets were fast catching up. Was the convoy strategy a chance to bring the Russians to heel? The question, ultimately, was not one of calling the Soviet's bluff but one of self-doubt about whether America herself dared to use the bomb.

Cooler, if not wiser, heads prevailed in Washington. The Allies turned with renewed emphasis to the airlift and the trickle of supplies to Berlin grew into a stream and finally a flood. It was not cheap in blood or treasure. American and British pilots died. American, British and German workers performed prodigies of labour in loading and unloading the aircraft. Day after day the transports rose from airfields in West Germany and flew the air corridors into Berlin. Often they were buzzed by Soviet aircraft. Often they flew in atrocious conditions. But the airlift worked.

The blockade of Berlin brought another dividend to the Western alliance, one which the Soviets failed to anticipate. The behaviour of the people of West Berlin was exemplary. It is not too much to say that their demeanour under heavy and continuous Soviet pressure wrote the passport for Germany's return into the West European family of nations.

The West Berliners were led by their elected mayor, Ernst Reuter. With Clay and Murphy he was a true hero of the blockade. He was an ex-communist well aware of what would befall him should the Allies give in to Russian pressure and leave the city. With serene courage he oranised meeting after meeting to protest against the blockade. The crowds that attended were infiltrated by spies from the Soviet sector noting the names of the West Berliners present. Overall, the Berliners' response to Soviet pressure and threats demonstrated a corporate sense of defiance not unlike that shown by Londoners during the German bombings of 1940.

The event that epitomised the Berliners' defiance of the Soviet Union was the demonstration organised by Reuter on 9 September 1949. It was not simply a demonstration, it was a victory.

The site chosen was the open space in the British sector opposite the gutted Reichstag. Reuter had hoped for an attendance of a few thousand or more. Two hours before the demonstration was due to begin, the streets leading toward the Reichstag were filled by the ordinary folk of West Berlin; women with children in arms, toddlers walking with their parents, old men, young men, many without a leg, a hand or an eye. They filled the space in front of the Bundestag and flowed into the streets around it. They cheered Reuter's defiance of the Soviets. They cheered the Allies. They cheered when a young man clambered to the top of the Brandenberg Gate and tore down the Soviet flag. They cheered a few scattered shots from the Soviet sector.

This was the most remarkable demonstration of defiant German stubborness of the cold war. It was impossible thereafter to look upon Germans, at least upon West Berliners, as anything but allies in the struggle with the Soviets.

When the blockade ended in May 1949, American and British and, to a lesser degree, French attitudes toward the West Germans had changed. The memories of 1933-45, the Hitler period, had not been dissipated. But as the Soviet military and political pressure mounted, exemplified by the take-over in Prague and the Berlin blockade, the Western powers sought some form of collective security that would balance the Soviet Union's growing military power. In the spring of 1949 there were two American divisions and a regiment of constabulary, and two British divisions in West Germany. The French army of occupation was ill-equipped and ill-trained. The Belgians and Dutch were negligible military factors.

Save for a few, Field-Marshal Montgomery among them, no-one at that time considered the rearmament of the West Germans as part of any organisation for collective security. Yet within a few years, West Germany, too, would take her place in the Alliance.

As a result of the Vandenberg Resolution of the United States Senate, planning for what was eventually to become the North Atlantic Treaty Organisation began in Washington in February 1949. The discussions were on the ambassadorial level with the United States, Britain, France, Canada, the Netherlands, Belgium and Luxembourg taking part. The negotiators faced three basic questions: Should the treaty deal with more than military security? What nations should be the signatories? What commitments should it contain? Acheson, who orchestrated the meetings, was anxious that the Allies should not go too far too fast in their planning lest they affront influential senators and the House Committee on Foreign Affairs.

It soon became apparent that, as the Soviet threat grew, other nations became interested. First Norway, then Denmark and Iceland, and finally Italy showed their interest in the treaty then being drafted and in joining the organisation.

The movement of the three Scandinavian states toward membership was especially significant. The Soviets had put outrageous pressure on all three, with Norway the first target. Norway, like Denmark, had learned in the Second World War that neutrality was a costly illusion. After some argument, both accepted the basic purpose of the treaty: it was to be a system of collective defence against attack.

The French proved awkward. They would not accept Norway as a member without Italy's admission. This was understandable, because Italy would help guard France's southern flank in the Mediterranean. Then, not for the first or the last time, General de Gaulle attacked the project that would bring Western Europe at least the promise of security. The North Atlantic Treaty, he proclaimed, was simply a device of the Americans to organise Europe in their defence. Fortunately, since de Gaulle was out of power, his diatribe had less impact than he anticipated.

Italy was a problem. It could not be considered geographically a North Atlantic state and its military capacities were low. But Acheson and his colleagues reasoned that an Italy isolated from the treaty and with a numerically strong communist party might be vulnerable to Soviet pressures. The West's intention was to bolster Italy's resistance to any Soviet approach, political, diplomatic or military, and, once the treaty was signed and Italy a full member, increase the flow of modern arms.

Portugal was a problem for another reason. No-one could doubt the country's strategic importance, located as it was near the entrance to the Mediterranean and possessing invaluable airfields in the Azores. The problem lay in the dictatorship of Dr Salazar, which was anathema to the Scandinavians and to the Labour government in Britain. The distaste for the Salazar regime had been exacerbated by the conclusion of an alliance between Portugal and Franco's Spain, a country which had earned the even deeper hostility of those governments anxious about Salazar's membership in a league of democratic states. In the end, strategic interests prevailed over political susceptibilities.

Italy, Denmark, Iceland and Portugal were invited by the eight original builders of NATO to join in signing the treaty. The invitation to Italy, which changed the geographical nature of the alliance, prompted anxious requests from Turkey and Greece that they, too, be included. The two governments, the first recipients of aid under the Truman Doctrine, felt abandoned. Two years later these two states were admitted to membership and became NATO's eastern flank in the Mediterranean.

By 18 March 1949, the treaty was ready for public exposure in the United States and the eleven other capitals. As might be expected, it met with sharp opposition from isolationist and conservative circles, especially over Article III, the guts of the pact. This bound the parties to develop their individual and collective capacity to resist armed attack by self-help and mutual assistance. Acheson, stoutly backed by Truman, carried the day.

On 4 April 1949 the North Atlantic Treaty was signed by the foreign ministers of the twelve governments involved. Here was another watershed in the global contest between the USSR and the United States. Soviet pressures, political, economic and military, had accomplished the seemingly impossible feat of promoting in peacetime a defensive alliance among the most powerful states of Western Europe. Once again a Western response more than matched the communist provocation.

Five years later West Germany joined, adding half a million men and over a thousand aircraft to the alliance. The inclusion of West Germany was part of a diplomatic package which gave the country full sovereignty, while the Germans in turn pledged themselves never to manufacture atomic, bacteriological or chemical weapons. A list of major weapons was also proscribed, although since then the West Germans have built, with NATO's sanction, at least one of the weapons on the list—tanks. By 1980, the West German contribution to NATO, somewhat scaled down in numbers of men and aircraft, constituted the strongest single force on the Alliance's central front.

The signing of the North Atlantic treaty in 1949 was quickly followed by Truman's designation of General Dwight D. Eisenhower as the organisation's commander-in-chief or, in the more grandiose wording of his title, Supreme Allied Commander. Eisenhower was the one soldier who enjoyed the confidence not only of European military men but of governments and parliaments as well. He would need this confidence, for the military and organisational problems he faced were tremendous. There were thirty Soviet divisions in central Europe as opposed to about six American and British divisions and twelve ill-armed French divisions. The American force of three and a half divisions was nearly doubled, the British added another two divisions and the flow of military supplies from the United States and from ordnance plants in Europe began to meet the inadequacies of the French and other NATO forces. The United States Navy strengthened the Sixth Fleet in the Mediterranean. The British fleet there was reinforced and the inclusion of Italy in the Alliance provided bases for these and other NATO fleets.

NATO grew and worked. In the decades of its existence, sixty-four Allied divisions in northern, central and southern Europe, plus supporting air and naval forces and tactical nuclear weapons, have deterred Soviet military aggression into Alliance territory.

It achieved what British statesmen, Churchill in particular, had long yearned for: a permanent American military commitment to Europe. Apart from Charles de Gaulle, no-one questioned the right of the Americans to take over the leadership of this alliance. The United States had drawn its citizens from every country in Europe. All the peoples enslaved by communism—including the Russians themselves—now had compatriots in America who nourished their longing for freedom. But outside Europe, a colossal shift in the power structure of the world was taking place, and here, in what came to be called the Third World, America's role was less clear. At a distance of more than thirty years it is hard to imagine the scale and nature of this shift of power. Great Britain was represented at Yalta and Potsdam not just because it had been in the war from the start, but because the British Empire covered something like a quarter of the earth's surface and included a quarter of the earth's population. The winding-up of this empire took place more rapidly and more completely than anyone could have believed possible at the time, and we can only understand the way the cold war has developed if we take note of some of the consequences of this dramatic shift of power.

Once, way back at that never-to-be-forgotten discussion between Stalin and Hitler's emissary, Ribbentrop, the subject of British rule in India had come up. It was ridiculous, said Stalin, that India should be controlled by so few people. British officials pricked up their ears at Stalin's remark when the record of it came into their hands after Germany's surrender. But nothing had come of it. Hitler and Stalin were both impressed by Britain's achievement in acquiring so vast an empire with such little effort. The danger to the British empire came not from these European dictators but from the one across the Atlantic Ocean. At Teheran, in 1943, Roosevelt had approached Stalin in his usual ingratiating manner and said that he had plans for India which he would like to share with him—privately, of course. 'The best solution to India,' said Roosevelt, 'would be reform from the bottom, somewhat on the Soviet line.'

What Stalin really thought of Roosevelt's suggestion is not on record. At Yalta, the American president made another approach, this time about the Far East. Matters in this part of the world, Roosevelt hinted, could best be settled between the two of them, that is, between the Soviet Union and America directly. But, ever cautious, Stalin warned that Churchill would 'kill us' if Britain were not included in the post-war system. Despite its humiliations in the war in Asia, the British Empire retained an appearance of strength at the war's end, even if it was an empty shell, and this shell probably suited Stalin's purposes better than what was to him the obvious alternative of an American world system.

In India, the end of British rule came with unexpected speed. The granting of self-government had been implied in India's participation in the war; but the terms under which it might actually be made proved insoluble. Discussions on India's future invariably foundered on the rivalry between Moslems and Hindus, and on the strange personality of Gandhi, known as the Mahatma or Great Soul. An advocate of non-violence in humanity's most violent age, Gandhi had spent all his days (2338 of them in gaol) devising various forms of civil disobedience to British authority, first in South Africa and from the end of the First World War in India, Gandhi's ascetic habits and a special quality of saintliness won him the devotion of India's masses and the respect of other Indian leaders who recognised in him a political force far greater than anything they could command. The Indian Communist Party, founded in 1925, made no impression whatever during Gandhi's lifetime.

The British were baffled by Gandhi. Churchill called him a seditious fakir and spoke of the nauseating and humiliating spectacle of his half-naked figure striding up the steps of the Viceroy's palace to parley on equal terms with the representative of the King–Emperor. British newsreels called him 'the little man from India in shawl and loincloth'. Lord Wavell, a kindly scholar–soldier who was last-but-one Viceroy, thought him a 'malevolent old politician'. Jinnah, the Moslem leader who was Gandhi's greatest political enemy, called him 'a cunning fox'.

Britain's new Labour government was no more able than its predecessors to make headway in resolving India's constitutional problem. If ideologically the socialists felt more committed to Congress leaders like Nehru, they were quite unable to understand the underlying conservatism of Gandhi, who pleaded for a deferment of independence in order that India might remain undivided. The Labour government's answer was to appoint a new viceroy, the vain and inexperienced, but glamorous, Admiral Mountbatten, who provided just the right image for a government-on-the-run. Previous viceroys had laboured conscientiously to provide rationally and disinterestedly for India's future. Mountbatten's contribution was to accelerate the programme for independence so that Britain might gain the credit for a good intention without incurring the cost of it.

An interim government had been formed in August 1946, with Nehru as prime minister. In February 1947, the British government announced that independence would come by June the following year. In March, Mountbatten was installed in New Delhi; by May he had decided on partition and a quick withdrawal of British troops; a month later he brought the date of independence forward by several months, naming midnight 14-15 August 1947 as the day on which it would take place.

The partition of India tore apart the centuries-old fabric of Indian life and released forces which neither Viceroy or Mahatma could control. Throughout northern India, in scenes of unbelievable savagery, different communities of Hindus, Moslems and Sikhs slaughtered each other in a bloodletting which accounted for some one million lives. On 30 January 1948 Gandhi himself was assassinated by a young Hindu fanatic as he walked to his evening prayer-meeting. Meanwhile, in orderly fashion, the British withdrew, their bands playing to the last and leaving their erstwhile friends, the princes and the rajahs, to make the best terms they could with India's new rulers. By the end of February 1948 the last British troops had gone.

To accommodate the ninety million Moslems whom Jinnah represented, but whose language he never learned to speak, the British allowed a new concept in nationhood to come into being. Pakistan, the name given to this new state, was based on a religious idea, namely that of an Islamic republic. Pakistan was itself divided into two separate entities, an eastern part centred on the Bay of Bengal, the future Bangladesh, and a western part which contained the martial tribes of northern India with whom the British had always felt most at home.

The end of British rule in India meant that the old-style European colonialism was finished everywhere, although it would take more than three decades for the process of decolonisation to work itself out. It was a process which added greatly to the number of pieces on the cold-war chessboard and, incidentally, completely changed the character of the United Nations. India herself was now a leading force in the politics of neutralism.

In Palestine, where Britain ruled under a League of Nations mandate after the eviction of the Turks in the First World War, the end of Hitler's war meant that Britain had to face another intractable problem: how to reconcile its commitment, made in the First World War, to provide the Jews with a national home with her economic and strategic interests in the Arab world. Modern Zionism had been born in the ghettos of Eastern Europe. It had gathered strength largely as a workers' movement, borrowing many elements from international socialism. The most forceful of the Zionist leaders, David Ben-Gurion, had first come to Palestine when the country was ruled by the Turks. He was a passionate admirer of Lenin, but a visit to Moscow in 1923 opened his eyes to the reality of Soviet communism. His conviction that one day the Jews would have their own independent state in Palestine seemed wildly unrealistic to the intellectuals of the Zionist movement, like Chaim Weizmann, who believed in going along with the ruling power, Britain, rather than antagonising it. Ben-Gurion would have none of this. When Hitler's extermination camps were uncovered, the Jews were able to present a more emotional case to the world than the Arabs, whose public image at this time was low. Britain's attempt to clamp down on the number of Jews allowed into Palestine was answered by Ben-Gurion with a call for unrestricted, if illegal, immigration and for the building-up of an underground Jewish administration, with its own military forces, all with an eye to a future state of Israel.

Thousands of illegal immigrants, many of them survivors of Nazi persecution, now sought entry into their promised land only to find themselves intercepted by British troops and returned, often forcibly, to camps in Cyprus and Europe. The spectacle of Jewish men and women, recent victims of the Nazis, being herded once more at bayonet-point behind barbed wire made devastating propaganda against Britain which the Zionists exploited to the full, especially in America.

In the Middle East, as everywhere else, President Truman inherited the legacy of Roosevelt's double-dealing. America's strategic interests, like those of the Western world generally, lay in maintaining the friendship of the Arab kingdoms which had enlarged their dominions when the Turks had moved out. Between the wars, Britain had filled the vacuum left by the departing Turks; but she was unable to continue the role without the support of the United States. This support was not forthcoming, nor was America herself prepared to fill the new vacuum which would be created if Britain withdrew. In the long run and viewed in the context of general decolonisation throughout the world, a Zionist state which depended largely on immigrants from Europe and international Jewish finance would come to appear as running counter to the tide of history, a last gasp of Western imperialism, as it were. But Truman was unable to dissociate himself from the political pressure of American Jewry. 'I do not have hundreds of thousands of Arabs among my constituents' he once said. Although he was angered by the unscrupulousness of the Zionists, and despite the advice he received from the State Department and other senior members of his government, he bent to Jewish arguments.

At the same time Britain was the target for a sustained programme of terror mounted by Jewish underground units. It is ironic to reflect that it was the Jews themselves who first introduced into the Middle East the systematic use of assassination and intimidation through bombings and machine-gun attacks against the established authorities. Lord Moyne, the British Minister in residence in the Middle East, was struck down in Cairo late in 1944. But the most spectacular incident was the blowing-up of the King David Hotel in Jerusalem in July 1946 by a terrorist group led by Menachim Begin, a future prime minister of Israel.

Harassed on all sides, unable to satisfy Arabs or Jews, sniped at by America and burdened by its many other troubles, Britain threw in its hand. In February 1947 she referred the problem to the United Nations. Terror and counter-measures continued. In July 1947, in a particularly distressing incident, Jewish terrorists kidnapped and cold-bloodedly murdered two British sergeants. In September, Britain announced it would shortly be giving up the Mandate and soon it named the date, 14 May 1948, when this would take place.

Once the future of Palestine became a matter of international debate it was inevitably turned into a factor in the politics of the cold war, which it has remained ever since. On 29 November 1947 the United Nations was due to vote on a proposal, strongly promoted by Zionists, that Palestine should be partitioned. Intense lobbying preceded the crucial vote with international Jewry mounting a formidable public relations campaign which threw the American government into confusion when it seemed that Truman was at odds with his own officials. Crude commercial pressures were applied to states which depended on American goodwill, such as Haiti, the Philippines and Liberia, the last being persuaded to support partition as a result of a hint that the American Firestone Tyre and Rubber Company might otherwise retaliate with economic sanctions. It has been alleged that several delegates were bribed by American–Jewish interests.

In the event, partition secured the necessary two-thirds majority, with the Soviet Union and America for once voting on the same side, something which naturally did not prevent the Soviet Union from subsequently switching its support to the Arab cause.

As 14 May 1948 approached and Britain prepared to leave, the armies of five Arab states stood poised on the frontiers of Palestine. Ben-Gurion was strongly advised not to proclaim Jewish independence for fear the Jews would be annihilated by the Arabs, who were more numerous and better armed. The highly respected General

Marshall, Truman's Secretary of State, pressed this view, intimating that United States' recognition of an independent Jewish state was unlikely.

Ben-Gurion, however, was not to be deterred. An opportunity like this, he believed, might never recur. The Jews owed it to their history to seize this supreme moment of destiny. Perhaps he was influenced by his old admiration for the way Lenin had acted in 1917. On 14 May 1948 he duly proclaimed the independence of the new state of Israel.

The Arabs attacked even as he was making his independence broadcast to the world. In the brief but savage war that followed, several Jewish settlements were overrun and for a time it looked as if the new state would die in infancy. But the Jews—now Israelis—held their ground. New weapons, secretly purchased before the end of the Mandate, arrived just in time to turn the tables on the Arabs. President Truman, in a surprise move, recognised the new state within hours of Ben-Gurion's proclamation. Fighting for their very existence, Israeli forces kept the road to Jerusalem open as a symbol of their racial claims in Palestine. The Arabs were worsted and forced to give ground. By the time an armistice was agreed on under United Nations auspices, Israel had found its nationhood.

Repercussions from this first Arab–Israeli war were felt immediately in Egypt, another area of special British interest which dated back to the opening of the Suez Canal in the previous century. During the war against Germany, the British had kept a tight hold over Egyptian affairs, building up huge bases along the Suez Canal and turning Cairo into the nerve-centre of Allied strategy for the Middle East. Egyptian nationalists welcomed the advance of Rommel's Africa Corps across the desert, but the British victory at El Alamein, in October 1942, put an end to their hopes. For most of the war, in fact and as a matter of convenience, Egypt remained neutral until, as a result of the Yalta Conference, it was agreed that she should declare war on Germany and so qualify as a founder-member of the United Nations.

Once the German war was over, Britain clearly had to go, which it did reluctantly and in stages, the last stage being the evacuation of its bases along the Suez Canal. In the process, Britain arranged for the Sudan—previously, the Anglo–Egyptian Sudan where the ghost of General Gordon hovered over Khartoum—to become an independent sovereign state.

The departure of the British left Egyptian affairs in the hands of King Farouk, one of the oriental potentates Roosevelt had visited on his return from Yalta. Farouk was a descendant of the Albanian adventurer, Mahomet Ali, who had wrested power from the Turks at the beginning of the nineteenth century and begun the process of giving Egypt a European-style face-lift. But circumstances had turned Farouk into a playboy and a weakling. He had been forced to toe the British line during the war and the corruption of his court had caused Egyptians to be despised by outsiders. The British called them 'wogs', a derisive term which stood for 'wily oriental gentleman' and which conjured up an image of an obsequious official who would do anything you asked him—for a price—or the cynical dragomen who haunted the bazaars and tourist spots, procurers of any form of vice desired by Western man.

Egypt's army had been one of those most heavily engaged in the 1948-9 war against Israel. Its poor performance was resented by many younger officers, who felt betrayed by their seniors and were deeply humiliated by British attitudes, especially the way Britain had dictated to them during the war against Germany. For ten years a group of these young officers, led by a certain Gamal Abdul Nasser, nursed their resentments and plotted revenge. Nasser later described how the British came to be hated by the Egyptians even more than the Ottoman Turks had been before them. He and his friends adapted an Egyptian curse formerly directed against the Turks: 'As a little child,' Nasser wrote, 'every time I saw aeroplanes flying overhead, I used to shout:

O God Almighty, I wish,
A calamity overtake the English.

In July 1952 the officers struck against Farouk and his government. The king's life was spared and he went into exile in the south of France. Nasser for a time remained in the background, the figurehead for the revolution being a respected Egyptian army officer, General Neguib.

Nasser's revolution had no programme or ideology. Its dynamic was Egyptian nationalism, he himself being the first ethnic Egyptian to rule in Cairo since the Pharaohs. Anti-British riots had flared up at intervals before the *coup d'état* against Farouk and Nasser himself was carried forward on a huge upsurge of popular feeling. But he had nothing with which he could satisfy this feeling, except to feed it with negative sentiment against outsiders, particularly the Israelis. Within Egypt, the revolution brought some tightening-up against corruption and vice, but its lack of any positive aim except a furtherance of Egyptian nationalism led to greater political repression than the Egyptians had experienced under the British or Farouk and to a rapid decline in the welfare of the people.

When Molotov visited Hitler in November 1940 France had fallen, the Germans were masters of Europe, and Britain, it seemed, was finished. Germany, Japan and Russia could dispose of the world between them. In the 1970s or 1980s, Hitler said, they would need to consider some kind of 'hemisphere defence' against the United States of America, but until then the rest of the globe was theirs for the taking. What would Moscow like? Without hesitating, Molotov answered for his master. Stalin often spoke of Russia's historic destiny as lying in Asia. Southward towards the Persian Gulf and neighbouring territories, said Molotov, was the natural direction for Russia to move. Many years would pass before these ambitions would be realisable; in the meantime, it was further east in Asia that communism was on the march.

4 Hot War in Asia

The collapse of a German order in central Europe had enabled Stalin to advance communist rule a thousand miles to the west of the frontiers of the Soviet Union. In Asia, the collapse of a Japanese order brought opportunities for communist aggression on an even larger scale. While the formation of NATO stabilised the situation in the West, so that the history of the cold war in Europe concerns politics, diplomacy and psychology rather than armed conflict, in the East, no such containment of communism was possible.

In February 1948, under cover of an Asian Youth Congress held in Calcutta, various Asian communist parties were ordered to get going with terrorism or insurgency. Gandhi's example of non-violence was not recommended by Moscow. At first, this outburst of communist aggression took the form of what appeared to be legitimate nationalist movements against the old colonial powers, movements which were in part satisfied by the granting of independence to the territories concerned. The communist elements were thus exposed for what they were and suppressed by the new national governments, although in some cases, as in Malaya, fighting against communist guerrillas continued for many years. Transfer of power went smoothly in Burma in January 1948 and in Ceylon (now Sri Lanka) in February 1948, and rather less smoothly in the Dutch East Indies, where Sukarno had proclaimed a republic on the island of Java in August 1945 and went on to form the unitary state of Indonesia, despite Dutch opposition. Malaya was eventually to become independent in 1957 and Singapore in 1958. In the Philippines, the communists had played an important part in resistance to Japanese occupation and they enjoyed some initial success after the war; but by 1954 they too would be defeated. The French empire in Indochina created a different kind of problem, one which was to lead to the Vietnam War and is best considered later.

All these events were initially dwarfed by the momentous happenings in China, a country which had entered its own nationalist revolution in 1911 under Dr Sun Yat Sen and which, largely for appearances' sake, had been considered a great power by the Western Allies, America in particular, in the Second World War. Two men, both legatees of Sun Yat Sen's movement, contended for power: Chiang Kai Shek, the Nationalist commander-in-chief, and Mao Tse-Tung, his principal communist rival.

China's Communist Party, in common with others, was a creation of the Comintern. But Mao Tse-Tung was not initially a dominant figure in Chinese communism. Early in his career, he developed a deep scepticism about applying the Marxist–Leninist principle of proletarian revolution in a country like China, with its overwhelming peasant population. He was proved right when a more senior communist, trained in Moscow, Li Li-san, tried to start a revolution by organising the workers and by attempting to seize Shanghai, Wuhan and other big cities. So complete was Stalin's hold on the Chinese Communist Party at that time that in July 1928 its Sixth Congress was held in Moscow and Li was made secretary-general on Stalin's orders. The policy Li tried to put into effect was Stalin's and Stalin was going by the Marxist–Leninist book. The Communists, however, were utterly defeated, and Li Li-san was made the scapegoat: accused of 'Trotskyism', he lost his job and was recalled to Moscow, where he spent many years.

Mao, who had toed the Moscow line reluctantly after criticising it, concentrated on organising the peasants into 'soviets'. He emerged as the undisputed boss of the Communist Party after the famous Long March of 1934-5, in which he led thousands of followers over thousands of miles to the caves of Yenan to escape from Chiang Kai-shek's pursuing nationalist forces.

Throughout the Second World War period, when the Japanese had invaded China, Mao Tse-tung and his followers were relatively isolated in the international communist movement. In effect, Mao was going his own way, fighting a guerrilla war against the Japanese, but also resisting Chiang Kai-shek's attempts to stamp out the communists, and building up his own power base. During this period, Stalin maintained superficially cordial relations with the anti-communist Chiang, who had received part of his training in Moscow and could be relied on to kill Chinese communists as much as Japanese.

The apparent lack of confidence between Stalin and Mao turned out however, to be deceptive. Understandably, Stalin had concentrated Russia's war effort upon the defeat of the invading Nazis. We cannot really tell what lay behind his policy in the Far East. His eleventh-hour decision to declare war on Japan on 8 August 1945, two days after the first atomic bomb had been dropped on Hiroshima, enabled the Soviet Union to take part in the Japanese surrender. By moving into China in the last few days of the war, the Red Army created the geopolitical conditions for Mao's subsequent defeat of Chiang's forces in the looming Chinese civil war.

By the time of Japan's surrender, in August 1945, most of Inner Mongolia and Manchuria were in the hands of Stalin's forces. The Soviets promptly removed most of Manchuria's industrial plant to the Soviet Union, but they were able to hand over to Mao and his military commander, Lin Piao, enormous stocks of arms and ammunition seized from the defeated Japanese.

For a moment, the Americans considered airlifting Chiang's forces to fill the vacuum left by the departing Japanese, but they chose, instead, to attempt to mediate between Chiang and Mao, with what ultimate purpose it is not clear. Because of his own mistrust of Stalin, Mao sent strong signals to Washington that he would favour American assistance if it were offered rather than Russian. We cannot tell how genuine this move was or whether, if followed up, it would have made any essential difference to Chinese communism. The Americans were not well served by their advisers in China, nor by pressure groups in the United States, and by continuing to support Chiang, they drove Mao into Stalin's camp. More than twenty years would pass, and much blood and tears shed, before this policy could be revised. As it was, armed by Moscow and by the weapons and supplies taken from the Japanese, Mao Tse-tung went on to defeat Chiang's nationalist forces. On 1 October 1949 he proclaimed the Chinese People's Republic. Immediate recognition came from the Soviet Union and its satellites. Mao rewarded Stalin by going to Moscow, where the Soviet dictator kept him waiting for weeks before deigning to receive him. On 14 February 1950 the two men signed a Thirty-year Treaty of Friendship, Alliance and Mutual Assistance. The terms for China were severe. A series of economic agreements followed, and swarms of Soviet technicians settled in China to supervise joint projects, mainly to build up China's industry.

Ten years later, the great rift between China and the Soviet Union split the communist world. But in 1950, China had accepted satellite status and a considerable degree of Soviet control.

The creation of this new and apparently monolithic bloc with a population already approaching a billion confronted the United States with a series of grave new problems. Not the least of these was a bitter public debate over 'Who Lost China?' Since the country had never been America's to win or lose, the debate was largely diversionary. But it illustrated a certain arrogant insensitivity in the United States towards other people, which was to be a constant impediment to the formulation of a successful global foreign policy. It also damaged the reputations and in some cases the careers of some gifted public servants. To many Americans, particularly in the Republican Party, a communist China was a more serious challenge to America's world outlook than a communist Europe, since a strong emotional element in America's tradition has always been a turning away from Europe. In this tradition, it was westwards that men went free and sought a new dawn, westwards across America, westwards across the Pacific.

But now upon this western horizon loomed the gigantic menace of a Red China joined in one huge land mass to the Soviet Union. All that remained, it seemed, of the old westerly dream was Japan, recently America's most detested enemy, and some islands salvaged from the disaster—notably, the Philippines, to which the Americans had granted independence in July 1946, and Taiwan, where Chiang Kai-shek had retreated with the remnants of his forces. Stalin had been refused a share in the occupation of Japan, and the country, with all its potential economic strength, was virtually an American dependency. But nearest to Japan on the continent of Asia was Korea, and in North Korea, by 1950, there was already a Soviet satellite state.

North Korea had come under Stalin's control in a manner that was almost fortuitous. The Pacific war had been fought by the Americans and their Western Allies, and it fell to two American colonels in the Pentagon to define the surrender zones in all theatres of the war. It was about midnight on the night of 10-11 August 1945, and they were given half an hour to do their work. One of them was Dean Rusk, who later became Secretary of State. The two young men placed a small-scale map of the Far East in front of them and in some haste drew a line dividing Korea along the 38th Parallel. As they saw it, this line offered an advantage to the US side, as it passed north of

Seoul and thus left the Korean capital under the control of the American Armed Forces.

At the very moment the two colonels were drawing their dividing-line, Stalin's forces were entering Korea, which the Japanese had annexed in 1910. The Soviets occupied Pyongyang on 24 August 1945. On 10 September the Americans accepted the surrender of the Japanese forces in Korea and the 38th Parallel duly became the dividing-line between the Soviet and the American occupation forces. Thus, as in Germany, surrender zones became zones of occupation, and zones of occupation became identified with the rival world systems which the cold war represented. On 15 August 1948, after general elections supervised by the Americans, a Republic of South Korea came into existence. On 9 September the same year, Kim II Sung, who was emerging as an oriental carbon copy of Stalin, proclaimed a Korean People's Democratic Republic in Pyongyang. Significantly, it claimed authority over the whole of the Korean peninsula.

Mao's victory in China left South Korea more vulnerable than ever to communist aggression. In deciding to order the North Koreans to invade the south, Stalin may have intended to outflank Mao's new regime. He probably assumed that the United States would not intervene since, on 12 January 1950, the American Secretary of State, Dean Acheson, had made a statement placing Korea outside the United States' defensive perimeter'. To Stalin the way seemed clear for aggression.

On Saturday 24 June 1950 the State Department received a cable reporting that North Korea had launched a heavy attack across the 38th Parallel which divided North and South Korea. This was not simply a patrol in force such as the North had launched in the past but the start of a major offensive. An armoured force was pushing fast toward the South Korean capital of Seoul and Kimpo Airport. It signalled the start of the Korean War.

Truman and his advisors were certain that the attack had been planned, mounted, supplied and instigated by the Soviet Union. The Administration acted promptly. Their first course was to push a condemnatory resolution through the United Nations, their second to send American troops to South Korea to stem the tide of invaders flooding south.

The Security Council met on the afternoon of Sunday 25 June. Jacob Malik, the Soviet representative on the council, had decided to boycott the body because of the presence of a Nationalist Chinese. He was in Moscow, so there was no Soviet vote and the resolution passed by a margin of nine votes to none, with only Yugoslavia abstaining. Malik's boycott was a serious political blunder. For it allowed the United States, under the aegis of the resolution, to rally other members of the United Nations to the defence of South Korea.

Halting South Korea's retreat and avoiding a *débâcle* was a good deal more difficult. From the start it was clear that only American troops were immediately available to do the job. But under an agreement with the Soviet Union, the last American occupation forces had been withdrawn from South Korea on 29 June 1949. The nearest troops were in Japan. Stalin had timed his move carefully.

The cumulative effect of other Soviet adventures in Czechoslovakia, Iran and against Berlin was of great importance in determining the United States response. Here was one of those 'just' wars which America could fight without compromising its liberal principles or offending isolationist prejudice. The prevailing wisdom in Washington was that although the invasion did not constitute a *casus belli* against the Soviet Union, it was clear that America must accept the Soviet–North Korean challenge or suffer a serious loss of prestige throughout the free world.

Even then, however, there were shadings of the United States' intentions. The President, Acheson, now Secretary of State, and others were determined that the North Korean attack should be halted and seen to be halted. Others in the military sought complete victory over the communists which might involve, as proved to be the case, an invasion of North Korea.

While the form and scope of American military intervention was under debate, Acheson and the State Department took another significant step. A second resolution was introduced into the Security Council calling on United Nations members to give South Korea such help as might be needed to repel the invasion and restore peace.

Again Malik was absent, and the resolution was adopted with Yugoslavia, again, dissenting and Egypt and India abstaining. This enabled British, Canadian and Australian units to fight alongside the Americans under the United Nations Flag.

After a hurried visit to the war theatre by Brigadier-General John Church of General Douglas MacArthur's staff, it was clear that the situation could not be restored without the large-scale intervention of United States troops. By 29 June, the military situation had worsened. The South Koreans had retreated over the Han River south of Seoul, the capital, which was now in communist hands. The gravity of the situation was underlined by a message from MacArthur, who had visited the front and, on his return to his headquarters in Tokyo, reported that the Korean retreat was a rout. The American commander asked for authority to send a regimental combat team to South Korea at once. This was to be the vanguard of a two-division force to be despatched as soon as possible.

It was soon evident that this original response to the invasion would not suffice. The divisions brought from Japan lacked combat experience, the logistical arrangements were faulty and the South Koreans proved of little help in stemming the tide of invasion. Again the cold war theme of Soviet action and an overwhelming American reaction appeared. On 15 July the President reported to Congress that additional men, supplies and equipment must be sent to MacArthur's forces, that the size and material support of America's armed forces must be increased 'substantially' and that the military strength of the nations associated with America in the Korean War must be bolstered by United States help.

The impact of this action was lessened by the first of a series of curious episodes involving MacArthur and the Nationalist Chinese. After a trip to Taiwan and, understandably, a hero's welcome from the Generalissimo, the Far East commander ordered three squadrons of fighters to Taiwan to assist in the island's defence. He did not think it necessary to inform the Defense Department of his action. This was followed by a message to the Veterans of Foreign Wars in which he attacked those who advocated 'appeasement and defeatism' in the Pacific. The long duel between the brilliant, volatile commander-in-chief and his superiors in Washington had begun. But MacArthur already was preparing for a counter-offensive, although, to the watchers in Washington who knew his assets, this plan seemed blatantly over-optimistic. But, not for the first time, MacArthur confounded his military critics.

MacArthur's great counter-stroke against the communists was the Inchon landing. He had realised in June, when he first visited the front, that the advancing North Koreans would depend, as they drove further south, on long and vulnerable lines of supply. This situation was the genesis of the Inchon landing well in the rear of the invading forces. If successful, it would put his troops in a position to recapture the lost capital of Seoul.

MacArthur liked the plan. It appealed to his sense of the dramatic. It savoured of the days of 'island-hopping' in the Second World War when his strategy, damned by many Americans, had proven victorious. But few others liked the idea. The Navy objected that it had been given the task of landing the ground forces in conditions that were highly dangerous; the sea-approach to the harbour of Inchon was through a narrow channel with a strong current and which, in addition, was studded with shoals and rocks. The tidal range was high and at the ebb the harbour became an enormous mud-flat. The Marine division, which was to make the landing with its flank covered by the Army's Seventh division, had similar objections. One of the most important objections, and the one to which MacArthur apparently paid the least attention, was that the withdrawal of the Marine division from the southern front would weaken the area.

Critics of the operation made their case at a meeting at MacArthur's headquarters in Tokyo on 23 August. The front in the south, they said, was just holding. Any diversion of effort would imperil its solidity. General Collins emphasised the folly of dividing forces in the face of a numerically superior enemy. The Navy emphasised the navigational and other dangers to a successful landing.

MacArthur, puffing on his inevitable corn-cob pipe, heard them out and then defended his plan with a mixture of military good sense and hyperbole. 'The very arguments you have made to me as to the impractibilities involved,' he said, 'will tend to ensure for me the element of surprise. For the enemy commander will reason that no-one would be so rash as to make such an attempt.' Then in his best mixture of mysticism and military reality he added, 'I can almost hear the ticking of the second hand of destiny. We must act now or we will die . . .'

Inchon was a resounding success. It surprised the North Koreans and their Soviet advisers, and forced upon them a withdrawal from their positions in the south. Seoul fell to the Americans, now accompanied by South Korean divisions whose discipline and weaponry had begun to improve.

The victory had another, darker side. It bred in MacArthur and his associates a conviction that there were no limits to what they could do in Korea and, more important, that any foreign intervention, most probably by the Chinese communists, could be handled by the Allies.

MacArthur's confidence was at its greatest during a meeting with President Truman on Guam. The general assured the president that victory had been won in Korea and that the Chinese communists would not attack. The general conceded that the People's Republic of China might be able to put 50,000 to 60,000 men into Korea but that without an air force they would be slaughtered. This must be considered one of the gravest under-estimates of military history.

MacArthur's confidence infected Truman. He returned to Washington satisfied with the military progress that had been made and convinced that the general was loyal to both the Administration and to the foreign policy of the United States.

At that point, in late August, the American and United Nations response to the North Korean invasion had clearly been successful. The military situation had been restored. At the time of the Inchon landing MacArthur had 65,000 American troops under his command. To meet his requests for reinforcements, the Defense Department had sent forces from the continental United States, Hawaii and Puerto Rico. Marine contingents had been pulled out of the Sixth Fleet in the Mediterranean and shipped to the Korean front.

The impact of these forces accelerated the dissolution of the North Korean armies. By 19 October, Pyongyang, the North Korean capital, had been taken and the broken enemy fled northwards towards the Yalu River, well beyond the 38th Parallel that had divided North from South Korea.

The stage was now set for one of the most dramatic episodes in the contest between communism and the West. It involved the defeat of an American army—to date, the only such defeat on the open battlefield in the tangled history of the cold war; the downfall of one of the greatest United States generals; and the arrival on the international scene of a formidable military power, the People's Liberation Army of the People's Republic of China.

MacArthur was determined to drive north and conquer North Korea. Neither he nor his subordinates paid much attention to the possibility of Chinese intervention, although ominous signs that this might occur were beginning to come from Peking. But even without those signs, the American commanders in the field and their political chiefs in Washington should have been more alert to the Chinese interpretation of the military situation. This interpretation was based primarily on the fact that an American or UN advance to the Yalu would place hostile forces on the frontier of Manchuria. This was, and is, China's most important industrial area. Once American aircraft were installed in North Korea, Manchuria's industrial plants and cities would be within easy range of American bombers. This was a risk the Chinese felt they could not run. Their determination was stiffened, although little stiffening was needed, by military advice from Soviet officers in the country.

The success of the Inchon landing prompted a spate of Chinese warnings which made it clear that any offensive into the area south of the Yalu would be regarded by Peking as a direct military threat.

Throughout the East–West contest from 1945 to the present an acute ear for the meaning of what the other side is saying or hinting is essential to success, military, diplomatic or economic. The American ear was stopped in the autumn of 1950 partly because of the over-confidence that followed MacArthur's victory.

Indications of Chinese bellicosity grew. After the South Korean forces had crossed the 38th Parallel, Chou En-lai, China's Foreign Minister, told K.M. Panikkar, India's ambassador in Peking, that if American troops followed, China would fight. When Pyongyang fell, Peking issued a warning that the Chinese people could not and would not tolerate an invasion of the North because they saw such action as a direct challenge to China's security.

At that moment in Washington two powerful schools of thought were in conflict, as they have been almost since the start of the duel with the East. On the one hand there were those who believed that by reconquering and stabilising South Korea the original aims of the United Nations intervention had been attained and that, a lesson having been taught, the West should now turn to the useful if undramatic task of rebuilding the economy of South Korea. In other words, that communism should be contained. The other school of thought, symbolised by General MacArthur and his supporters in the United States, was hellbent on carrying the fight into the communists' camp: in other words, that communism should be rolled back. Armoured by the righteousness of their belief, they were already moving to that end. MacArthur had begun planning for the conquest of North Korea immediately after his meeting with the President in Guam.

A factor which weighed with MacArthur and eroded some of the opposition to his policies in Washington was a low estimate of the communist Chinese military capabilities and the serious doubts over the sincerity of Chinese warnings. Also, American military intelligence in this arena was poor.

Inspired by what now seems an almost unbelievable over-confidence, MacArthur was determined to move north to the Yalu. He had been successful in the Inchon landing, and elsewhere, in dividing his forces. Proposing now to do it again, the division was particularly awkward. His X Corps was to be transported hundreds of miles by sea around the Korean peninsula to Wonsan on the east coast. From that port it would proceed to occupy north-east Korea north of the Yalu. The other major formation, the Eighth Army, was to remain on the west coast and push into north-west Korea. There would be a gap of twenty to fifty miles between the two forces. Headquarters assumed that the country in the gap was too rough to allow large-scale enemy operations. In the event, both the Eighth Army and the X Corps had to divert strong forces to safeguard their open flanks in the gap.

The division of MacArthur's forces, whatever the enemy strength, known or presumed, and whatever influence guerrilla activity would play on the open flanks, was a cardinal mistake that violated the doctrine of unity of command sacred to all armies. But MacArthur was intransigent. General Walton H. Walker, the commander of the Eighth Army, and three major-generals protested the Allied alignment. But, in those days, who could argue with MacArthur, the conqueror of Inchon? He rejected their arguments because, he said, the Taeback range of mountains, the spine of Korea, separated the two forces and made an advance on two unconnected fronts the only feasible strategy.

MacArthur was about to experience the most serious defeat suffered by a United States army since the Civil War. It need not have occurred. The West's aims in Korea could have been consolidated, the strategic balance in north-east Asia stabilised. But these goals were not achieved.

Washington could have intervened and did not. A directive from the Joint Chiefs of Staff on 27 September forbade the employment of non-Korean forces in the provinces bordering on China and the Soviet Union. MacArthur paid no heed. On 24 October he told his commanders to 'drive forward with all speed and full utilisation of their forces'. The weak response from the Joint Chiefs was that these orders were 'not in consonance' with their directive of the previous month.

MacArthur was a master of military politics. His disarming reply was that the revered General George C. Marshall, who was now Secretary of Defense, had agreed that he was to be 'unhampered' in his operations. In any event, MacArthur argued, the South Korean forces in his command were so weak that his orders to push his American troops forward were justified.

The conflict between MacArthur and Washington, which was to distort and complicate America's efforts to check communism in Asia, thus reached another critical point. Resentment was deep in Washington, both in the Defense Department and the State Department, but the general could not be effectively challenged. He was the victor, the war-winner. All that happened in the first few days of the attack into the region south of the Yalu appeared to support his strategy and his overweening confidence. By 26 October 1950 his forward units were at the Yalu.

This must be considered the high point of the American and United Nations' effort in Korea. It was also a focal point in the cold war because it led to the armed intervention of an enemy of far greater consequence than the North Koreans. Having entered the cold war in this way, for nearly a quarter of a century afterwards China exercised a significant, if largely illusory, influence on American military planning. To look ahead: it is highly probable that United States' strategy in the Vietnam War would have taken a more positive course had it not been for the fears, fed by interested parties at the United Nations, of Chinese intervention.

The first Chinese intervention, lasting roughly from 25 October to 7 November, turned the war around. Units of South Korean troops were smashed, and the Americans had to give ground. Then, as suddenly as they had appeared, the Chinese withdrew from the battlefield into the shelter of the hills. But the importance of the advent of the Chinese was not immediately grasped by MacArthur. He believed it was only an attempt by the PLA to rescue the shattered forces of North Korea. This view, totally inaccurate, possibly resulted from a lack of information on the strength of the Chinese forces. Intelligence had erred again. The G-2 estimate on 1 November was that there were about 60,000 Chinese in North Korea. In fact there were about 180,000.

The Chinese concentration in North Korea must be considered a logistical masterpiece. Moving by night and lying low by day in cleverly camouflaged and well-scattered bivouacs, the Chinese went undiscovered by intelligence and unnoticed by the few reconnaissance flights which were able to penetrate the heavy cloud layer in the north.

Although the size of the Chinese forces was not known in Washington, it was obvious to the National Security Council and to the President and his advisers that MacArthur and his command had been caught napping. Tempers were not improved by MacArthur's words and actions.

The Chinese attack across the Yalu, the general declared with his customary hyperbole, was 'one of the most offensive acts of international lawlessness of historic record . . .' Deploring the enemy's 'privileged sanctuary in Manchuria', MacArthur ordered General G. E. Stratemeyer, his Air Force commander, to destroy the bridges over the Yalu which linked Sinuiju and Antung. MacArthur believed that supplies were moving to the Chinese over these bridges.

His orders to Stratemeyer provoked a counter-order from Washington cancelling the operation. All air attacks within five miles of the frontier were banned. MacArthur protested bitterly. The traffic over the bridges, he claimed, threatened 'the ultimate destruction of the forces under my command'. As had happened before, Washington yielded to the imperious commander. On 8 November the Fifth Air Force attacked the bridges and towns on each side of the river with 300 fighter-bombers. The bombing attack had little impact on the campaign. It can be assumed that it reinforced Chinese fears over the danger to Manchurian industry arising from American air-bases in North Korea.

Conventional military wisdom, speaking through General Omar Bradley, the Chairman of the Joint Chiefs of Staff, held that MacArthur's troops would be able to hold their positions against a new Chinese onslaught. But the general insisted that there were to be no operations against Chinese bases in Manchuria, MacArthur's 'sanctuary', because the British had been assured that this strategy would not be pursued. London, like half a dozen other capitals, feared that attacks by ground or air forces into Manchuria would escalate the Chinese military effort and perhaps bring the Soviet Union openly into the conflict.

This apprehension about possible Soviet action was a powerful factor in the relationship between Washington and other NATO capitals. The Europeans' fear was certainly exaggerated. But Western Europe was almost defenceless, the major NATO build-up had not yet begun, many military men predicted that if the Soviets did move they would strike into West Germany.

Incredibly, hours of discussion of military options ended with MacArthur free to pursue, within certain limits, whatever strategy he chose. He was forbidden to bomb Manchuria, but he was free to take other military steps. Since the commander-in-chief had now clearly recovered his confidence, it should have been clear to the White House and the National Security Council that he would choose to resume the offensive northward.

Two factors prevented the Administration from taking a harder position towards MacArthur's new plan; neither it nor MacArthur had any idea of the true strength of the Chinese forces, and the Republicans, who had made substantial gains in recent Congressional elections, were abusing the Administration for its restraint of the national hero.

Despite the misgivings of two of his senior and experienced commanders in the field, one of them expressed in writing, MacArthur ordered a second advance to the Yalu. The result this time was disaster.

The temperature that winter in Korea never rose above zero. The cold stunned the Americans, but did not seem to have the same effect upon their opponents. In great strength, the Chinese forces rose out of the ground and the advance was checked. The Chinese followed with a full-scale attack, throwing thousands of infantry against the Americans in their hilltop positions. The Chinese, as they were to do throughout the fighting, accompanied their attack with a cacophony of sound, drums, bugles, whistles and gongs. The Americans threw back the attacks because of their greater firepower, but it was evident that a further advance was out of the question. Worse was to come. Renewed heavy Chinese attacks destroyed three South Korean divisions, split MacArthur's forces and threatened to cut off large numbers of American troops. The United Nations were again driven to retreat, with British Commonwealth regiments and American units fighting a rearguard action to prevent the retreat turning into a rout.

MacArthur finally realised the gravity of the situation. He sent a message to the Security Council of the United Nations reporting that he was under attack by more than 200,000 Chinese and that the Allies face 'an entirely new war'. But more than messages and florid communiqués were needed to save the situation.

A stand was made. American artillery hammered the Chinese, inflicting casualties of a magnitude for which the PLA was unprepared. The 'human wave' attacks disintegrated under the fire of modern military served by trained gunners. Although the Chinese were ultimately victorious, the cannonade had a lasting effect on the soldiers of the PLA. It taught them that the tactics that had been so successful again Chiang Kai-shek's nationalists and, to a lesser degree, against the Japanese were out of place on a modern, high-intensity battlefield.

But the stand could not go on forever. Under continual pressure, MacArthur's Eighth Army was forced into full retreat, a fact trumpeted to the world by the massive communist propaganda machine in Moscow, Peking and the satellite capitals of Eastern Europe. The communists, after scoring a series of political successes, except for the setback at Berlin, had now produced a startling military victory.

But, as the next few days demonstrated, the PLA lacked the means to exploit their victory on this sector of the front. MacArthur had ordered a retreat back to the 38th Parallel, the old dividing-line between North and South Korea. It was 120 miles to the south, and the withdrawal could have turned into another disaster by a foe equipped for rapid pursuit. The Chinese were not so equipped. They had exhausted their ammunition and other supplies. They had taken very heavy casualties. To keep up pressure on the retreating Allies was beyond their capabilities.

At this critical point in the first war between communist and non-communist forces MacArthur's behaviour was extraordinary. Having ordered a withdrawal to the narrow waist of the Korean peninsula, he then announced that it could not be held because of the inhospitable terrain, inadequate forces and logistical difficulties. Some positive and immediate action must be taken, he proclaimed, otherwise 'steady attrition leading to final destruction can reasonably be contemplated'.

The defeat in Korea was a milestone in the chain of events which eventually brought about MacArthur's removal by Truman. The Administration, feeding on the general's optimism, had been as surprised by the reverse as the general and his staff had been. Senior officers in the Pentagon had begun to think the hitherto unthinkable: the withdrawal of all UN forces in Korea.

To this crisis, MacArthur added provocation. He sent messages to friends in the United States complaining of the inhibitions placed on him by the Administration. No blame lay with him and his staff for the defeat. The guilty were elsewhere: in the State Department, in London, in the Administration itself.

Meanwhile things went from bad to worse. A British rearguard evacuated Pyongyang, the only communist capital ever held by the West, on 5 December. Accompanied by hordes of terrified refugees, the troops shifted south to the 38th Parallel.

The fate of MacArthur's X Corps in the north-east was now critical. American Marine and Army units fought a desperate march to the coast where they were evacuated by sea under cover of aircraft from seven carriers of the Fleet. Casualties were high and the suffering was terrible, but the damage inflicted on the Chinese forces by superior American firepower was unbelievable. By Christmas, the whole of North Korea lay once more under communist control.

The defeat of the American and UN troops in North Korea was a decisive event not only for the Korean War but for the wider political contest between communism and non-communist states. From the military angle, an Asian army had defeated a much better equipped Western army in a series of hard-fought battles and had driven the Westerners more than 250 miles down the Korean peninsula. Not only had the American army and its allies been defeated but the best-known of all American generals had been defeated.

From that point on, the Korean War's character changed drastically. There were no more full-blooded offensives. Instead there was a period of steady retreat, of hard-fought defensive battles, such as that fought by the British on the Imjin River, and finally a series of well-prepared, methodical advances that recovered much of the territory lost in the retirement. But, 'Never again bright morning'. The war could not be lost. But given the political restraints imposed by Washington, it was not going to be won in the MacArthur or any other manner.

The defeat had a peculiar psychological impact upon the American people. More than half of those polled thought that the Third World War was just around the corner. This war phobia was translated into a substantial increase in the defence budget. The Administration had asked for $13.5 billion for 1951. The figure was quadrupled to $52 billion. Like so many other communist successes, before and since, the ultimate result was to strengthen the American military position.

The course of the winter campaign and the subsequent political discussions on the next step had two effects that were little noted at the time. The United States and its UN allies did not even consider a new effort to liberate North Korea from its communist masters. And, although the United States was the primary atomic power in the world, there never was any serious consideration by President Truman of what came to be called 'massive retaliation'. The campaign taught Truman and his advisers the limits of power. Others took longer to grasp the lesson.

After the defeat in North Korea MacArthur found himself increasingly at odds with the Administration. He did not like the policy of containment which was at the basis of UN military strategy. He saw a negotiated peace which left North Korea in communist hands and the Chinese undefeated as a disaster for the country he loved. He believed that there must be a showdown with communist China; and, in the event, he was willing to risk his position—and his soldiers—for his beliefs.

MacArthur, and all other theatre commanders, had been told on 6 December that all their public statements must be cleared by Washington. The general, as was his habit, paid no attention. He issued a military appraisal of the situation which, in fact, was an attack on the policies of the President and the UN and an outright challenge to Peking.

The statement infuriated the White House. Worse was to follow. The Administration was moving toward negotiations for peace in Korea on terms that would be an anathema to MacArthur. On 20 March the general replied to a letter from Representative Joe Martin. MacArthur in his reply fuelled all the old controversies with the White House.

'It seems strangely difficult for some to realise that here in Asia,' MacArthur wrote, 'is where the communist conspirators have elected to make their play for global conquest, and that we have joined the issue thus raised on the battlefield; that here we fight Europe's war with arms while the diplomats there still fight it with words; that if we lose this war to communism in Asia the fall of Europe is inevitable; win it and Europe most probably would avoid war and yet preserve freedom. As you [Martin] pointed out, we must win. There is no substitute for victory . . .'

The letter was read on the floor of the House of Representatives on 5 April. It was seen at once by Democrats and Republicans alike as a challenge to the foreign policy that the President and Secretary of State had fashioned since the defeat in North Korea. Coming from the commander-in-chief, the words seemed to be a demand for the extension of the war in Asia, something that neither the political nor the military powers in Washington sought. The opinion of the Joint Chiefs of Staff and of General Marshall, the Secretary of Defense, was unanimous. MacArthur must go. Marshall, indeed, having read all the exchanges between the Administration and the commander-in-chief, concluded that MacArthur should have been fired two years earlier.

The final action took place on 11 April 1951. From the White House came an announcement which began: 'With deep regret I have concluded that General of the Army Douglas MacArthur is unable to give his wholehearted support to the policies of the United States government and of the United Nations in matters pertaining to his official duties. In view of the specific responsibility imposed on me by the Constitution of the United States, and of the added responsibility which has been entrusted to me by the United Nations, I have decided that I must make a change of command in the Far East. I have, therefore, relieved General MacArthur of his commands and have designated Lt-General Matthew B. Ridgeway as his successor . . .'

MacArthur's dismissal aroused a political storm. But it was a storm that blew itself out in the United States. Appearances before Congress and private talks with Senators and Representatives, news conferences and speeches all hurt the Administration. But they did not hurt it as much as they would have had they emanated from General Headquarters in Tokyo and a serving soldier of proven abilities. In the end Truman was the victor. The war went on. But it was the war that Truman wanted to fight; his war, not MacArthur's.

By the time a truce was signed in Korea, in July 1953, the North Koreans and the Chinese had suffered two million casualties. But communism does not concern itself with human suffering. Viewed from Moscow, Korea was a useful experiment. The men in the Kremlin knew how to bide their time, and they could always return to the attack in Korea if circumstances looked propitious, no matter how long they might have to wait.

Under Stalin, communist rule had extended itself from the River Elbe in Germany to the South China Sea. There were many other possibilities for extending it further in South-east Asia, for attempting further subversion in the West through the large and well-disciplined communist parties of France and Italy, for returning to sensitive areas like Iran. Although Tito's Yugoslavia might be accounted a tactical set-back, the response of the West to the cold war posed no serious threat to the communist system itself. NATO was a defensive alliance only, and the United States had shown it would not use atomic weapons in the pursuit of offensive political goals.

Stalin died on 5 March 1953. According to his daughter, it was a terrible death which followed upon a stroke. The tyrant's end shook the world, so accustomed had everyone become to the terror of his name. But Stalin was not a Genghis Khan or a Tamurlaine, nor even, as recent scholars have tried to make out, a latter-day Ivan the Terrible or Peter the Great. He was the product of a system of power which of necessity has to spread itself or die. Stalin's heirs soon found it convenient to denounce Stalin for what they called 'the cult of personality', blaming him for all the crimes to which they themselves had been willing accomplices. They revived the term Stalinism to mask the inexorable continuity of communist development, to mask indeed its anti-human nature from which the Russian people have been the first and foremost sufferers. But in this 'deStalinisation' process there was never a hint of criticism over Stalin's foreign policies, except for the mistake over Yugoslavia. Thus Stalinism, a term first coined by Trotsky's clique in its feud with Stalin, is, in truth, implicit in Leninism; as Stalin liked to put it: 'Stalin is Lenin in our day.' Just as Lenin himself had revived the Tsarist secret police, so Stalin took over the permanent terror which had become part of the Soviet way of life. He refined it and extended it but he did not create it. Terror, indeed, was inherent in the system of government Lenin erected on the foundation of Marxism; it was inherent in his élitist party, with its monopoly of political power and its totalitarian tentacles spreading over every aspect of life—culture and entertainment, production and employment, religion and travel, both within and outside the USSR.

It has always been misleading to regard the Communist Party as a political party in the normal sense of the word. It is an atheistic order, an apparatus of power, stretching downward and outward into all sectors of society to enforce the decisions taken by the two dozen or so men at the top—originally the Political Bureau (usually called the Politburo), then the Presidium of the Party's central committee, then again the Politburo. Ideology is a weapon, and no more; no-one in the power structures can afford to believe in it. Power for the power's sake alone is the communist rule.

We shall never know for certain whether Stalin contemplated an invasion of Western Europe in his last years. With American forces tied up in Korea, he must have been tempted to do so but refrained, perhaps for fear that such open aggression would provoke nuclear retaliation at a time when the United States was undergoing political convulsions with fierce Republican attacks on Truman's administration, spearheaded by Senator McCarthy. In any case, the threat to the free world would be maintained in all its rigour by his successors, only they would try a different style of cold warfare, calling it peaceful co-existence.

PART 2
THE KHRUSHCHEV YEARS:
PEACEFUL CO-EXISTENCE

5 'You've Never had it so Good!'

Stalin had ruled over the Soviet Union for twenty-five years. For many ordinary Russians his death came as a shock. Despite the fearful conditions of life under communism they had come to regard Stalin as their indispensible leader, the-more-than-mortal master of their destiny.

Among the small clique who were his intimate cronies in the Kremlin, the shock was tempered by a life-and-death struggle for the succession. Theoretically his heirs formed a collective leadership, but gradually one man succeeded in gathering the reins of power into his own hands. He was a round little man with a most expressive face, as ready to grin as to scowl, to shake his fist as to fling his arms wide in an embrace.

Like all his colleagues, Nikita Khrushchev had been Stalin's unconditional and obsequious servant. He was a good organiser, very hard-working and endowed with natural intelligence. But he was no intellectual, and he uncritically accepted Marxism as the obvious answer to the questions raised in his own mind by the hardships his family had undergone in the coal-mining area of the Donbas. As a young communist, he had enthusiastically endorsed Stalin's purges and ruthlessly carried out Stalin's orders as party secretary in the Ukraine in 1938. A successful political commissar during the Second World War, he emerged from the siege of Stalingrad as a lieutenant-general. This did not save him from a spell in near-disgrace in 1946-7, which might well have ended with his death but which he survived through a mixture of zeal and sycophancy.

In his taped memoirs, Khrushchev paints a vivid picture of Stalin's later years, with his growing paranoia, interminable dinner parties in which all the guests had to take turns to taste every dish in case it had been poisoned and the constant fear of incurring the dictator's displeasure. Yet, when Stalin died, Khrushchev wept. 'After all,' he told

Averell Harriman, the American diplomat, 'we were his pupils and owed him everything. Like Peter the Great, Stalin fought barbarism with barbarism, but he was a great man.'

Two months earlier, the dictator had had a number of doctors arrested on charges of plotting to kill Soviet commanders. Most of them were Jews, and a major purge, with strongly anti-semitic overtones, was undoubtedly on the way when Stalin died. On his death, the doctors were released, and even those who, like Khrushchev, had wept, also breathed sighs of relief.

Initially, Khrushchev's main rival was Malenkov, who became Premier the day after Stalin died, but was forced to give up his post as First Secretary to the Communist Party's central committee. In the Soviet Union, and in general in all communist regimes, the party boss is more important than the head of government. It was as party boss that Stalin had achieved supreme power, although he later found it expedient, for his international wartime relationships, to become Premier as well. Khrushchev took over this key party job on 20 March 1953.

Malenkov was supported by the old guard of the party, including the veteran Foreign Minister, Vyacheslav Molotov, and Lazar Kaganovich. On Khrushchev's side was Marshal Bulganin, one of the deputy Premiers.

To begin with, Malenkov had hoped to use Lavrenty Beria, the much-feared head of the MGB (later the KGB), to consolidate his own power, but he was talked out of it by the others. Terrified that they themselves might be arrested on Beria's orders, Khrushchev and the others arranged for Beria to be seized at revolver's length by Marshal Zhukov and other top military figures. He was expelled from the party on 10 July and executed just before Christmas.

Malenkov was forced to yield the premiership to Bulganin on 8 February 1955. Bulganin and Khrushchev then embarked on a series of joint travels abroad, quickly achieving fame and even some popularity as 'B and K'—a kind of travelling circus act which the international public welcomed after the grim austerities of the Stalin period.

In 1957 Khrushchev faced a serious challenge to his authority in the Presidium (as the Politburo was known at the time), where Malenkov was still a power though no longer Premier. He met it by invoking an obscure party statute requiring such disputes to be settled by the entire central committee. With great resource he organised an airlift of distant members from all over the USSR and won the day.

Malenkov, Molotov and Kaganovich were promptly declared to constitute an 'anti-party group' and banished to distant places, but not executed: Stalin really was dead. Later that year, on 26 October, Khrushchev dismissed the prestigious Marshal Zhukov as Defence Minister. Twice Zhukov had served him well: by arresting Beria, and by organising the airlift of central committee members that gave Khrushchev his majority. Zhukov had won a considerable personal following, but there were reports that he was planning to seize power for himself. The reports were probably fabricated, but they gave Khrushchev the excuse to get rid of him.

On 27 March 1958 Khrushchev at last felt strong enough to rid himself of Bulganin as well, and took over the Premiership on top of his job as the party's No. 1. Four days later, the Supreme Soviet (a rubber-stamp Parliament) approved all Khrushchev's appointments. His power was now at its peak. It was to last until October 1964, a period which in retrospect may be regarded as a kind of interregnum in the Kremlin's approach to the cold war.

In the United States, Dwight D. Eisenhower had become President in January 1953, two months before Stalin's death, having beaten Adlai Stevenson, the Democratic Party's presidential candidate, the previous November. Eisenhower's inauguration introduced a period characterised by an appearance of American domination, superficial though that proved to be in a number of instances, and of a confidence verging on complacency among the people of the United States. Americans tend to look back on Good King Ike's Golden Days as a time of tranquillity after the storms of the Truman era. For the eight years that the Republicans were in office an immensely popular President supported by an astute Secretary of State, John Foster Dulles, led the Western world in the global struggle with communism.

Eisenhower and Dulles were a strangely assorted pair. The President was a national hero, supreme commander of the triumphant armies in Europe, the first commander of NATO, a man with the ability to inspire both confidence and affection. His Secretary of State seldom inspired affection, although he did win respect. A corporation lawyer, Dulles' avocation was international affairs, and he had served the Truman administrations with distinction in that field. By birth and education he belonged to that small group of Eastern élitists which had contributed so many able men to the winning of the war and the containment of the Soviet Union in the first post-war years.

Recent research has destroyed one of the myths that surrounded the two men. This was that Eisenhower was the soft-spoken searcher for peace in the world while Dulles was a sort of diplomatic Patton, prone to intemperate defiances of the Russians. The truth as revealed by Eisenhower's diaries and other studies is that the making of foreign policy rested far more with the President than with his Secretary of State. Politically it was advantageous for Eisenhower to assume the role of president of all the people while Dulles's belligerence toward communism maintained the Administration's good standing in the right wing of the Republican Party and among southern Democrats.

Dulles suffered from what was then called by his critics 'Pactomania'. There seemed to be no problem within his view that could not be eased, if not settled, by the creation of a political and military alliance to meet the communist challenge. Behind these alliances lay American nuclear power which, so the Administration advertised, could be used in a strategy of 'Massive Retaliation' against any military challenge.

In Stalin's day the cold war had turned into a duel between Moscow and Washington, with Truman responding to the Soviet dictator's moves in a series of American initiatives which largely determined the pattern of post-war development in the free world—notably, the Truman Doctrine, Marshall Aid and the formation of NATO. During the Khrushchev years, while the duel remained ultimately one between the two superpowers, both Moscow and Washington were distracted by changes in the power structure of the world. Although the communist bloc seemed monolithic, Tito's defection posed one threat to Soviet leadership, while increasingly the Kremlin had to take account of its huge communist associate in Asia. It was during Khrushchev's time that the momentous break between Moscow and Peking took place, the consequences of which have still to be fully worked out. Nevertheless, in 1960, the year the break took place, the leaders of eighty-one communist parties, including the Chinese, were able to meet in Moscow and put their signatures to a declaration which is of immense importance to our understanding of the cold war.

The most significant point in this Declaration concerned 'peaceful co-existence', which was the phrase used in Lenin's time to describe the interim period between the Russian Revolution and the collapse of 'capitalism', and which Khrushchev adopted as his main propaganda offensive.

The 1960 declaration put a new gloss on it. As with all communist statements, it was an exercise in political semantics, providing both reassurance and menace. The two key passages on peaceful co-existence were these:

By upholding the principle of peaceful co-existence, communists fight for the complete cessation of the cold war, disbandment of military blocs and the dismantling of military bases, for general and complete disarmament under international control, the settlement of international disputes through negotiation, respect for the equality of states and their territorial integrity, independence and sovereignty, non-interference in each other's internal affairs, extensive development of trade, cultural and scientific ties between nations.

These soothing calls for the end of the cold war, and for peace and freedom were, however, nullified by the following passage:

Peaceful co-existence of countries with different social systems does not mean conciliation of the socialist and bourgeois ideologies. On the contrary, it means *intensification of the struggle* of the working class, of all the communist parties, for the triumph of socialist ideas. But ideological and political disputes between states must not be settled through war.

The communists who drafted these words, and those who listened or read them, needed no translation. The message was instantly clear. It meant that the cold war which the West was waging against the communists must stop, but that the ceaseless war which the communists were waging against the West and all other countries must go on, and be intensified, until final victory went to the forces of communism.

The 1960 declaration also launched an important new ideological concept, termed 'States of National Democracy'. In retrospect, it can be seen that this curious label was invented to fit the peculiar case of Cuba, where Fidel Castro had recently come to power by revolutionary methods largely his own and without the help of the local communist party. Here was a regime which was clearly 'revolutionary' and 'anti-imperialist', but which was not yet 'socialist'.

There were other candidates for the label: Burma, Egypt (where the local communist party was banned), and in black Africa, Ghana, Guinea and Mali (all of them anti-Western but without a communist party between them). By calling these countries 'States of National Democracy', the communists were signalling that they qualified for aid and advice, until such time as, according to Leninist principles, they took the road to 'socialism'.

Washington, too, had problems with its allies. Marshall Aid promoted the recovery of European nation states whose sense of national identity took many different forms. Unlike the communist bloc, the Western alliance thus contained a diversity of national interests which were not always in accord with the priorities of American foreign policy. The Middle East was changing fast and presented many points of possible conflict. But much of Eisenhower's time was taken up with the Far East, in a seemingly interminable and futile series of crises over small islands off the coast of China. To America's European allies, Red China was a less immediate threat than the Soviet Union. Although Britain had no love for Chinese communists, Prime Minister Attlee's government had given Mao's regime diplomatic recognition, much to the chagrin of the China lobby in the United States. But the Americans had backed Chiang Kai-shek and were therefore committed to waging the cold war against Peking and Moscow simultaneously.

In retrospect, much of the effort Eisenhower and Dulles expended seems wasted. But it is now forgotten how important the Chinese threat then seemed and what a large part it played in American politics. In retrospect, too, American diplomacy in Indochina appears inept and shortsighted, too cautious to help the French, too indecisive to avoid the eventual disaster of the United States' own involvement in Vietnam in more adverse circumstances.

As in Stalin's day, then, the cold war was being waged on many different fronts, psychological as well as geographic. But its basic pattern was often obscured by the kaleidoscope of events which constitutes human history. The Khrushchev years lasted from 1953 to 1964, eleven years which spanned the presidencies of Eisenhower and Kennedy. They took the world from a generation with memories of the war against Hitler to a generation which looked towards landing a man on the moon.

For the British, the loss of empire was less of a psychological shock than might have been expected, perhaps because the realisation of what had happened was masked by the scares of the cold war. For the same reason, what amounted to a social revolution at home produced remarkably little unrest. But after five years in office, Britain's Labour government ran out of steam. Austerity, rationing, the drabness of post-war life, doctrinaire policies and increased government controls—these all robbed socialism of its utopian appeal. In elections in February 1950, the socialists just scraped home, but Prime Minister Attlee had a difficult time running the country with a small majority in the House of Commons and with colleagues who were always inclined to be fractious. Bevin was ailing. In March 1951, he resigned and a few weeks later he died. In April 1951, the silver-tongued Aneurin Bevan, architect of Britain's national health service, resigned in protest at the imposition of charges for doctors' prescriptions. By October 1951, Attlee had had enough and he called for another election.

Churchill, meanwhile, was still alive. His slogan of 'Set the people free!' caught a national mood. The Conservatives won the election and Churchill became Prime Minister for the second time. He was almost seventy-seven, long past the age when most men seek power, and he remained in office until April 1955, when he handed over to Anthony Eden, for so many years his heir-apparent. By then Churchill had celebrated his eightieth birthday. He had attended King George VI's funeral in February 1952 and seen Queen Elizabeth crowned with romantic pomp in June the following year. From her he received a knighthood in the Order of the Garter, which enabled him to remain a commoner while participating in the colourful ceremonies which, the British fancied, inaugurated a second Elizabethan age.

A proper assessment of Winston Churchill must wait until the archives of his second premiership are thoroughly researched. In terms of public opinion, or his appearance in the media, an underlying theme of this book, it seems that he had become more than ever an image, programmed like a waxworks figure to growl and gesture and go through the motions of presiding over a government for the sake of photographers and newspaper correspondents. He had made little impact on British politics as leader of the opposition and his contribution now that he was again head of the government was negligible. For some of the time a stroke removed him from affairs altogether, when the day-to-day business of government was apparently conducted by members of his family. Often he was unable to recognise the members of his own cabinet. He played no part in the conduct of the cold war except to appear when required by photographers. Much more than during the war against Hitler, Britain's foreign policy became Eden's exclusive territory.

The truth is that the political scene to which Churchill returned in 1951 was so different from the one he had known at Yalta as to make him seem like a dinosaur who had strayed into the wrong geological age. Perhaps the old man himself was confused by what had taken place. The man who had once warned of the danger of letting Soviet power reach into the heart of Europe had been proved right after all. Franco's Foreign Minister, Count Jordana, had expressed this fear three weeks after the battle of Stalingrad, although his views carried little weight at the time, as Spain had a division of troops fighting on Germany's eastern front. But in the changed atmosphere of the cold war, Franco's Spain was eligible for rehabilitation in the West— except among die-hard liberals. In November 1950, the United Nations revoked the trading restrictions on Spain which had been imposed in 1946, leaving the way open for the trade and military agreements of the Eisenhower era.

Tito was another candidate for revaluation. the outcast of 1945-6, who had been soundly condemned in American newspapers and newsreels for the shooting down of unarmed American aeroplanes, was accorded flattering press interviews. In March 1946 Churchill had placed Yugoslavia behind the Iron Curtain, but in March 1953 he was on hand to welcome Tito to Downing Street, Tito's first state visit to a Western democracy.

But the most spectacular change in the alignment of states concerned the two defeated Axis powers, Germany and Japan. 'If Germany did not exist, it would be necessary to invent it,' Count Jordana said in his famous interview with the British ambassador. In the Far East, the existence of Japan was a similar necessity.

From the day he had received the formal surrender of the Japanese upon the battleship *Missouri* on 2 September, 1945, until his dismissal by Truman in April 1951, MacArthur had been the virtual dictator of Japan. But if, in the person of MacArthur, the American presence in Japan was highly visible, it was mostly thanks to the person of the Emperor Hirohito that it was able to take effect. Hirohito had ascended the Chrysanthemum Throne in 1926 and he had been forty at the time of Pearl Harbour. Instead of being indicted as a war criminal, as the Australians and British would have liked, Hirohito became MacArthur's willing instrument in the democratisation of Japan, broadcasting on the radio on 1 January 1946 to deny his own divinity and thereafter visiting factories and cities in a crumpled suit and felt hat in a complete reversal of imperial tradition. Through the Emperor a new constitution was promulgated, and the Japanese people were encouraged to undertake the process of national regeneration which made them, three decades later, one of the leading industrial powers of the world.

Myopic, self-effacing and quietly courteous, Hirohito was the antithesis of the theatrical American general, Douglas MacArthur. But each needed the other to turn around the attitudes generated in their countries by the recent hostilities, which had reached their climax in the use of atomic bombs. Nothing could have aided this process more than Stalin's adventure in Korea. Not only did the Korean War stimulate Japan's economy, it produced among the Japanese people a response, similar to that of West Germans to the Berlin blockade, which entitled Japan to a place in the anti-communist system. In 1951, in San Francisco, President Truman promulgated a peace treaty which came into force in April 1952, Japan then being incorporated into one of Secretary Dulles's regional defence pacts. Court scholars had earlier given Hirohito's reign the title 'Enlightened Peace', a choice which seemed inappropriate in the years of strident Japanese militarism when the Emperor was most often pictured as a resplendent figure on a white horse. But from 1945, when Hirohito came into his own, the title proved singularly apt. Japanese communists tried to disrupt this process through street-disturbances and terrorism, but by 1964 Japan's recovered status was symbolised by the choice of Tokyo as the scene for that year's Olympic Games.

In West Germany, as in Japan, recovery of national morale was helped by developments in the cold war, notably the Berlin blockade. But the recovery was closely associated also with the personality of Konrad Adenauer, a relic of the old imperial Germany which Bismarck had created and which had gone down in the First World War. In 1917, at the age of forty-one, Adenauer had become the chief executive, or ruling mayor, of Cologne, a position of considerable power which he used conscientiously until forced out by the Nazis in 1933. Adenauer then retired, his political life apparently over. In 1944 he was rounded up in one of the last Gestapo purges of the war and confined in miserable conditions, expecting to be shot. But the Americans arrived first. Knowing his past, they asked him to assist in restoring life and order to the shattered city where he had once been the ruling mayor. But Cologne lay in the British occupation zone and Britain's socialist leaders were hostile to Adenauer. In October 1945 they dismissed him, a slight which Adenauer never forgave Britain.

In the West, public animosity towards Germans, which for a time knew no bounds, was partially sated by the verdicts of the Nuremberg War Tribunal, as a result of which ten Nazi leaders, including Ribbentrop, were hanged in October 1946. But the destruction of German cities and the sufferings of ordinary German men and women during the first winters of peace made a strong impression on European statesmen like de Gaulle and Churchill, who shared a sense of Europe's historical destiny. When the Western occupying powers allowed political activity to start up again, Adenauer turned to the formation of a new political party, the Christian Democratic Union, or CDU, reminiscent of the old Catholic Centre party of the Weimar Republic, in opposition to the socialists who were led by Kurt Schumacher, a veteran opponent of the Nazis, and who were naturally favoured by British socialists. Throughout the tense months of the Berlin blockade, Adenauer took a leading part in the constitutional arrangements which led to West Germany's first elections in August 1949. His tireless efforts paid off; the CDU won the elections and on 15 September 1949 Audenauer became the first Chancellor of the new Germany.

He was then seventy-three and he went on to dominate West Germany's political life for the next fourteen years, winning elections in 1953, 1957 and 1961. His Asiatic features, the result of a car accident which affected the setting of his cheek bones, were among the most compelling images of the cold war, expressing an undeviating opposition to making any concessions to Soviet power. In 1953, the year of his first electoral triumph, of his first official visit to America when Eisenhower did him the honour of playing the old German national anthem, and the year, too, of the East German uprising, *Time* magazine named him Statesman of the Year. In 1955, the tortuous diplomacy successfully completed by which West Germany won sovereignty and the right to re-arm within NATO, Adenauer undertook to visit Moscow, one of the most testing experiences of his life. It yielded nothing except the return of German prisoners-of-war who had been incarcerated all this time in Stalin's death camps. The Soviets at first denied their existence. In the end, less than 10,000 of the million or so whom Stalin had taken prisoner were found alive to return to their homes.

In 1963, Adenauer was forced to step down; he was too old to contribute further to the political life of the new West Germany. But his achievement had been extraordinary. Although he owed much to cold war developments, his own skill, patience and iron fortitude won for West Germany the respect of its former enemies. Thanks to his own past, he demonstrated that national socialism was more closely allied to Soviet communism than to Germany's conservative tradition. Despite the attempts of communist agents to smear Adenauer's Germany with apparent neo-Nazi tendencies, it was in East Germany that visitors found the most disturbing reminders of the Nazi era. Adenauer himself went out of his way to make amends to the Jews in the form of a reparations agreement with Israel, an arrangement which caused uproar in Jerusalem but which gave the economy of the new Israeli state a much-needed stimulus. Ben-Gurion and Adenauer became good friends. In the end, the concessions which Adenauer dreaded the West might make became the centre-piece of the policy of his socialist opponents when eventually they came to power in Bonn under Willy Brandt.

France, meanwhile, was also slowly recovering from the war. In January 1946 General de Gaulle suddenly resigned his powers, expecting to be called back by popular acclaim to rebuild the country as he wanted without the interference of the old political parties, the *politichiens* as he contemptuously called them. But the political system he so depised succeeded in becoming a third force between the communists on one extreme and, on the other, de Gaulle's own Rally of the French People, a populist movement he launched as a direct challenge to the Fourth Republic. Disappointed, de Gaulle allowed the RPF to fade away while he withdrew to the seclusion of his home at Colombey-les-deux-Eglises to write his memoirs and brood on his country's embroilment in colonial wars. Meanwhile the French economy was quietly brought under control and the seeds of future growth planted, including the decision that France would have her own nuclear programme. Although outsiders laughed at the regularity with which the governments of the Fourth Republic came and went, the achievements of these years provided the necessary base for de Gaulle's own manoeuvres once he was back in power.

By 1958, however, he was seemingly a forgotten man. In that year the threat of civil war loomed over France because of events in Algeria, where French settlers, numbering about one million, were fearful that the government in Paris would make a deal with Algerian nationalists. The threat would not have been serious but for the support the French in Algeria received from units of the French army, and especially its famed paratroopers, led by General Massu.

For de Gaulle it was now or never. He made no specific promises. 'I have understood you,' he said to the Algerian colonists, leading them to believe he would champion their cause. In the event, he betrayed them in the interests of France, and so he became the target of a 'Secret Army' of assassins and saboteurs. But de Gaulle was in a hurry. In 1958, when he returned to power, he was sixty-seven and he might not have much longer to live. As it turned out, he ruled France for eleven years, forging a new constitution—that of the Fifth Republic—and pursuing a maverick course in international affairs, which angered and bewildered his friends and enemies alike.

Of communist parties outside the Soviet bloc, the French is the most obedient to Moscow and, after the Italian, the largest. De Gaulle's view of communism has been described by one of his biographers as 'historical pessimism'; that is, he regarded the ultimate success of communism as inevitable, but not because of its ideological importance. To preserve the integrity of France, therefore, he believed he had to keep her in the mainstream of communist development while denying Soviet ambitions. His policies certainly placed French communists in a dilemma, since de Gaulle's initiatives were in line with the Kremlin's objectives—such as the break-up of NATO and ending the American connection—but they brought the French Communist Party no nearer to power within France. Although French communists, like the Italians, were pledged to the parliamentary road to power, de Gaulle's constitution was designed to give the President of France freedom of manoeuvre whatever happened in parliamentary elections. In the extraordinary crisis of 1968, the Communist Party showed no desire to bring de Gaulle down. They rightly saw that they had to dissociate themselves from the students and other extremists on the left in order to remain a respectable political force. Thanks to them, an apparent Gaullist defeat was turned into a victory which gave the Gaullist party the biggest majority in French parliamentary history. The communists succeeded in retaining their position as the main power on the left.

'War is against our enemies, peace against our friends,' de Gaulle is quoted as saying. Had he been invited to Yalta or been admitted to the post-war system which America and Britain planned, no doubt the course of the cold war would have been different. In the crisis of 1960, when Khrushchev came to Paris full of bluster, de Gaulle's strength of character deflated the Soviet leader and bolstered the morale of the Anglo-Saxons, Eisenhower and Macmillan. But such lofty control of the situation was needed within the Western alliance, not as a kind of *maquis* operating on its flanks, which is where de Gaulle chose to place it. His international forays thus grew increasingly eccentric, like his excursion into Canada in 1967 when he outraged the government in Ottawa by his cry of 'Vive le Québec libre!' Irritating to his allies though these forays may have been, probably greater damage was done to the anti-communist cause by his decision in 1966 to remove France from NATO, though not from the Alliance. But the history of the cold war is not yet finished, and who can say whether de Gaulle's underlying fear of a Soviet-American settlement at the expense of Europe may not be proved right?

After their election victory under Churchill in 1951, the Conservative Party remained in power in Britain for 13 years, until October 1964, winning elections in May 1955 and October 1959, and increasing their majorities each time. For the first part of this period the dominating figure was not Churchill but Eden, whose experience of foreign affairs was of great value to the West in the initiatives of the Eisenhower–Dulles era, and notably those which brought West Germany into NATO and enabled France to disengage from Indo-China. In the Korean peace negotiations, too, Eden was able to make some amends for what had happened after Yalta. There were some 132,000 Chinese prisoners in United Nations hands and 62,700 of them were unwilling to be repatriated. Eden rejected the communists' demand that they all be returned. 'It would,' he told the House of Commons, 'clearly be repugnant to the sense of values of the free world to send these men home by force.'

But Eden's view of Britain's role in the world belonged to the past. His diplomatic skill was apparently resented by Dulles, a factor

which contributed to the Suez *débâcle* in 1956, when Eden attempted
to pursue an independent British policy in the Middle East. Its failure
caused Eden to resign in January 1957, his health ruined.

His place was taken by Harold Macmillan. Partly by adroit use of
the British Royal Family as travelling salesmen for Britain, and partly
by exploiting wartime friendships with Eisenhower and others in the
President's circle, Macmillan succeeded in restoring Anglo–
American relations, badly damaged by the Suez affair, and reconciling the British people to their changed position in the world.

To some a rather comical figure, with drooping moustaches and
drooping eyelids, Macmillan remained Britain's prime minister for
seven years. During the war he had been Churchill's political representative in the Mediterranean, where he alternated between bouts
of fruitless activity and laziness. He continued to be something of a
ditherer in the seven years which coincided with Khrushchev's years
of power in the Kremlin.

Having no clear idea of what Britain's role in the world should be,
Macmillan went on a tour of Africa in 1960 to discover, as he put it,
that 'a wind of change' was blowing through the continent. The old
Punch cartoonists would have described this observation as a glimpse
of the obvious, but the new mass media took to Macmillan's pose as a
philosopher–statesman of the Edwardian era. Behind his old Etonian
tie, he cultivated an image of imperturbability which increasingly
became a kind of music-hall act. He became Supermac, unruffled as
far as the cameras could make out by Khrushchev's shoe-banging
antics in the United Nations, although if de Gaulle is to be believed
he was reduced to near-panic when the Soviet leader broke up the
summit in Paris in 1960.

Macmillan's chief contribution to the history of these years was
the election slogan 'You've never had it so good!' which brought him
a personal triumph in 1959. The slogan no doubt reflected a sense of
relaxation in world affairs after the tensions of the Stalin era of the
cold war, but at the same time it appealed to a mood of escapism
which seemed to overtake Britain during the following decades.
Macmillan took the British into the 1960s into an atmosphere of fun-
seeking fantasy which the media described as 'swinging'. *Lady
Chatterley's Lover* became the most talked-about book of the decade,
schoolboy jokes and smut became the most sought-after programmes
on television, the Beatles and the Rolling Stones became national
heroes, honoured by the Queen, treated deferentially by the

Establishment, idolised by the young. But when stories of high-living scandal touched members of his government, Macmillan eventually had to go.

As the 1960s went by, the British seemed more preoccupied with discovering a new permissive way of life than with the continuing struggle of the cold war. 'Great Britain has lost her empire and has not yet found a role,' said America's former Secretary of State, Dean Acherson, in 1962. De Gaulle twice rebuffed Britain's attempt to enter the European Common Market. Decolonisation went on apace in Africa. South Africa left the Commonwealth and went on her way in 1961. In 1963 independence came to Kenya, the land of the white settlers, and the reins of government passed to Jomo Kenyatta whom a British governer had recently described as 'the African leader to darkness and death'. Now, one and all revered him as Mzee, the Old Man, a paragon of wise statesmanship. The same could hardly be said of Idi Amin in Uganda, although even here some white men were ready to bend their knees in respect, just as in the former French colony of Oubangui-Chari they co-operated in the grim farce of crowning the Emperor Bokassa in robes copied from those of Napoleon Bonaparte. In the Congo (now Zaire) some tribes resorted to cannibalism to proclaim their newly-won freedom; elsewhere they merely slaughtered each other almost to the point of extinction, as they had been doing for centuries before the white man first arrived.

So enfeebled had Britain become, in 1965 the socialist government of Harold Wilson was unable to prevent the white Rhodesians, under Ian Smith, from declaring their own independence, a regime which was to last until 1980 when the Marxist, Robert Mugabe, took over. Instead, Britain began to liquidate its remaining commitments east of Suez. By the end of 1967, the last troops had left Aden, creating another power vacuum which the Soviets were quick to exploit. In 1968 the British moved out of the Persian Gulf, leaving the Shah of Iran as the West's champion in the area. Meanwhile in 1965, Winston Churchill died, aged ninety. His funeral gave the British the opportunity for a final celebration of past glory.

At the time, then, the Khrushchev years of the cold war gave an overall impression of hope, as though both sides recognised that 'peaceful co-existence' was the only course open to them. But in retrospect it can be seen how illusory this impression was and how damaging to Western morale the idea of ever-increasing prosperity would be. For this reason, Macmillan's election slogan 'You've never had it so good!' has more than a passing interest. Like the glamour of Kennedy's tenure of the White House, it struck a false note in a world where the grim struggle for global mastery went on unabated. In the course of a long campaign, many tactical mistakes are inevitably made and can be corrected without too great a loss; but it seems as if during these years several wrong decisions were taken which would profoundly affect the West's position in the cold war, decisions which were based on a fundamental misunderstanding of what was truly at stake. Not the least of these was the projection of energy needs and supplies based on the assumption that Middle East oil would continue indefinitely to be cheap and plentiful.

But at this point, we have to admit that modern history moves into journalism. We do not have sufficient records or information about the recent past to be truly objective, and hindsight may deceive us today over how things will look tomorrow.

In a later chapter we shall have to consider the significance of the media in the cold war. Western memories are short, Western hopes of ever-increasing affluence are always buoyed up by fresh promises. When Macmillan made his election boast, only six and a half years had passed since Stalin's death, a period which accounts for little in the time-scale of communist planners but which in democracies is likely to include at least one general election, when radical changes often occur, as with de Gaulle's return to power in France. It is worth noting that Molotov was still among Soviet policy-makers in 1955, a prominent figure in cold-war diplomacy ten years after the Yalta conference and sixteen years after his notorious Nazi–Soviet Pact which precipitated the Second World War.

Nevertheless, in the aftermath of Stalin's death some change was desperately sought for, both inside the Soviet Union and outside, and Nikita Khrushchev was history's instrument in seeing if change was possible.

6 'We Will Bury You!'

The absolute power that Stalin wielded in the USSR had extended to the world communist movement. Despite occasional ripples of dissent, his word was law. If he decreed a change of line, it was binding on the French Communist Party and equally on Indonesian or Chilean communists. The world movement was a huge and obedient instrument of Soviet foreign policy, executing Lenin's original directives, initially through the Comintern and after the Second World War through the Soviet International Department.

Khrushchev severely damaged this monolithic instrument, although he did not entirely destroy it, and he shook the Soviet empire to its foundations, although again without destroying it. And it may well be that he had no choice in the matter. All the Soviet leaders, Khrushchev included, were deeply implicated in Stalin's crimes. Had they declined to play their allotted part they would have been purged or liquidated as so many others were. But all of them lacked Stalin's monstrous dimension. They were incapable of administering a permanent terror, although they were not about to dismantle the police state which alone kept them in power.

They had to be careful, for if they had hinted that the system itself was at fault, their own hold on power would have been fatally weakened. So the entire blame had to be put on Stalin for perverting the system to his own ends. Khrushchev took it upon himself to carry out the inevitable demolition job when the Communist Party of the Soviet Union (CPSU) convened for the first time since the war in its Twentieth Congress, in February 1956. On 25 February he delivered a speech of enormous length—it ran to some 26,000 words and was obviously a composite effort and not written by Khrushchev alone—to a hushed assembly of the party faithful, including a fair number of foreign communists.

The speech was not intended for publication, and is therefore usually referred to as Khrushchev's 'secret speech'. But so many copies of it were in circulation that the American CIA, in a notable 'scoop', was able to get hold of a full text, which was published by the State Department on 4 June 1956 and is universally admitted to be authentic.

At Stalin's instigation, said Khrushchev, thousands of innocent persons had been executed. Extensive torture had been used to extract confessions from the innocent. Ethnic minorities had been ruthlessly and unjustly deported in the Soviet Union during the war. Khrushchev told his stunned audience the inside story of the 'doctors' plot' concocted by Stalin shortly before his death. He touched another raw nerve by giving them the background to the so-called 'Leningrad affair', which many of these present remembered. Some months after Stalin's right-hand man, Zhdanov, had died in 1948, his most prominent followers in the Leningrad district, headed by Politburo member Voznesensky, had simply disappeared. All of them, said Khrushchev, had been arrested on charges trumped up by Beria, and summarily shot with Stalin's approval.

When it came to getting 'confessions', Khrushchev added, Stalin's methods were simple: 'Beat, beat and beat again.'

The impact of Khrushchev's words was tremendous. Strictly speaking, hardly anything he said was 'news' in that much of it had been published in some form or the other in the 'capitalist' countries by such defectors as Viktor Kravchenko (whose powerful book, *I Chose Freedom*, appeared in 1946). What Khrushchev had to say nevertheless shocked his audience, and it is important to understand why. So long as Stalin's crimes were disclosed by the 'bourgeois' press, or by 'traitors', the entire membership of the world communist movement simply ignored them or dismissed them from their minds. As George Orwell would have said, these were 'unfacts'.

But it was a different matter when the boss of the Soviet Communist Party, in the original home of the Revolution, the repository of Marxist–Leninist truth, described the atrocities of the regime under Stalin. Communists everywhere were henceforth forced to recognise that facts which they had previously denied or ignored were true all the time. The secret speech called in question the infallibility of the mother-church of Marxism–Leninism.

But there was more to it than that. In the course of his speech, Khrushchev even appeared to discard two of the best established dogmas of Leninism: the inevitability of war between communism and capitalism, and the inevitability of violent revolution before socialism could be introduced in any country. Before his overthrow, Malenkov—conscious of the terrible destructive power of nuclear weapons—had taken a risk by declaring that another world war would destroy civilisation. In so doing, he had violated the Leninist precept that only 'imperialism' would be destroyed in a general war—in other words, that the victory of communism was historically inevitable. Khrushchev had used this lapse in his campaign to discredit Malenkov. And now he was taking it over as his own.

As for revolutionary violence, Khrushchev now said that in certain circumstances the transition to socialism might be achieved by parliamentary means. Moreover, he publicly discarded yet another dogma, which owed as much to Stalin as to Lenin: that of 'proletarian internationalism', or the view that Moscow's way must prevail over all others in achieving socialism and communism. He praised the Chinese People's Republic and even Yugoslavia, and found a saying of Lenin's to quote: "All nations will arrive at socialism, but not all will do so in exactly the same way.' Was Khrushchev, then, inviting non-Soviet communist parties to go their own way?

One of those who thought he was doing just that was the Italian party boss, Palmiro Togliatti, who had spent many years in Moscow and, like Khrushchev and the others, had approved of all Stalin's crimes and even carried out some of them himself (for example, by transmitting Stalin's order for the torture and liquidation of the Catalan Trotskyist leader, Andrés Nin, during the Spanish Civil War). Now, on hearing Khrushchev's words, Togliatti coined the term 'polycentrism' to describe a state of affairs in which each individual party would find its own way to power according to local conditions, and not necessarily act only on Moscow's orders.

One foreign communist leader, above all others, read reports of Khrushchev's secret speech with particular outrage: the Chinese leader, Mao Tse-tung. At first sight, this may seem paradoxical, since Mao had ignored Stalin's advice and found his own way to power in China through peasant revolution in defiance of Marxist–Leninist precepts. Indeed, he had had so little reason to love Stalin that he did not attend the dictator's funeral, sending Premier Chou En-lai instead.

However, Mao owed his shattering victory in the Chinese civil war largely to Stalin's belated invasion of Manchuria at the end of the Second World War and to the delivery of huge quantities of captured Japanese arms and equipment, by the Soviet invaders. Under his pact with Stalin, he had accepted a kind of satellite status for China. Mao Tse-tung, on the other hand, was intensely proud to be Chinese and considered himself the heir of China's ancient civilisation and its traditional claim to be 'the centre of the world'. When Stalin died, he considered himself to the the senior personage in the communist world. He reckoned that Khrushchev ought to have consulted him before shattering the myth of Stalin and discarding sacred dogmas one after the other.

The maximum impact of Khrushchev's speech, however, was felt much nearer home, in the Soviet satellites, or colonies, of Poland and Hungary. Already, in June 1953, the workers in East Berlin had taken advantage of a relaxation of the communist regime that followed Stalin's death to riot and shout anti-government slogans. The collective leadership in Moscow had sent in tanks and troops to crush the incipient uprising.

Now, in the wake of the Twentieth Party Congress, trouble of a far graver kind faced Khrushchev and his colleagues. Both in Poland and Hungary, the established communist regimes challenged the authority of the Soviet overlords. Both regimes, of course, owed their existence to Soviet power, and it was this fact that made their defiance so dramatic.

Before the war, Stalin had invited twelve leaders of the Polish Communist Party to Moscow, then had them executed, between 1937 and 1939, along with hundreds of rank-and-file members. One Polish communist leader escaped death, however, because he happened to be in a Polish gaol at the time. This was Wladyslaw Gomulka, and it was he who challenged Stalin's successors in 1956. Popular discontent had been building up below the surface, and in June thousands of factory workers attacked the headquarters of the security police and of the local Communist Party. In October, the central committee of the Polish Party (which now called itself the Polish United Workers' Party) met and sacked all the Stalinists in its Politburo. These included the Polish Soviet citizen, Marshal Rokossovky, who was Defence Minister. That day, 19 October, Khrushchev, Molotov and other Soviet leaders had flown to Warsaw to warn Gomulka not to go too far in his liberalising policy. In a major speech on the 20th, however, Gomulka denounced Stalinism and the cult of personality and called for a Polish road to socialism. In doing so, he was merely echoing Khrushchev's secret speech, but he was nevertheless running an enormous personal risk, for as he spoke,

Soviet tanks were closing in on Warsaw and Soviet warships were gathering outside the Polish port of Gdynia. He got away with it, however, and the Soviet leaders, having failed to browbeat him, went back to Moscow and called off the military threat.

In the very similar crisis that broke out a few days later in Hungary, the Soviets crushed the Hungarian people with maximum force. The fatal difference between the two situations was that Gomulka kept his act of defiance within bounds, whereas the Hungarians totally lost control of the crisis.

The Hungarian regime was one of the most brutally oppressive in the Soviet empire—so wretched that even the Russians were worried. When the Hungarian ambassador to Moscow reported that there would be a revolution unless the Stalinist party boss, Matyas Rakosi, was removed, the collective leadership in mid-July sent the old guard Bolshevik Mikoyan to Budapest, where he personally presided over a Hungarian central committee meeting which sacked Rakosi.

At first, however, things were no better, for Rakosi's successor, Ernö Gerö, was also a Stalinist and the oppressive measures continued. On 23 October, more than 200,000 demonstrators marched through the streets of Budapest, demanding freedom and the return of the softer-line Imre Nagy, who had been gaoled by Rakosi but freed on the 13th. Next day (the 24th), Nagy became Premier, and Gero—still the party boss—called out the Hungarian army. However, both the army and the police started handing over their weapons to the revolutionaries, and the Soviet forces (called in, it was later learnt, by Gerö) began to fire on them. On the 25th, Gerö was forced out and was replaced by Janos Kadar who, like Gomulka in Poland, had once suffered gaol and torture at the hands of the Stalinists.

With the revolution spreading throughout the country, the Soviet forces withdrew on 30 October after Nagy had given Moscow assurances that all would be well. Carried away, or swamped, by the revolutionary fervour all around him, Nagy publicly pledged free elections and the ending of the one-party dictatorship. Some days later, he went further, denouncing the Warsaw Pact and calling on the United Nations for assistance. But the Soviet retreat was a feint and the United Nations a broken reed. Khrushchev and his colleagues had already decided that they were going to move in again to crush the revolt, and they did so on 4 November. Three fresh divisions were sent to Hungary and Soviet tanks and artillery went into action in Budapest. In a week's fierce fighting, marked by some notable tactical mistakes, more than 30,000 Hungarians were killed. The Soviets were said to have lost 7,000 men. Nagy was forced to step down, in favour of Kadar. He was later executed, after a secret trial, with General Pal Maleter and other leaders of the revolution. Maleter, who had been invited to the Soviet embassy ostensibly for discussions, was handed over to the executioners by his host the Soviet ambassador, whose name is better known today than it then was: Yuri Andropov.

On 14 November, Soviet forces crushed the last pocket of resistance. Kadar settled down to the thankless task of cautious long-term liberalisation, while taking care not to incur Soviet displeasure. Years later, the consensus was that he had largely achieved his aims. It was still a communist regime but a much more relaxed one than formerly. In Poland, too, something remained of the hopes aroused in the heady days of defiance. In 1980 these feelings came to the surface again in widespread workers' strikes which forced the Polish authorities to allow the creation of free trade unions and to recognise the place of religion in national life.

It is interesting to note that behind the scenes the Chinese communists played an important part in urging the Russians to crush the Hungarian revolution. That at least became their version of history. In his taped memoirs (*Khrushchev Remembers*, Vol. 1, pp. 418–19), the Soviet leader records that a special Chinese delegation led by the then Chinese President, Liu Shao-chi, wavered, at first advising against military action, then rallying behind the Soviet decision to send the army back into Hungary. Earlier, the Chinese had advised against Soviet action in Poland, on the ground that the Polish communists were utterly dependent upon Soviet support against the Germans and would not leave the Soviet camp.

China had evidently ceased to be a satellite: you do not consult satellites, you tell them what to do. Yet they were still unmistakably in the Soviet camp and went along with the Russians in preserving the unity of the empire, at whatever cost.

Yet the great Sino–Soviet rift was now not far away. Before dealing with it, let us look at the international scene, and at Khrushchev's way of conducting the cold war against the non-communist world.

The Soviet Drive continues

When Stalin died, his expansionist policy had come to an apparent halt nearly everywhere. His blockade of Berlin had failed, and there seemed no immediate prospect of getting the Allies to abandon Germany's former capital. In Korea, the war Stalin had provoked had bogged down in an uneasy truce and there was no hope now of achieving his original war aims. NATO had established itself and the Marshall Plan had brought growing prosperity to Western Europe. American power was successfully re-asserting itself.

In South-east Asia, the insurgencies instigated by Stalin in the immediate post-war period had either been defeated or were being brought under control. In one area only, communism could still be said to be advancing, and that was French Indochina, where a communist party had been active since 1930, directed by one of the most remarkable figures of our time, the Vietnamese leader Ho Chi Minh.

Ho had been in Moscow's pay for many years. He was a founder-member of the French Communist Party in 1920. He studied Marxism–Leninism and revolutionary methods in Moscow's 'University of the Toilers of the East' in the 1920s, until Stalin sent him to South China as a Comintern agent in 1925. The little man with the traditional goatee and the gentle voice was a professional revolutionary in East Asia for years.

In 1930 he initiated his own revolutionary machine, the Communist Party of Indochina. There are, however, two things to note about this particular party. One is the name: not the CP of Vietnam, or Laos or Cambodia (the three neighbouring countries of the Indochina peninsula), but the CP of *Indochina*. This was a clear signal that Ho intended to 'liberate' the whole of France's Indochina empire and rule over all three countries in the name of communism. The other thing to note is that although Ho Chi Minh was a nationalist (he took the name of 'Nguyen the Patriot' for his revolutionary work), his party was an integral part of the Comintern's apparatus, directed from Moscow.

Ho was a great master of the 'united front' technique. In 1941 he gathered his Vietnamese followers in Kwangsi province, in south China, and created the Vietminh—a contraction of a lengthy string of names meaning League for the Independence of Vietnam. Later, he created a whole series of other fronts, according to needs, and set up communist parties under deceptive names in Laos and Cambodia.

In prolonged negotiations with the French, Ho tried to persuade them to hand over their Vietnamese territories to his party. During the Second World War, many of these French colonial officials remained loyal to their Vichy government, and so they maintained an uneasy collaboration with the Japanese. Meanwhile, Ho's colleague Vo Nguyen Giap, an authentic military genius, was training guerrillas. On 19 December 1946 the Vietminh struck, with a general massacre of French people in Hanoi, capital of Vietnam's northern province on Tonking. So began a long and bitter war, one which was to overshadow even the Korean War in its impact on the cold war.

Ho was personally ambitious, but he was also a loyal Comintern agent. He was greatly helped by Mao Tse-tung's victory in the Chinese civil war and the arrival of Chinese communist forces along the northern border of North Vietnam meant easier supplies for Ho and his commander-in-chief, General Giap. The Vietminh political and military organisation steadily gained the upper hand over the French.

Although Giap's technique of 'people's revolutionary war' owed more to Mao's example and writings than to Lenin or Stalin, Ho's political methods reflected his orthodox Moscow training. Taking a leaf out of Stalin's book he ostentatiously announced the dissolution of the Communist Party of Indochina in 1945 (as Stalin had 'dissolved' the Comintern in 1943), but soon revived it as the Vietnamese Workers' Party (Lao Dong Dang). Meanwhile, he set up front organisations on the Soviet model and created and controlled the People's Revolutionary Party in Cambodia and the Laotian People's Party in Laos.

To assist him, the Soviets used their forum in the UN and mobilised the vast resources of the world communist movement's propaganda machine. A major part was played by the French Communist Party in systematically undermining French morale on the home front (where revolutionary wars are won or lost). In the end, the Soviets made a massive and decisive contribution to the Vietnamese Communist defeat of the French garrison at Dien Bien Phu in North Vietnam by sending supplies of modern artillery and other arms and equipment overland via China.

As the struggle for Indochina was nearing its climax, the Big Four foreign ministers met in Berlin in January 1954 to consider German reunification, a peace treaty for Austria and other problems. The meeting ran into the usual deadlock and adjourned on 18 February. It was agreed, however, that it should resume on 26 April in Geneva, to deal with the problems arising out of the Korean and Indochina wars.

By the time the Geneva conference convened, the French were in dire straits at Dien Bien Phu, being surrounded, mercilessly pounded by Soviet artillery from the hills around them and dependent on uncertain air supplies. At home in Paris, morale was low, and as early as 9 March the government of Joseph Laniel had indicated that it was ready to discuss a peace settlement. Although President Eisenhower declared on 24 March that the defeat of communist aggression in Indochina and elsewhere in South-east Asia was crucial to the United States, the Americans declined a French request of air assistance to the defenders of Dien Bien Phu. The fortress fell on 7 May.

A new Premier, the French socialist Pierre Mendès-France, came to office with a pledge to end the fighting within a month or resign— a pledge he was able to fulfil at the last moment by the subterfuge of 'freezing' the clocks at midnight on the night of 19–20 July in the negotiating chamber in Geneva.

The Vietnamese communists had hoped to be awarded about three-quarters of the national territory, but under pressure from their Soviet allies they had to content themselves with about half, with Vietnam to be partitioned on the 17th Parallel. As usual, the Soviets thought globally, and Indochina was only one of their current concerns. Possibly a still more important concern to them at the time was a proposal for the creation of a European Defence Community (EDC) which would have involved the re-armament of West Germany.

The EDC proposal was shortly due for consideration in the French National Assembly. As a Jew, Mendès-France was instinctively against German re-armament, and in return for Molotov's agreement to the partition of Vietnam on the 17th Parallel, he undertook to kill the EDC project. Both sides of the bargain were kept, and on 30 August 1954 the French parliament rejected the EDC treaty. The net outcome of the Geneva settlement was that the communist hold on the northern half of Vietnam was given international recognition and that West German rearmament was forestalled, though only temporarily, as it turned out.

As usual, Soviet foreign policy was conducted on a variety of levels, of which diplomacy was only one. Agitation and propaganda also played their part, as did espionage and subversion, the arms build-up and aid to surrogates in distant places (such as Korea and Vietnam). On the whole, however, the period of the struggle for power in Moscow (1953–8) represents a relative lull in the expansionist drive of the USSR. During this time, the collective leadership in Moscow made a number of conciliatory gestures to the West, though without neglecting opportunities created during the Stalin era, as in Vietnam, or by exploiting differences within the Western powers, as in Egypt. As soon as Khrushchev had all power in his hands, he felt sufficiently self-confident to resume the forward march of Soviet communism, which he did with increasing truculence between 1958 and 1962.

The 'B and K act', mentioned earlier, really got into its stride in 1955. Three times that year and again in the spring of 1956, Bulganin and Khrushchev went on much-publicised trips abroad. Both men drank a great deal in those days, and showed it; the ribaldry and alternations of bonhomie and belligerence gave good copy to the hordes of journalists who followed their peregrinations.

The most striking instances of conciliation were over Austria and Yugoslavia, although both cases served the broader interests of Soviet policy. The Soviets had consistently turned down all Western proposals for a peace treaty with Austria and rebuffed UN resolutions to the same end. On 8 February 1955, however, Foreign Minister Molotov surprised Western governments by declaring that under certain conditions Soviet troops could be withdrawn from Austria. At the beginning of May, the foreign ministers of the USSR, the United States, Britain and France met in Vienna, and on the 15th, after unusually short negotiations, they announced agreement on a State Treaty guaranteeing the sovereignty of a neutralised Austria.

This sudden end to Soviet intransigence puzzled many observers, but has to be seen against the background of looming military confrontation in Europe. The Soviets maintained armed forces in Rumania and Hungary under Stalin's peace treaties with those countries, which declared that these forces were needed 'for the maintenance of the lines of communication of the Soviet Army with the zone of occupation in Austria'. The Soviets, however, had decided to set up a military alliance in Eastern Europe as an answer to NATO, which would provide a fresh and permanent excuse to keep their forces in

Rumania and Hungary. Austria was therefore no longer needed as a pretext, and the enforced neutrality of that country would remove Western occupation forces from a country bordering the Soviet empire.

Following the failure of the European Defence Community, the Western Allies in October 1954 had invited Germany to join NATO. This decision was formally implemented on 9 May 1955, and five days later the Warsaw Pact was announced. The following January, the Warsaw Pact decided to set up a new East German army.

Moscow's decision to seek a reconciliation with Yugoslavia was a remarkable example of the new flexibility made possible by the death of Stalin. It was the first venture of Premier Bulganin and party boss Khrushchev into the arena of international summitry. In a speech at Belgrade airport on arrival, Khrushchev made the *faux-pas* of blaming the rift of 1948 on Beria (which went down badly, since Tito knew as well as Khrushchev that all the hostile decisions against Yugoslavia were taken by Stalin in person).

Khrushchev did, however, offer a full apology for past offences. The visit was less than a complete success, and the course of Soviet–Yugoslav relations was uneven over the ensuing two years. Having burnt his bridges with Moscow in 1948, Tito was willing to be friends again, but not to rejoin the Soviet bloc: his own concept of non-alignment had become more congenial to him.

The other 'B and K' trips in this period were to the Geneva summit meeting in July 1955, to India for a six-weeks' tour in November and December, and to Britain in April 1956. The Geneva summit enabled Khrushchev to meet President Eisenhower for the first time, along with Anthony Eden of the United Kingdom and Edgar Faure of France. It was essentially a public platform for the proclamation of rival positions that were already known in advance of the conference. Bulganin called for an all-European system of collective security and arms reductions, together with the prohibition of atomic weapons under an unspecified system of international control. All foreign forces should withdraw from Europe and both German governments should take part in collective security arrangements on a basis of equality.

President Eisenhower and his Western colleagues called for the re-unification of Germany through free elections and tabled a proposal for 'open skies' inspection of Soviet and American territory by aircraft of their respective countries; which the Soviets rejected out of hand. He also brought up the subject of international communism, which Bulganin declined to discuss on the ground that state-to-state relations had nothing to do with relations between communist parties.

On 19 July, when the summit conference was scarcely 24 hours old, the Soviets released a bombshell: the signature of an Egyptian trade agreement with Czechoslovakia, under which Egypt would receive large quantities of arms and military equipment, to be paid for in deliveries of Egyptian cotton over the following years. In effect, President Gamal Abdel Nasser had mortgaged his country's cotton crops for years ahead in return for arms.

The deal had in fact been negotiated by Dimitri Shepilov, at that time the editor of *Pravda*, the Soviet party daily. The following year (1 June 1956), in recognition of his diplomatic skill, Shepilov replaced Molotov as foreign minister. Strictly speaking, the deal was a spectacular Soviet incursion into the Arab world, made possible by the reluctance of the Western powers to sell arms to Egypt in its confrontation with Israel. But the device of presenting it as a Czech arms deal was designed to deflect possible criticism of the Soviet Union. Possibly as a sequel, Moscow announced on 12 August that the Soviet Union was to reduce its armed forces by 640,000 men because of the post-Geneva 'relaxation of international tension'.

A follow-up conference of the Big Four foreign ministers, in Geneva in late October, nevertheless began and ended in deadlock. The cold war was settling down into a long-term confrontation.

The 'B and K' visit to India, during which they attracted a spectacular welcome, was designed to establish the Soviet Union's credentials as the champion of peoples struggling for their freedom against 'colonialism', and was marked by vituperative Soviet attacks on Britain as the former colonial power of India.

The Soviet leaders had rightly calculated that the British Prime Minister, Anthony Eden, would not renege on the invitation to visit Britain which he had extended to Bulganin and Khrushchev in the euphoria of the Geneva summit. The calculation was correct and the visit went ahead as planned. At his most truculent, Khrushchev publicly demanded the lifting of the Allied ban on the delivery of strategic materials to the Soviet Union and boasted of new Soviet 'guided missiles with a hydrogen head that can fall anywhere in the world'. (On 8 August, 1953, Premier Malenkov, as he then was, had announced that 'the United States no longer possesses a monopoly of the hydrogen bomb'.) Ahead of their visit to Britain the Soviet leaders had sent General Serov, head of the secret police, to supervise security arrangements. The arrival in Britain of Beria's successor touched off a storm of press and other public protests and Serov had to cut off his trip and go home, to the apparent astonishment of the Soviet leaders.

The British visit was marked, or marred, by an extraordinary incident during a reception for the two visitors given by the Labour Party Executive in the House of Commons. The Labour leader, Hugh Gaitskell, presented his guests with a list of the names of some two hundred East European social democratic politicians who had disappeared, and asked them to find out what had happened to them. Gaitskell, of course, knew, as Bulganin and Khrushchev did, that all had been shot. George Brown (later Lord George-Brown) engaged in a slanging match with Khrushchev, who later described social democrats as 'enemies of the working class' and told Eden, half in jest, that he was thinking of joining the Conservative Party.

Later that year, the Soviet leaders were faced with the crisis in Poland and Hungary which we have already described. But it so happened that a crisis within the Western alliance erupted at the same time as the Hungarian uprising, when Britain and France sent an expeditionary force to Egypt to topple President Nasser after his decision to nationalise the Suez Canal Company. The story of the Suez crisis is told more fully in the following chapter, since it belongs to the problems arising within the Western alliance. However, it enabled Moscow to score a notable propaganda victory.

At the height of the Suez crisis Premier Bulganin sent notes to Britain, France and Israel (which had invaded Egypt), threatening to rain rockets on their territory and send volunteers to help the Egyptians unless they halted their military action.

Almost immediately, the Anglo–French expedition was called off, and the Israelis stopped in their tracks. The Soviets naturally took the credit for stopping the fighting, but the fact is that the British decided to call the whole thing off in the face of severe financial pressure from the United States. The public were not immediately aware of the true facts, and the Soviets took the credit at minimum cost.

Nearly a year later, on 5 October, the Soviets scored a far greater propaganda victory, backed this time by genuine substance, when they fired an earth satellite, Sputnik I, into orbit. A few weeks later,

Sputnik II was fired into outer space, this time with a dog as its passenger. This Soviet triumph, the first of its kind in history, demonstrated to the whole world, and above all to the Americans, that whatever its backwardness in some respects, the Soviet Union possessed the most powerful rockets in the world.

A year later, armed with this knowledge and brimming with self-confidence after eliminating all his rivals in the struggle for power in the Kremlin, Nikita Khrushchev went over to the offensive, with the standard combination of threats and military might. His chosen objective was West Berlin. Ten years earlier, Stalin had failed to subdue the West Berliners or force the Allies out of their occupation sectors. Since then, the very existence of the West Berlin enclave had become more and more intolerable to the communist side. As an island of capitalist prosperity in the surrounding drabness of a collectivist State, it acted as an irresistible magnet to the East German people. Every month, nearly 30,000 'voted with their feet' by seeking refuge in West Berlin. With every refugee who crossed over, the validity of the communist system was further undermined.

On 27 November 1958, Khrushchev delivered a six-months' ultimatum to the Western allies. During that time, he said, West Berlin should be turned into a free city, if necessary under UN supervision, and for that period there would be no interference in Western traffic to Berlin. If nothing was done during the six months, however, the Soviets would hand over all their functions in West Berlin to the East Germans, with whom, in future, the Allies would have to deal.

Predictably, the formal answer of the Western powers, issued on 31 December, was that the four-power agreements on Berlin were not obsolete, and that Russia was responsible for discharging its obligations.

Khrushchev, though bold enough to issue an ultimatum, was not bold enough to do anything much when the Allies called his bluff. He was no Stalin. The Allies stood firm and on 27 May 1959, after an abortive meeting of the four foreign ministers in Geneva, the ultimatum, almost forgotten by now, was allowed to expire quietly.

The Soviet leader was soon to show, however, that he was not prepared to give up as weakly as the course of his ultimatum might have suggested. The main objectives of Soviet foreign policy in the post-Stalin era emerged with some clarity during this period. these were:

to end the special status of West Berlin, to isolate West Germany from its allies, to flatter General de Gaulle into the belief that he could settle European affairs without reference to the United States, and yet to build a special relationship with the Americans on the basis of joint superpower responsibility for the peace of the world.

Although Chancellor Adenauer of the German Federal Republic had visited the Soviet Union in September 1955, he and his government were the target of unremitting hostility on the part of the Soviet press and radio, whereas the Soviet ambassador to Paris, Mr Vinogradov, cultivated warm relations with de Gaulle. As for Eisenhower, Khrushchev toured the United States, complete with his family and a large retinue of officials, for two weeks in September 1959. It was the first time a political boss of the Soviet Union had come to America, and he was greeted with a mixture of apprehensiveness and natural curiosity. The media recalled that in 1957, in an interview with an American television company, he had declared: 'Your children will live under Communism.' Then again, in a casual but much-reported remark, he had said to the American people: 'We will bury you.'

He had never bothered to explain just what he meant by these four threatening words, which could have referred to a nuclear war which the Russians, but not the Americans, would survive; or merely to his standard view that communism would outlast capitalism. He was taunted with his own words while in the United States and insisted several times that he had not meant them literally. Taking no chances, the Catholic Cardinal Cushing urged the faithful to 'pray in the street, pray any place' while the Soviet leader was in their midst.

At the end of his tour, Khrushchev spent three days with the President in the mountain lodge of Camp David in the Maryland hills. In the final communiqué, Eisenhower made a small but significant concession to his Soviet guest, in agreeing to a resumption of talks on Berlin without the usual clause linking this question to that of German reunification. Otherwise, nothing came of the talks except the intangible 'spirit of Camp David', a recurrent myth of the cold war which was to be blasted a year later.

The Sino–Soviet dispute

At this point we must turn to an event of major significance in post-war history: the rift between the Soviet Union and the Chinese People's

Republic. Although Mao Tse-tung had accepted satellite status for China in his hour of economic need after the long years of war and civil war, this was not a situation that could be expected to continue indefinitely. The size of China, in territory and population, made it impossible for the Russians to treat the Chinese as they treated the subject-peoples of Eastern Europe. In any case, now that China was unified under central rule for the first time in many years it was natural for Chinese communists to aspire to a role of their own on the world stage.

Their 'people's volunteers' in the Korean War demonstrated the effectiveness, though at high cost, of 'human wave' tactics in warfare, even though they had intervened on Stalin's behalf. In diplomacy, their first essay was at the Geneva talks on Korea and Indochina in 1954, where the able premier and foreign minister, Chou En-lai, played a prominent part. With his cosmopolitan background of studies in France and Germany, and an urbane and handsome presence, he was well qualified to present an emollient image of the new China.

In June, during a lull in the conference, he slipped off to New Delhi, where he met Prime Minister Nehru, and publicly endorsed the 'five principles' which Chinese and Indian diplomats had drafted in Peking some weeks earlier. Since these 'principles' have caused as much public confusion as any other official document since the Second World War, they are requoted here:

(1) Mutual respect for each other's territorial integrity and sovereignty.
(2) Mutual non-aggression.
(3) Mutual non-interference in each other's internal affairs.
(4) Equality and mutual benefit.
(5) Peaceful co-existence.

In this new atmosphere of friendship (which was, incidentally, short-lived), the Indian and Chinese leaders, along with the leaders of twenty-seven other African and Asian countries, went to Bandung, in Indonesia, for a conference in April 1955. The so-called 'Afro-Asian' movement was born at that time, and the point of interest in this context is that the Russians, although their vast empire stretched into Asia, were not invited. Khrushchev was considerably irked by this exclusion, and set his Soviet subversive apparatus in motion. With the help of local communist parties in various countries, the

Soviets set up Asian Solidarity Committees. In 1957, an Indian communist was sent to see Nasser of Egypt and persuaded him to convene an Afro–Asian Solidarity Conference in Cairo. At that time, the Chinese still accepted the Soviet leadership of the world communist movement, and raised no objections to Russia's entry into the Afro–Asian movement, as it were, by the back door. Later, as the rift between the two communist giants solidified, the Chinese started accusing the Russians of racism and imperialism.

Although Mao had kow-towed to Stalin in 1950, and restored the military balance in Korea, the Soviet Union's economic aid to China was on a meagre scale. Within months of Stalin's death, the collective leadership in Moscow made amends, by sending an army of specialist advisers to various parts of China, where they supervised the building of factories and power stations. Mao and his colleagues applauded this start, but they wanted the Russians to go further, and concentrate whatever help could be spared for the Third World on China. Instead, Bulganin and Khrushchev embarked on major aid schemes in Egypt (the Aswan dam), India and other non-communist countries.

All this left Mao Tse-tung profoundly displeased. We have already mentioned his displeasure at Khrushchev's failure to consult him when he smashed Stalin's idol and swept away so much of Leninist dogma at the Twentieth Party Congress in 1956. Although the Soviets did seek Chinese advice in the Polish and Hungarian crises that year, they did not seek it in the Middle East crisis of 1958, when the Americans and British intervened in Lebanon and Jordan, respectively. Worse still, Khrushchev had gone to America to visit Eisenhower at a time when Mao was advocating maximum hostility towards the United States. To add insult to all this injury, he had taken a neutral (and later a pro-Indian) stand in the dispute between China and India over Himalayan borders.

The last straw seems to have been the flat refusal of the Russians to part with the secrets of nuclear know-how to the Chinese. In his taped memoirs, Khrushchev accused the Chinese of helping themselves to the spare parts of Soviet missiles, among other misdemeanours. Suddenly, in 1960, the Soviets withdraw all their technicians and advisers from China, leaving the Chinese to their own devices, with unfinished projects in various places.

Despite this treatment, the Chinese Communist Party sent a delegation to Moscow at the end of that year for the major conference of eighty-one parties, mentioned in Chapter 5, where the policy of 'peaceful co-existence' was formally adopted. But it was to be the last time the communist parties of the Soviet Union and China were to participate in a joint exercise of this kind. Henceforth, the Soviet Union became a permanent target for Chinese abuse; and vice versa. The favourite Chinese epithet for the Soviets under Khrushchev was 'revisionist', and for the Chinese from the Soviet side, 'Stalinist'. Later, the Chinese were to dub the Russians 'social imperialists' and 'hegemonists'.

As part of the developing rift, the Chinese revived long-standing claims to territory seized by the Tsars in their westward expansion and incorporated by Lenin into the USSR. Desultory talks on these problems were conducted over the years, punctuated by border clashes between the two armies.

The Sino–Soviet rift was undoubtedly a major reverse for the Soviet Union, and in particular for Khrushchev. The monolithic communist land mass was broken, and henceforth the Soviets, instead of using the Chinese as instruments of their policy, found themselves competing for influence as the Chinese set up rival parties or groups as far afield as Europe and Latin America.

7 Massive Retaliation

Stalin's death and the messages of peace which his successors immediately began to propagate did nothing to persuade Eisenhower and Dulles that the danger to the free world had passed. The Western leaders replied to the new Soviet line with tough statements. But for those then charged with the military defence of the West, there seemed to be a remarkable lack of determination to clothe the words with deeds.

Only in one part of a troubled world was the United States prepared to do more than exhort and preach. This was in Korea. The truce talks had been broken off. There ensued an inconclusive war which pitted American air power against weak Chinese air and ground opposition. American losses, of course, were far less than they had been in the dreadful winter of 1950–51, but men died, the operations devoured equipment and money. Again, the death of Stalin appears to have altered the situation.

Chou En-lai, China's Foreign Minister, returned to Peking after attending Stalin's funeral markedly more pliable than he had been in the previous winter. He announced that China was prepared to resume the truce talks, including the repatriation of prisoners-of-war: a thorny issue which had blocked progress. Eisenhower's reaction was cautiously optimistic. Dulles suggested that peace was possible if the communists would agree to a frontier well north of the present battlelines. This was unacceptable to the Chinese and to the North Koreans.

The Administration's dilemma, one that was to occur repeatedly over the next twenty years, was that it could not focus all its attention on Korea alone. Ho Chi Minh's insurrection in French Indo-China, the eruption of a new rebellion in Laos, new insurgency against the British in Malaya, all had to be considered by the White House. In these circumstances it is not surprising that the Administration chose force over further haggling with the Chinese and their North Korea clients.

American bombers heavily attacked the hydro-electric power plants on the Yalu River on 10 May, an operation that would have delighted MacArthur. Three days later the bombers fulfilled a more unorthodox mission. Most of the water needed for the cultivation of rice by North Korea was stored in more than twenty irrigation dams. Attacks on such dams had been condemned at the Nuremberg trials and great had been the outcry during the Second World War when the Germans had attacked dams in the Netherlands. But for three days American bombers pounded these dams and devastated scores of square miles of North Korean farmlands.

We do not know, we probably never will know, the effect of these two major bombing attacks on the Chinese and the North Koreans. We do know that before long the communists adopted a more conciliatory tone toward some of the issues under debate with the UN and the truce talks were resumed. In this instance the United States had used military power to bring about a desired political result.

The divison of Korea, like that of Germany, was a legacy of the Second World War, part of the deal Roosevelt had struck with Stalin at Yalta. Because of its proximity to Japan, Korea was of special strategic importance to the United States—and, for that matter, to the Soviet Union as well. The strategic importance of Indo-China lay in what came to be called the 'falling dominoes' theory, an important doctrine which Eisenhower formulated when the battle for the French fortress of Dien Bien Phu was at its height. Surrender by the French, warned the President, would have dire consequences. 'You have a row of dominoes set up,' he told a news conference, 'you knock over the first one, and what will happen to the last one is the certainty that it will go over very quickly.' The President went on to express his fear that losses in Indo-China, Burma and Malaya might lead to new threats to Japan, the Philippines and even Australia and New Zealand.

Critics of his and succeeding administrations had a great deal of sport with the 'falling dominoes' principle. The fact is, however, that after South Vietnam fell to the North Vietnamese in 1975, Laos and Cambodia soon fell to communism and Thailand lies vulnerable to new aggression.

The factor that saved South-East Asia from being taken over lock, stock and barrel by Soviet communism was one that neither Eisenhower nor Dulles could have imagined: the split into mutually hostile ideological and national enemies of Peking and its allies and the Soviet Union and its allies. Vietnam today, while clearly ambitious to become the primary power in South-East Asia, is held in check only by the presence of large Chinese air and ground forces close to its northern frontier.

Eisenhower's dilemma was that the geo-political dimensions of a strategy to counter the falling domino theory must inevitably fall upon a superpower. None of America's allies had the resources to undertake the global containment of communism, while the political commitment of the old colonial powers, Britain and France, was to their electorates at home. Although the British were slowly gaining the upper hand in Malaya, it was clear that the French could not master the situation in Vietnam on their own, and the political implications of American military intervention to assist them were unacceptable, both to the French and ultimately to the Americans themselves. For the assumption was that behind Ho Chi Minh's forces lay the army of Red China, a military power for which the West, since Korea, has had an exaggerated respect. The Central Intelligence Agency considered that Chinese retaliation as a result of American entry into the war was an even bet.

Although the President gave serious consideration to a plan for an American air strike against the Vietminh to save Dien Bien Phu, code-name 'Operation Vulture', it was recognised that air power alone would probably not suffice to deter the Vietminh, even if the strike were an atomic one. Eisenhower's military advisors argued that American combat troops would sooner or later have to be deployed, and here the United States ran into another difficulty in its cold war strategy. With the French and to a lesser extent the British pressing for a political solution—ultimately secured at the Geneva Conference—America might find itself fighting alone in a land-war in Asia, something which American politicians could not support so soon after the experience of Korea. Truman's nightmare, in other words, was Eisenhower's also, although Eisenhower at least had no MacArthur to contend with.

The first major political change came when ex-Emperor Bao Dai named Ngo Dinh Diem to become Prime Minister of the South Vietnam that would emerge from the Geneva Conference.

Eisenhower and Dulles remained strongly opposed to any settlement in Indochina that made concessions to the communists. Their resolution on this point was stiffened by pressure from the China lobby and other interested groups in Congress who were bitterly opposed to anything they could interpret as appeasement. The temper of the Congress was illustrated by the passage of a bill, by 390 to 0, that stipulated that no foreign aid funds should be used on behalf of governments committed by treaty to maintain communist rule 'over any defined territory of Asia'. The British and French were the obvious targets.

Meanwhile, Colonel Edward Lansdale had arrived in Saigon charged with the mission of undertaking 'paramilitary operations against the enemy' and 'waging political–psychological warfare'. Diem, therefore, from the outset had some American military support although at that point it was on a small scale, and was designed to improve South Vietnam's internal security.

The *impasse* at Geneva led Winston Churchill to renew his urgings to Eisenhower for a summit conference with the Russians. The President, however, while wishing the Prime Minister well in any bilateral talks with the Soviets, was unwilling. Instead he returned to an old theme; why did not the United Kingdom join the United States in a firm stand against the communist Chinese?

When on 21 July the final agreement was signed between France and the Vietminh, the United States remained aloof, declaring it was not prepared to join in the Final Declaration, as it was submitted to the conference. However, the Administration did pledge that it would refrain from the use of force or the threat of force that might disturb the agreement, and that it would view the renewal of 'aggression' as 'seriously threatening international peace and security'. The Final Declaration called for an election to unite Vietnam. This the Administration endorsed.

The Geneva Conference's results left the United States in a position of diplomatic isolation. Whereas most of the governments concerned saw the Final Declaration as a major step toward peace, Washington's opinion was that the communists had taken a major stride toward the control of South-East Asia. Intelligence told the President that neither the French nor the Vietnamese were capable of establishing a South Vietnam strong enough to resist pressure from the North.

To Washington, the danger in Indo-China seemed part of the greater threat posed by communist China. The confrontation between Chiang Kai shek and Mao Tse-tung had not ended with the defeat of the former in the Chinese civil war. There were two Chinese republics; the People's Republic of China on the mainland

and the Nationalist Republic established in Taiwan by Chiang after his flight from the mainland. Taiwan enjoyed the protection of the United States Navy's Seventh Fleet, under an order issued by President Truman, but Chiang had been instructed by the President not to provoke the PRC. Had the nationalists been confined to Taiwan itself, the confrontation might have been avoided. But nationalist soldiers also had established themselves on a string of islands off the mainland's coast. The most important were the Matsus, including the large island of Quemoy off the port of Amoy. On 3 September the Administration was informed that the People's Liberation Army on the mainland had begun shelling Quemoy.

Since Eisenhower's inauguration the Nationalists, supported by the United States, had been carrying on something approaching a guerrilla war against the mainland. American officers were training and advising Nationalist troops in raids and in clandestine operations by land, sea and air against the PRC. The Nationalist air force, liberally supplied with American equipment, now operated from a string of airfields built with American funds. The extent of the American involvement was not widely known, although even if it had been, it is unlikely that there would have been any serious protests. Eisenhower and Dulles enjoyed widespread support in their campaign against communism. Moreover, the psychological wounds inflicted on American self-esteem by the Chinese victories in Korea were still raw and the Chinese communists were an enemy, as important an enemy to many as the Soviets.

The offshore islands were an important geographical element in the Allied military effort against the mainland. They were bases for raids on the mainland and for radar installations. At a time when very little was known about conditions in the PRC, the information brought back by the raiders was of great importance. Although often inaccurate, especially when it dealt with popular attitudes toward the communist regime, the information did serve to open a window, however, slightly, on the new China.

The shelling, which killed two American officers on Quemoy, posed a new and serious policy problem for the Administration. The decision-making process was complicated by renewed pressure from the China lobby and from the Republican right wing for some meaningful American response. The response would have to appear to be more definite than the treaty which Dulles was cobbling together at the time. This was the South-East Asia Treaty Organisation, a Far East imitation of NATO, whose members included the United States, Australia, Britain, France, New Zealand, Pakistan, the Philippines and Thailand. Thailand was the only signatory that could be considered part of South-East Asia and Pakistan and the Philippines the only other Asian nations. The treaty was yet another example of Dulles's 'pactomania'. It alienated other Asian nations, it failed, in the Vietnam War, to rally European members to America's side and it gave Americans a false sense of unity against further aggression in the area.

The Secretary of State, who had been in Manila selling SEATO, left for Taiwan to reassure Chiang that he was not alone. Eisenhower in Washington had the more difficult job of reconciling expert advice with political expediency.

To begin with, there was a difference of opinion among the Joint Chiefs of Staff about what should be done. The Chairman, Admiral Arthur W. Radford, Admiral Robert Carney, the Chief of Naval Operations, and General Nathan Twining, the Air Force commander, believed that the loss of the islands would destroy Nationalist morale. In consequence they recommended that United States' forces should be employed to hold the islands. In effect this meant putting American air, sea and land forces within shooting range of the People's Liberation Army which had amassed strong forces in the provinces facing Taiwan. The only dissenter was General Matthew Ridgeway, who opposed any attempt to defend the islands. The CIA's report was pessimistic. It forecast that the offshore islands would fall quickly to the communists and that Taiwan would be the next victim unless there was a major American military intervention.

The debate that followed between the President and his advisers marks a turning point in the history of the cold war. By now the Administration had accepted Churchill's dictum that a balance of terror existed in the world. As Eisenhower put it, 'there is no longer any alternative to peace'. America's monopoly of atomic weapons had gone and with it America's ability to force the Soviets to back off, as in the Berlin blockade. Whether the communist Chinese could have been intimidated by the threat of nuclear annihilation was not a realistic option for Eisenhower because of the close alliance which then existed between Moscow and Peking. It would be assumed that an attack on China would bring about war with the Soviet Union—in effect, the nuclear holocaust which would destroy civilisation. There is some evidence that Mao Tse-tung actually sought this outcome, believing that China would survive the holocaust better than anyone else, both in the sheer numbers who would escape a nuclear attack and because her economic development was still at the relatively primitive stage from which recovery would be easier than for the advanced societies of the West, the Soviet Union included. Possibly some intimation of the danger to Soviet interests in Mao's attitude prompted Khrushchev to sever his ties with Peking. But no-one in the West had any idea of the impending rift before it happened. Nor can we be certain, even now, how lasting it will be.

For Eisenhower, there always remained, of course, the resort to bluff and with Dulles huffing and puffing about the world, an element of bluff persisted in America's actions in the China Sea; but in their innermost councils the American leaders knew you could not bluff with nuclear weapons. Their value as a deterrent lay precisely in not bluffing, but keeping them as a last resort in defence of America's vital interests. Also, America's allies had to be considered, and if a policy involved nuclear bluff they would have to be told, which necessarily lessened the chance of the bluff succeeding.

Of course, this raises at once the question of what constitutes a vital interest. The balance of terror inevitably gives an advantage to the political aggressor. He can always probe for weak spots, test responses, pull back if necessary, occupy where possible, and always be safe in the knowledge that only a madman on the other side will invite 'mutually assured destruction'—the phrase which would later be coined to describe this state of affairs.

During Eisenhower's administration, much time was spent and many scares encountered in defending Taiwan, which at the time was judged to be essential to America's strategic security. In 1955 Dulles drew up a mutual defence treaty between Chiang Kai-shek's regime and the United States, and in a special message to Congress, the President told the Chinese, and an uneasy Europe, that the United States had to 'remove any doubt regarding our readiness to fight, if necessary, to preserve the vital stake of the free world' in a free Taiwan and to engage in any operations required to maintain that freedom. In private and in public Dulles underlined the fact that in a Far East war America would have to use tactical atomic weapons.

Dulles's verbose bellicosity understandably worried America's allies. Fearful though they were about the dangers of communist aggression, the majority felt that Taiwan was not a suitable cause for war and Chiang hardly a symbol of embattled liberty. While politicians and military leaders, notably the ineffable Admiral Carney, vied in issuing warnings of the danger of war, Allied governments went about disengaging their states from involvement in an atomic war over Taiwan and the offshore islands. The fact that the offshore islands certainly could not be considered vital to American interests increased the Administration's dilemma.

Indo-China and Taiwan remained constant preoccupations of Eisenhower's administration, who held to the belief that a master plan for military conquest in Asia had been hatched in the Moscow–Peking axis. But in Moscow at this time Khrushchev was establishing his own power-base and in the aftermath of Stalin's cold war ventures the new Soviet leadership was anxious to propagate the idea of 'peaceful co-existence'. Theirs was more of a waiting game, of exploiting situations which arose from the changed power structure in the world caused by the disappearance of the British Empire. Throughout Eisenhower's time in the White House, the Middle East was in ferment, and his first crisis in the region came in Iran, where the Shah, Mohammed Reza Pahlevi, a youthful playboy, found himself dominated by an elderly and charismatic Premier, Mossadegh. Events in Iran seemed to mirror those in Egypt, where King Farouk had been driven out of the country in the *coup* that was engineered by the then-unknown colonel, Gamal Abdul Nasser.

The foundations of Western influence throughout the area were weakening. The Egyptians denounced their treaty of friendship with Britain. The Iranians decided to nationalise the Anglo-Iranian Oil Company. There were rumblings of discontent with the *status quo* from Syria and Iraq. In North Africa, the Algerian war of independence against the French gathered momentum from this upsurge of Arab nationalism.

This was a situation for which the Eisenhower administration, indeed any American administration, was singularly ill-equipped to deal. As long as the United States was able to draw the oil it needed from the Middle East, Washington had been content to let the British, then the paramount power in the area, enforce stability by political skills and military force. But by the 1950s it was clear that although the political skills might be present, Britain's martial strength was ebbing fast around the world.

About this time a significant alteration in the United States' attitude toward Britain began. Since 1945 and the end of the Second World War, the Americans had regarded Britain as almost an equal partner in the West. But Britain's economic weakness, the abandonment of empire and the drastic reductions in her armed strength changed the American view. Ironically, it was Eisenhower, probably the most popular American in Britain, who presided over this change and who, five years later, was to try the Alliance to breaking point.

There can be little doubt that the new American attitude toward the British and the consequent British resentment contributed to a general weakening of the West's position in the crises that were to come. When action was taken in Iran it was largely American. Eisenhower was alarmed by Mossedegh's movement toward the Soviet Union and his embrace of the Iranian Tudeh (Communist) Party. He found this 'very ominous' for the United States. The Central Intelligence Agency, with some help from the British, now attempted to get rid of Mossadegh and instal a more pliable premier. The first attempt failed. The second succeeded, and a General Zahedi succeeded Mossadegh. In August 1953 the Shah, who had fled the country, returned and remained as a staunch friend of the United States until he was ousted in 1979.

The disposition of the Anglo-Iranian Oil Company was highly advantageous to the American oil industry. Five major companies were given a 40 per cent holding in the company which thereafter would operate the nationalised oil industry. The British and Royal Dutch Shell, most of whose shares were owned by the British government, got 54 per cent. Peace, as Eisenhower noted in his diary, reigned in Iran. What he did not note was the wave of political arrests and the suppression of the press that followed Mossadegh's ousting.

On balance, however, the United States had responded vigorously to the possibility of a Soviet intervention in Iran. Eisenhower and Dulles both drew confidence from the result. Their belief that British power in the Middle East was ebbing and that the British were highly unpopular in the Arab world was confirmed. These attitudes were to strain the Western Alliance almost to breaking-point when the centre of Middle East tension shifted to Egypt.

Dulles, in his ceaseless endeavours to strengthen the containment of communism, had, with Eden's help, organised what was called the Baghdad Pact, which at the outset consisted of no more than a treaty of mutual assistance between Turkey and Iraq. Britain soon joined. The Soviets, still focusing on Western policy in Germany, had time for little more than blusterings in *Pravda* about 'imperialist machinations' in the Middle East which, they noted, was close to the frontiers of the Soviet Union.

Nasser, the new Egyptian leader, now entered the international arena in an ominous guise. He had been humiliated by a particularly wounding raid by Israeli paratroopers in Gaza. But he was in no condition to respond. The Egyptian army and air force had neither the weapons nor the ammunition to prevent further Israeli strikes. Nasser first sought aid from the United States. The numbers and the value of the weapons sought was small. But Nasser was engaged in organising a military alliance among Arab states and the obvious target for the alliance could only be Israel, America's protégé in the Middle East. So the Administration was reluctant. Nasser went elsewhere—to the Soviet Union. So began a Soviet involvement in Egypt which was to last from 1954 until 1972, and which was to supply Egypt with the arms with which it fought three wars against Israel.

There was one last opportunity to turn the situation around. Nasser's dream was the completion of the High Aswan Dam on the Nile which, he was convinced, would provide water for new farms and power for rural electrification. To this end he sought United States' and British financial aid. By early 1956 Eugene Black, President of the World Bank, had reached substantial agreement with Nasser on the financing of the project.

But the plan for American aid foundered. In vain Dulles told selected Congressional leaders that the plan was part of a general Administration policy to check the infiltration of Soviet communism into the Arab world. The plan was bitterly attacked by the Israeli lobby in Washington, and these attacks were supported by large elements of public opinion who, without knowing the intricacies of Middle East politics, generally favoured Israel in its struggle for survival.

The year 1956 had begun badly and matters were to get steadily worse. While Dulles and other Administration leaders were fighting to win approval for American participation in the dam project, Nasser sent notes to Washington and London requesting changes in the conditions attached to the original aid proposals. Even then, it is probable, Egypt could have been held in the Western camp, had the

Egyptian President been given at least an indication that the West was studying his proposals for change. But no answer was given. the Administration did not appear to be hostile, Dulles even praised Nasser's 'independence' despite the arms deal. But no answer went out.

This was partly due to Egypt's unexpected diplomatic recognition of the People's Republic of China. In the atmosphere of 1956 this was almost as much of a crime by Nasser as his willingness to obtain arms from the Soviet Union. Egyptian recognition of China, the earlier arms deal, the enmity of the pro-Israel lobby in Congress and the sympathy felt for Israel by a large section of public opinion all contributed to the final decision. The United States repudiated its offer to help Egypt build the dam.

The time chosen was inopportune. On 18 and 19 July Nasser was on the island of Brioni conferring with two other leaders of neutral nations, Josip Tito of Yugoslavia and Jawarhalal Nehru of India. These leaders were still smarting from some off-the-cuff criticisms of neutralism made by Dulles a few days earlier. Nasser, personally, was angered by the wording of the note which cancelled American aid. It criticised Egypt's economy and doubted the country's financial reliability. Both criticisms were fair but it was not the time to say them. Nasser was angry, he regarded the whole affair as an insult to himself and to the Egyptian people. He soon found a way to retaliate, one which had the gravest consequences for Western unity. On 26 July he nationalised the Suez Canal Company.

Britain, which also had repudiated its promise to help finance the dam, held 44 per cent of the stock in the company. The British holding was by far the largest single share and the company was profitable, but it was not profit and loss that concerned Britain. Although the old empire in the east had disappeared, transit through the canal remained essential to British interests. Two-thirds of the United Kingdom's crude oil imports went through the canal and about a third of all the ships using the waterway were British.

To the British and to a lesser degree the French, the Egyptian action, though legal, was close to being an act of war. The French were then passionately anti-Arab and their feelings toward Nasser were not improved by their belief that the Egyptian leader had given help to the rebels in Algeria. The Anglo–French attitude toward Nasser was also infused with memories of the 1930s, when Eden, then British Foreign Secretary, had opposed the Conservative government's policy of appeasement of the dictators, Hitler and Mussolini. Indeed he had resigned from Neville Chamberlain's government. Now, as Prime Minister, he saw in Nasser a successor to these dictators, a man who must be stopped lest he plunge the Middle East and perhaps the world into a third great war. At that early date, late July, the British Prime Minister was already considering the use of force against Nasser to regain the canal.

It is arguable that the diplomatic exchanges from 31 July 1956 and the start of the Suez adventure damaged relations between the Western 'Big Three' more than any other deliberations in the history of the cold war. On all sides there were deceit, half-truths, secret plans never divulged to old allies, misconceptions and misunderstandings.

In Washington Eisenhower's anger grew as he realised that, whatever was said in London and Paris, the British and French were intent on war against Nasser. The two European powers were at first confused and then shocked by Eisenhower's seeming inability to grasp the importance of the Suez Canal and the wickedness of Nasser. Dulles, for whom Eden had developed a strong distaste, was Eisenhower's agent in the negotiations. In contrast to what he regarded as the 'gunboat diplomacy' of Britain and France, the Secretary of State produced the Suez Canal Users Association, which was to be the instrument for collective bargaining with Nasser and for mutual assistance among the Western powers should the Canal be blocked.

The rift between the Americans and the British, the triumphant allies of the Second World War, widened. Eden saw the new association as a necessary tactic to curb Nasser, but warned the House of Commons that if Egypt interfered with it, Britain would feel free to take other courses. Dulles, under prodding by Eisenhower, announced that the United States would not use force. This had a reassuring ring for the American electorate, from whom Eisenhower was seeking a second term.

Israel, smarting from Egyptian attacks, now entered the picture. The Israeli army and air force had been in action against Jordan, but to Ben Gurion and his colleagues the true enemy was Egypt. By the middle of October, the British, French and Israeli governments had evolved a plan of operations; Israel was to attack Egypt in the Sinai Peninsula, the British and French were to demand that the combatants retire from the canal area and then send in troops to 'protect' the canal.

Eden approved the plan. He also decided not to inform Washington. The British cabinet was solidly behind him.

Israeli paratroops attacked in the Sinai on the morning of 29 October. Symbolically, the attack was supported by French air force fighters. The President got the news in the midst of a day of campaigning, he did not know that other Israeli forces were poised to drive deep into the Sinai toward the Suez Canal. The conflict between the United States and its two allies became heated. Eisenhower sent Dulles to the United Nations with an appeal to stop the fighting and a threat of sanctions against Israel. The President in his campaign appearances found that his decision not to countenance force, even British, French and Israeli force, against Nasser was warmly received. In the end American financial pressure rather than UN resolutions in New York or Labour Party protests in London brought the Anglo–French operations to a halt. But the outcome left the West divided more seriously than it had been at any time since the start of the cold war and diverted Western attention from a far more ruthless operation undertaken by the Soviet Union in Hungary.

The Hungarian revolution brought the Eisenhower Administration into the realities of central European politics. For four years the Republicans had been taking a hard line orally about what they would do to free the enslaved peoples of central Europe. Eisenhower had declared that America never would desist in its help for the people of 'those shackled lands', and had stressed the use of every political, economic and psychological means to maintain the spirit of freedom.

Suddenly he and Dulles were up against the real thing. If the promises of the past four years meant anything, the United States would act to 'roll back' communism in central Europe. This had been trumpeted throughout the region by Radio Free Europe. In Dulles's first speech to the American people in January 1953 he had told the Soviets' captive nations 'You can count on us'. Understandably the Hungarian rebels expected help. They got none.

To many people it might seem as if the West's ability to intervene in Hungary had been fatally compromised by the Anglo–French action in Egypt. But viewed objectively, it is clear that Eisenhower would never have ordered American military intervention in Hungary or anywhere else behind the Iron Curtain. Such an act, whatever the excuse, would have been a declaration of war. Better then than later, posterity may argue. But the restraint placed upon the offensive use of America's military power against the Soviets in Europe had been implicit ever since the Yalta Conference. Stalin knew it; Khrushchev knew it; the men who would succeed Khrushchev knew it. And now the enslaved people of Eastern Europe knew it too. They would have to find their own way forward out of the nightmare of communism.

Some moral confusion may have existed in Eisenhower's mind over the use of force in the pursuit of political goals, and his re-election campaign may have added to this confusion. But, as we have seen, he had already resorted to force to bring about a political solution in Korea, and, once re-elected, he would come to see that using force is a necessary responsibility for a world power.

From Cairo to the Persian Gulf, Western power, once represented by Britain and France, had vanished. The United States, the only Western power with its prestige in the area untarnished, except in Israel, had to find a means to fill the gap. For although the Administration bubbled with self-congratulatory comments after the ceasefire in the Canal, it was only too aware that Khrushchev had threatened Britain and France with rocket attacks and that the Russians were already taking advantage of the situation with promises of further military aid to Nasser, whose troops had been badly mauled by the Israelis, and with encouraging approaches promising economic aid to other Arab states. At the same time American sanctions against Israel had alienated the one state that might be counted upon as an ally in the Middle East.

American diplomats in the area reported fears that the Soviets were set upon overthrowing governments moderately friendly to the West and that the situation was most acute in Syria and Lebanon. The immediate American reaction was to send the Sixth Fleet into the eastern Mediterranean and to ship weapons to the threatened governments. Whether these actions prevented Soviet take-overs is unknown. In the event 1957 saw a return to something approaching tranquillity in the region.

Tranquillity, however, did not reign in intelligence circles. For not only had the Soviets launched an artificial satellite but they had tested at least four intercontinental ballistic missiles, which raised their military potential by a quantum jump. This view was reinforced by the *Gaither Report*, published by the Advisory Committee of the Office of Defence Mobilisation. This said that the Soviet Union was superior to the United States in weapon technology and that an increasing threat would become critical in early 1959 or 1960. The report offered little support for the new American position, promoted by the Suez fiasco, of world policeman.

The United States' ability to play that role was to be tested in Lebanon, where a turbulent political scene had been exacerbated by the intention of Camille Chamoun to amend the constitution to provide him with a second term as President. Chamoun's announcement of his intentions sparked riots in Beirut and Tripoli, with much of the violence directed at United States' diplomatic and propaganda installations. The view of Eisenhower and Dulles was that the rioting was communist-inspired, and it represented simply another manifestation of the international communist conspiracy against global stability which the United States upheld. The situation was made no easier by the support given to the rioters by Syria and Egypt and by a well-reported feeling that the United States was insinuating itself into Middle East affairs to replace the British and French. One popular story was that the CIA was behind Chamoun's move.

The American reaction was more military than political. The Sixth Fleet was again ordered into the eastern basin of the Mediterranean. Small arms, ammunition and some out-of-date light tanks were despatched to Beirut. Chamoun told the UN that the rioting, which had now expanded into a rebellion, was instigated and supported by the Egyptian and Syrian governments, then briefly joined in the United Arab Republic. But the trouble was not confined to Lebanon.

On 13 July 1958 Iraqi army officers killed King Faisal and his uncle Abdul Illah in Baghdad. Nuri es-Said, a firm friend of the West, was torn to pieces by a mob. Iraq was the only Arab state that had signed the Baghdad Pact which Dulles had seen as a bulwark against communism in the Middle East. America's position in the Middle East was disintegrating rapidly. Nasser was judged to be behind the murders in Baghdad and the Soviets were believed to be behind Nasser. There was a hurried consultation in the White House. To the President and his advisers there seemed to be no alternative to action. On 15 July the Marines landed in Lebanon and two days later 2,500 British paratroops landed in Jordan to shore up the regime of King Hussein, which had also been under heavy attack.

The subsequent expansion of Soviet influence in the Middle East had no direct impact on Jordan and only an indirect and ephemeral effect on troubled Lebanon. The two interventions thus can be considered a gain for the West in the cold war scorecard. But the price was high; other Arab states reacted indignantly. The Soviet Union's diplomats and propagandists in the area at once set to work portraying the Anglo–American operations as a revival of Western imperialism. The American explanation that the Marines had saved 'tiny Lebanon' from communist domination carried little conviction in Cairo, Baghdad and other Arab capitals. But Eisenhower's action in 1958 begs the question: had he backed the British and French two years earlier at Suez, how different would the subsequent history of the Middle East have been?

The Eisenhower Administration had two and a half years of life remaining. They were not easy years. Khrushchev's confidence was rising and new opportunities for provoking strife appeared in Cuba and Laos. Eisenhower and Dulles, now mortally ill, did their utmost to hold the line and on critical matters, like the future of Berlin, the Western Allies stood united and firm. But the advent of General de Gaulle to power in France in 1958 was to disturb the Alliance, while for propaganda reasons, if for no other, some breakthrough in East–West relations was eagerly sought by other Western leaders like Harold Macmillan of Britain. After Khrushchev's twelve-day visit to the United States in 1959, Eisenhower agreed to another summit meeting, scheduled for Paris in May 1960.

Four years earlier the United States had begun to fly a particularly effective photographic-reconnaissance aircraft, the U-2, over the Soviet Union from bases in Turkey and Pakistan. The U-2 was a valuable and necessary intelligence arm. It also carried with it a definite risk. The Russians who knew about it might somehow shoot one down. But the Administration continued to employ it, although the first American satellites were near deployment. The rationale was that, in view of the continuing Soviet advances in missiles, America must have information.

On 1 May 1960 a U-2 piloted by Gary Powers was shot down over the industrial centre of Sverdlovsk. Although the military consequences were negligible, the political results were vast. When Eisenhower, accompanied by his new Secretary of State, Christian Herter, arrived in Paris for the summit meeting he learned through Macmillan that Khrushchev believed that the President had 'betrayed' him by the use of the U-2. Further statements demonstrated the Soviet leader's outrage. An immediate result of his outrage was a series of diplomatic notes from Moscow to the governments of countries on the perimeter of the USSR protesting at the siting of U-2s, which applied only to Turkey and Pakistan, and a warning of Soviet displeasure for any other countries that provided bases for the United States.

The conference broke down. The only formal meeting provided the stage for a long, bitter diatribe by Khrushchev against the United States, which stated that no further meeting of the Big Four would be necessary and, almost as an afterthought, informed Eisenhower that the President would not be welcome in the Soviet Union, to which he had been invited during Khrushchev's visit to the United States. Thus perished the President's last essay in international summitry.

Eisenhower, the old soldier, left office confident that he had held the line against international communism. He remained convinced to the end of the domino theory. Indeed he explained this to the incoming president on the day before the latter's inauguration.

But although the line might have been held in the eight years between 1952 and 1960, it is clear that the communists had registered considerable gains. They had established a foothold in the Middle East, first in Egypt and, latterly, in Syria and Iraq. In central Europe, the Russians had demonstrated that they would use their armed might to subdue any movement that threatened communist power. East Germany, Poland and Hungary were all obedient members of the Warsaw Pact; the 'roll-back of communism' and 'massive retaliation' had taken their places among the propaganda slogans of history. What Eisenhower's eight years in the White House had proved, if proof was necessary, was that the world would not stand still in a *status quo* acceptable to both Soviets and Americans.

Although Kennedy had campaigned vigorously on the issue of the supposed United States' nuclear inferiority, the limitations on presidential initiatives in the cold war were the same for him as for Eisenhower. A change-over in American administrations is a particularly sensitive time in foreign affairs, as communist strategists are well aware. The problems bequeathed by Eisenhower were as serious and demanding as those he himself had inherited from Truman eight years previously. Whatever the outward glamour of the new face in the White House, cold war realities remained unchanged. In Cuba and Indo-China warning lights were flashing.

8 Khrushchev versus Kennedy

American Presidents cannot choose their priorities, they must cope with immediate, urgent problems. No sooner was John F. Kennedy inaugurated in January 1961 in a mood of supreme national confidence than America suffered a humiliating disaster in Cuba, a tragicomedy we call the Bay of Pigs.

Two of Dwight Eisenhower's decisions established the dilemma before the new President took office. On 17 March 1960 the then-President, Eisenhower, ordered the CIA to assemble a group of Cuban exiles, including adherents of President Fulgencio Batista, the leader deposed by Castro. This was a political decision aimed at assembling a broadly-based political opposition to the new Cuban ruler. The second decision was to direct the CIA to recruit and train a force of Cubans that could engage in a guerilla war against the new regime.

At the outset the first decision posed only superficial problems. Miami, then as now, was filled with refugees. Many of them had been prominent in the old pre-Batista political parties, and they sought re-establishment of the Cuba they had known before the dictator came to power. Others were hard-line anti-Castroites. Five groups vied for leadership, and out of these the CIA recruiters formed the Democratic Revolutionary Front (Frente Revolucionario Democrático).

One of the first and most favourable outcomes from the American point of view was a statement by Manuel Antonio de Varona, a pro-Batista Prime Minister, that any new government that supplanted Castro's would restore the properties seized by the Castro regime to their American and Cuban owners.

The front was little more than a political facade. The fighting was to be done by the refugees which the agency was recruiting among Cuban refugees in Central America and Florida.

By intelligent manipulation the CIA had obtained permission

from President Miguel Fuentes Ydígoras of Guatemala to establish a training camp and an air base in his country. The original CIA plan, which in retrospect has much to commend it, was to filter small groups of guerrillas into Cuba. There they would establish resistance areas to which, it was hoped, dissatisfied Cubans would flock. The theory was that as these resistance groups prospered they would present a challenge to Castro comparable with that which he had offered Batista. Eisenhower approved the expenditure of $13 million for the programme, stating explicitly that no American military were to take part in any combat operations.

The plan was changed. The CIA became convinced that the recruits had been penetrated by Castroites. They found it difficult to communicate with the scattered bands of guerrillas already operating in Cuba. In the gradual expansion of Soviet influence in the Cuban army and the transfer of Russian arms to that force they saw a barrier to effective popular resistance. The alternative was to train and arm a force that would land on the Cuban coast. It was to be supported by air power, there were a few B-26s from the Second World War available, and it would have artillery and all the available weapons of conventional warfare. The Army sent a team to train the chosen guerrillas in the techniques of landing operations.

This shift from a modest resistance operation to a more ambitious landing on the Cuban coast reflected the supreme confidence of not only the CIA but the American government and people of that period. It was to be a confidence that was to be eroded by the next ten years, but in January 1961, when John F. Kennedy, took office it was strong, a key element in the national outlook on the cold war.

The CIA's 'army' assumed a life of its own, the Agency men who supervised the training were understandably apt to favour those Cubans who were amenable to their plans rather than those who had strong ideas about the political structure of a liberated Cuba. But all the Cuban personnel were greatly heartened as new weapons flowed into the camp and as American officers intensified the training.

The military training, however, was accompanied by some critical mistakes. The Cubans were led to believe by the American trainers, Army officers as well as CIA officials, that their force was only one of many that would land to overthrow Castro. To this false concept they added their own conviction that, once they did land, thousands of Cuban patriots would rise to assist them in the defeat of the anti-American dictator. As so often happens in war and politics, those who disseminated and believed this were in a sense guiltless. Information from within Cuba was scanty, but in the eyes of the exiles it was clearly a communist dictatorship; armed uprising *had* been successful against other dictatorships. With the United States behind them how could they fail?

The American dilemma was clear. If the landing was to be successful, there would have to be powerful American support, although much of this could be obscured by vicarious operations. But, if the landing failed, the American responsibility and support would be evident and the Administration's role that much harder to explain.

Operations such as the Bay of Pigs do not exist in isolation. Quarrels within the Cuban leadership, CIA doubts about defections and, above all, intelligence reports that Castro was about to receive jet aircraft from the Soviet Union which would be flown by Cubans trained in Czechoslovakia, quickened the pace. By March Kennedy was confronted with the choice of unleashing the invasion or withdrawing. The decision-making process was not eased by a sudden switch in operational plans. The landing site finally selected was the Bay of Pigs, where there was an airstrip and the protection of swamps.

The testimony of refugees is seldom a sure guide to military action. The CIA during this waiting period was smothered in requests for arms from Cuban anti-Castroites and emboldened by reports of the tens of thousands of Cubans prepared to turn on the dictator as soon as, in the Spanish phrase, the invaders 'raised the shout'. Clearly these messages had an effect on Allen Dulles, the Director of the CIA, and his colleagues. Just as clearly they were the sort of reports that should have been investigated before the invasion armada embarked.

The Kennedy Administration was in a hole, one that it had dug. No President could proclaim a national willingness to fight for freedom, and prepare, as he was doing, to send troops to fight in Laos half a world away, and then fail to answer the call of 'freedom-fighters' on his own doorstep. There were strong voices outside the Administration pleading for caution and restraint. But the pressures within the Administration for action grew daily. Toward the end of the internal discussions it was evident that the President and his colleagues recognised and accepted the risk that the United States would be implicated in the adventure and blamed if it failed.

D-day was set for 17 April 1961. It is not to the credit of the United States that, up until the debarkment, the officers and men of the brigade were stuffed with stories of other landings and of heavy American support in the form of aircraft and reinforcements. Perhaps such lies were necessary to stimulate a force of 1,400 men, only 135 of whom had military experience, destined to land on a hostile coast. But they were lies nonetheless. The brigade's original mission was to hold the beachhead for three days. By the end of that period, it was assumed, on dubious authority, that thousands of rebels against Castro would have rallied to the cause and the march on Havana would be a victory parade rather than a military operation.

Seven ships carrying the brigade set out from Nicaragua. Eight B-26s attacked Cuban airfields harbouring the Castro air force of about 29 aircraft, none of them Soviet-made. The results, the returning pilots said, had been decisive; there was extensive damage. But the next day's reconaissance flights showed that only five aircraft had been destroyed. The CIA declared that the Cuban air force was 'almost non-existent'.

Kennedy had now directed the brigade to make for the Bay of Pigs and land on the beaches. To support the troops a second air strike had been arranged. In theory this strike would originate from the airstrip on the beachhead. But since this strip had not yet been secured—the first infantry were not yet ashore—the world would get the impression that it had come from Nicaragua and the United States would bear the onus. Kennedy cancelled the second strike. It was the first step toward disaster.

Ironically, the first of the frogmen to land on Cuban soil to mark the beachhead boundaries was an American. So much for the orders of two American Presidents against overt involvement in the adventure. As the frogmen went about their business, men of the brigade dropped from their transports into the landing crafts and set out for the shore. As always happens with inexperienced troops, some of the landing craft lost their way, and others foundered with the men swimming for the shore. It was realised, too late, by the CIA directors of the mission that an opposed landing at night from the sea is the most difficult of military operations.

Castro's froces reacted promptly and effectively. The ship carrying ten days' supply of ammunition for the brigade was sunk by a

Cuban air force Sea Fury. Other ships were damaged and harassed as soon as the little squadron put out to sea. The brigade's air support materialised in the form of some B-26s, and Castro's T-33s, training aircraft now armed with machine guns, shot down four of these out-of-date bombers. On the ground, things went a little better. The invaders dug in, supported by a few tanks, mortars and recoilless rifles, while Castro's forces, unable to cross the swamps, pushed down the single road leading to the beachhead.

The situation continued to deteriorate. The B-26s tried another attack on the main Cuban airfield but could not locate it in the early morning haze. Castro's tanks reached the battlefield well ahead of the expected time. Above all, the popular rising against Castro, on which the CIA and the Cuban leaders had placed such high hopes, did not develop. The brigade was on the beach alone, and each minute saw the reinforcement of the defending forces.

Step away from the sand, the heat, the flies, the wounded and the dead. The United States is faced with one of the many tough decisions of the cold war. Those people fighting and dying there on the beach were sponsored by America. Are they to be supported? Why not send in the Marines? The temptation before the young President was a serious one, but he resisted it. The principal reason that emerges from the writings of those who, like Arthur Schlesinger Jr, were with him was that the Cuban people had failed to respond to the invasion. In view of this, the United States by sending in the Marines would be trying to impose an alien rule upon the Cubans. But failure at the Bay of Pigs meant that Kennedy would have to face a far graver crisis in Cuba eighteen months later.

The brigade's position worsened rapidly. There were now about 20,000 Castro troops led by tanks and supported by artillery closing in on the thin lines that held the bridgehead. Unless there was a prompt and powerful American military intervention the brigade and the whole adventure were doomed.

There was one last attempt to retrieve the situation. Like many such attempts, it was too little and too late. The President authorised the flight of six unmarked jets from the Navy's carrier *Essex* which was lying off Cuba. The planes' mission was to protect a flight of non-American B-26s, sent from Nicaragua to bomb the Castro forces on the beachheads, but, like all the operations after the first day, this also failed. The Navy's jets were an hour late for the rendezvous over the beachhead. The B-26s, their pilots very tired after three days of operations, went in unprotected and were badly mauled.

By now the situation was hopeless from Washington's standpoint. The best the White House could offer was plans for a rescue mission that would pick the remnants of the brigade off the shore. But the brigade, hammered by Castro's artillery and savaged by his tanks, gradually lost all coherence. Some men escaped into the Escambray mountains, but the majority were taken off to Castro's prisons.

Thus the Bay of Pigs ended in disaster and recrimination within the United States government. The effect on America's position in the cold war was bad, but, as we shall see, this was temporary. It was bad because of the repercussions overseas and because it led to the first of those many 'house-cleanings' that have gradually emasculated the CIA.

Cuba, Laos, the continuing war in Vietnam were important but peripheral problems for Kennedy. His central, abiding problem remained—the Soviet government and its policy. On 6 January 1961 a speech by Khrushchev had outlined the view of the world from the Kremlin.

It was a tough, truculent speech because, as Arthur Schlesinger pointed out Moscow in early 1961 'had its own euphoria' comparable with that which had swept through the Democratic Administration after the President's inaugural speech.

To the Soviet leaders things were going their way. Industrial production was rising at a rate faster than that in the United States. The Soviet Union had developed the hydrogen bomb and had taken a lead over the United States in long-range missiles. Abroad, revolutionary movements were seen to prosper from Cuba to Vietnam. The Soviet Union, through its security agreement with Egypt, had established a foothold in the Middle East.

Despite these Soviet gains there was a note of prudence in Khrushchev's speech. The Russian leader shied away from the idea of world war or even what he called 'local wars'. But to the concern of the Americans and their allies he came down strongly for Soviet support of wars of national liberation, which he interpreted as popular risings against imperialists and colonialists. 'The communists,' he said, 'support just wars of this kind whole-heartedly and without reservation and they march in the van of the peoples fighting for liberation.' This passage is one of the most revealing in the literature of the cold war. What it meant was that the Soviet Union intended to support wars such as those then being waged in Algeria and Vietnam and to support Cuba and other newly independent countries whose policies were anti-American and anti-Western.

One passage in Khrushchev's speech had an immediate message for the White House. It dealt with Berlin. The Western position there was 'especially vulnerable' Khrushchev said, and the American, British and French governments must realise that 'sooner or later' the occupation regime (in the three Western sectors) 'must be ended'.

The threat was one that the Eisenhower Administration had heard. If the West did not accept 'the real situation' then the Soviets would sign a peace treaty with the German Democratic Republic.

The ghosts of Yalta were at work again. Whatever faults the newly installed Administration could find in the foreign policies of the Eisenhower government, it could not deny that it had been warned by its predecessor. Biting the bullet, the President, his advisers and a host of bright young men from industry and academia turned to the problem of national defence. Grand strategy was reviewed, steps were taken to improve the strategic nuclear forces and to raise the levels of weaponry and training in the tactical air forces.

The Seventh Fleet was ordered into the South China Sea. Combat units in Okinawa were prepared for deployment. In Thailand, across the Mekong river from Vientiane, Marines and helicopters appeared. In March, Kennedy asked for a supplemental $650 million for the defence budget.

Khrushchev responded to these moves by a conciliatory gesture in Laos. But, as is characteristic of Soviet cold war tactics, a Soviet concession in one area was accompanied by a challenge elsewhere. Khrushchev decided the time was ripe to test the young American President face to face.

From the Soviet standpoint, Kennedy's handling of the Bay of Pigs affair had been weak. In the same situation Khrushchev would have 'thrown the book' at Castro's forces, calling on all the military resources necessary. That Kennedy had not done so appeared to the Soviet leader a sign of irresolution. So Khrushchev suggested that he and Kennedy should meet at Vienna in early June. the President had already scheduled a trip to France to talk to de Gaulle, his most difficult ally.

The Vienna meeting opened in discord and closed on a sombre note. Khrushchev complained that the Soviet Union had tried for years to establish friendly relations with the United States, but that its efforts had been barred by the anti-communism of Dulles. Communism, however, had won around the world and no power could halt its development and expansion.

Kennedy's rebuttal was that the United States and its allies were not attempting to stifle communism in the countries that had embraced it, but only to offer an alternative in countries associated with the West where the communists were attempting to eliminate freedom.

But Khrushchev took full advantage of the young President's discomfiture in Cuba. When Kennedy tried to persuade Khrushchev to stop trying to alter the *status quo* by supporting anti-Western revolutions all over the world, he was treated to an illuminating lesson in political semantics. Khrushchev explained that in his eyes, the *status quo* meant allowing the communist revolution to go ahead, whenever it occurred, all over the world. And he accused the American President of being the one who was trying to alter the *status quo* by interfering with the revolutionary process.

From ideology, the discussion moved to Berlin and the peace treaty which Khrushchev proposed to sign with East Germany. The Soviet Union, said Khrushchev, would 'never' under any conditions accept American rights in West Berlin after the treaty was signed. Moscow was determined on its course and the responsibility for any violations of the treaty would be heavy. The final exchange was sombre.

Khrushchev: 'I want peace, but if you want war, that is your problem.'
Kennedy: 'It is you and not I who wants to force a change.'

The Soviet leader repeated his charge that it was up to America to choose between peace or war. The Soviet Union, he said, would certainly accept any challenge. His decision on the treaty was irrevocable. He would sign it in December.

Kennedy: 'It will be a cold winter.'

The President returned to Washington where the Administration prepared for a military confrontation. American diplomacy required the backing of increased defence funds, new weapons and an expanded programme of civil defence. National Guard and Reserve units were called up. America's commitment to Berlin was confirmed in an address by the President to the nation.

For his part, Khrushchev came away from the Vienna meeting convinced that the President of the United States was no match for him. As he saw it, the Bay of Pigs was the American equivalent of Hungary in 1956 for the Soviets. Since the Americans had shown they were not tough enough to see the matter through in Cuba, he concluded that they would not take action if the Soviets challenged them in Berlin.

In August 1961 Khrushchev put his conclusion to the test and proved his point triumphantly. Recognising that he could not physically evict the Allies from West Berlin without risking a nuclear war, Khrushchev decided instead to seal off the three Western sectors from the Soviet sector of the city in order to halt the steady flow of refugees which was draining East Germany of much-needed skills.

On the night of 13 August, teams of East German navvies protected by Soviet tanks split the city into two by building a wall and placing along it the intimidating apparatus of an Iron Curtain frontier. As Khrushchev had calculated, the Western Allies did nothing. After the event, President Kennedy sent Vice-President Lyndon Johnson to West Berlin to make a speech assuring West Berliners of American support, and a protest note went to the Kremlin. Having gained his objective in East Berlin, Khrushchev allowed the question of a treaty with East Germany to lapse.

The Berlin Wall demonstrated an uncomfortable fact of cold war politics. As the crisis subsided, both sides could congratulate themselves on the outcome. In propaganda terms, the Soviets appeared to have climbed down over the peace treaty while the Wall stood as a visible monument to the failure of communism. But in terms of power, it produced actual results in stemming the flow of refugees and skills which had been so damaging to East Germany. Further, in the eyes of the world it seemed as if the Soviets could indeed act with impunity. The advantage once again had gone to the political aggressor. The Soviets knew that time, aided by Western media, would rob the adverse propaganda of its force. On the other hand, what had the Western Allies actually done? Some 1,500 American soldiers had driven down the autobahn to West Berlin without hindrance, but they had not knocked the Wall down. Although West Berliners greeted Johnson, and later Kennedy himself, enthusiastically, all the rhetoric in the world would not breach the Wall. Its construction had closed one more door on freedom and forced the reality of their divided country upon all Germans.

In a letter to Kennedy, Willy Brandt, the socialist Mayor of West Berlin, complained of the feebleness of the West's response. Maybe the conviction was borne in on him and on other Germans at this time that West Germany would henceforth have to pursue a radically different policy towards the Soviets from Konrad Adenauer's, a change Brandt subsequently effected when he became Chancellor.

We must assume that Khrushchev also read the Western response as weak. At this time the Soviets were ahead in space technology and were pressing forward with nuclear tests in violation of previous agreements. In the autumn of 1961 they exploded a fifty-megaton bomb, the largest thus far. (One megaton equals one million tons of TNT.) Khrushchev's success in Berlin may thus have emboldened him to embark on his most audacious move to date, the emplacement of nuclear missiles on Cuba, ninety miles from the continental United States.

No-one knows why Khrushchev took this risk. It marked a sharp divergence from Soviet practice. No missiles had ever been deployed on the territory of the East European satellites. None had been given to China during the period of military and political co-operation between the two communist giants.

Whatever the genesis of the move there could be no doubt about the danger for America. With a range of about a thousand miles, they would be able to strike at a number of cities in the southern and south-eastern United States and just about double the Soviet offensive capacity against American targets. Had they been allowed to remain America's diplomatic and military position in the world would have been seriously weakened.

From CIA reports Kennedy knew that something unusual was happening in Cuba. In August 1962 there were already about 5,000 Soviet military advisers and training personnel on the island, but more were arriving each week. With them came shipments of heavy construction equipment and electronic devices. The intelligence estimate was that Khrushchev had decided that Cuba must have protection against external attack. The Soviet leader may also have concluded that with the Bay of Pigs incident fresh in the world's memory, no outside power could object if the Soviet Union provided serious military assistance to its Cuban allies.

The Administration had taken the precaution of doubling the number of flights over Cuba by U-2 photographic reconaissance aircraft. In early September, Soviet merchantmen sailed from Black Sea ports carrying forty-two nuclear missiles, technicians and operational crews. On 14 October a U-2 flight brought conclusive evidence of a Soviet missile on the ground at San Cristobal, together with a launching pad and storage for other missiles. Soviet diplomats solemnly denied that anything unusual was afoot. The crisis had begun.

Kennedy and his advisers considered America's options. The immediate alternative seemed to be between an air strike against the nuclear bases or their acceptance. But so grave was the situation that all other possibilities had to be explored.

Meanwhile, the Administration gathered its military resources. About 40,000 Marines scheduled to participate in an exercise were held in the Caribbean area. The 82nd and the 101st Airborne divisions of the Army were alerted for immediate deployment. In all, the Army assembled about 100,000 troops in Florida and the Air Force brought in tactical fighter squadrons from bases all over the country. About 14,000 Air Force reservists were recalled to fly transports in the event that airborne operations were required.

As invariably happens in the planning of operations, the military raised the operational level for any strike against Cuba. The limited strike thus far envisaged, the Pentagon held, would leave many Soviet assets in Cuba untouched and, moreover, there was no certainty that all the Soviet missile bases had been identified. Much better, the generals and admirals argued, that the United States launch a larger attack that would eliminate all the bases.

Opposition to this proposal developed rapidly. Some experts on the Soviet Union held that since the American attack would certainly kill Russians in Cuba, Moscow might be prodded into any one of a dozen responses, including a nuclear attack. Specialists on Latin America argued that a massive strike would destroy America's position in the Western hemisphere. Others said that an American attack would be regarded in Europe and elsewhere as an excessive response; a sledgehammer to kill a fly. One telling argument was that Soviet retaliation might take the form of an attack on West Berlin, where the Soviets held most of the military cards and the United States very few. The least we could expect, advocates of this idea argued, was a new blockade of Berlin. Kennedy let these arguments flow over him. Slowly, almost imperceptibly, he was attracted to the idea of a naval blockade of Cuba. But since a blockade is an act of war under international law, the Administration called it a quarantine.

In a televised address Kennedy alerted the nation and the world at large. The Administration's object, he said, was to remove a nuclear threat. He had taken initial steps, including the blockade (quarantine). He had also appealed to Khrushchev to 'abandon this course of world domination'. The speech had no immediate effect on the Kremlin.

In Cuba, Soviets and Cubans were labouring to complete the bases for the 42 missiles. Ilyushin-28 bombers were being assembled on Cuban airfields. About 25 merchant ships were heading toward Cuba from Soviet ports. On the American side the Pentagon had assembled 90 surface ships, eight aircraft carriers and 68 fighter and bomber squadrons. On 27 October Kennedy gave the Soviets forty-eight hours to remove the missiles or face an American invasion.

As the big carriers heaved in the long rollers off Florida and American fighters and bombers standing ready for instant action, Khrushchev realised that his gamble had failed. The United States *was* prepared to risk war over the missiles. A diversionary attack on Berlin would evidently bring the further risk of a nuclear strike on the Soviet Union. American sea and air power, far greater than anything the Soviet Union could mobilise at that date, stood between Khrushchev and his objective.

On 28 October Khrushchev surrendered. In the last in a series of letters to Kennedy, by turns conciliatory and blustering, Khrushchev said that the Soviets would halt work on the missile sites and that the weapons themselves would be returned to the Soviet Union. All he asked was that the United States halt U-2 flights over Cuba, a gesture to placate Castro.

Few victories of the cold war seemed more complete and this was how the Western world greeted it.

But much has been learned about the Cuban missile crisis since it took place. One important fact is that the President was able to act with the necessary firmness because of strong evidence provided by a high-level Western spy in the USSR, Colonel Oleg Penkovsky (later executed), that, contrary to the prevailing belief, the United States was far stronger in ballistic missiles than the Soviet Union. The other facts that emerged later concern the nature of the deal that brought the crisis to an end after the world had apparently stood on the verge of a nuclear confrontation. Khrushchev had indeed been forced to withdraw the Soviet missiles. But on his side, Kennedy had given a solemn undertaking to make no further effort to bring down the Castro regime in Cuba; and he had promised to remove American missiles pointed at Soviet targets from Turkey. The first of these undertakings enabled the Soviets, some years later, to bring the Castro regime completely under their control. The second was, in its way, a betrayal of America's NATO allies.

Although the missiles in Turkey had outlived their military usefulness, Kennedy did not consult his allies about removing them. The negotiations were conducted in the greatest secrecy between the Soviet ambassador and the President's brother, and Kennedy insisted that no mention of the deal should be made. The missiles in Turkey would only be shipped back at America's convenience some months later, and Kennedy gave no hint of what had happened to Britain's Harold Macmillan, with whom he appeared to be in constant touch. As a result, NATO's ultimate strategic safeguard against Soviet aggression now lay in America's intercontinental missiles.

Although it did not seem like it at the time, because of the nuclear stakes, the Cuban crisis had once again rewarded the political aggressor. Khrushchev indeed appeared on Soviet television to announce the result as a victory. He had abided by the standing communist rule: 'What we have is ours; what you have is negotiatiable.'

In ruling out an invasion of Cuba, Kennedy had accepted that the Monroe Doctrine was a thing of the past. The way was now clear for the Soviets to use Cubans as mercenaries in Africa, something the American President did not foresee when he gave Khrushchev his guarantee. Furthermore, the United States failed to anticipate another consequence of its victory.

The reverse in Cuba had taught the military leaders of the Soviet Union the importance of sea power to a superpower. Khrushchev, from the outset of his rule, had been an advocate of nuclear weapons, and the build-up of what the Russians call 'Strategic Rocket Forces' owed much to his support. Now the admirals and generals began to challenge his strategic approach. There had been, it is true, some effort to transform the Soviet Navy from a force chiefly armed and trained for coastal defence in the past ten years. But the idea of creating a genuine 'blue water' navy expanded in the aftermath of the Cuban missile crisis.

But in the immediate aftermath of the crisis Western prospects in the cold war looked bright. As 1962 ran into 1963, the Kennedy Administration had to grapple anew with the continuing problem of Vietnam. The President and his advisers were optimistic about the outcome.

When Kennedy entered the White House America's commitment to Vietnam was already seven years old. The basic approach of the Administration was still that of Dulles: the world was split into two blocs, communist and anti-communist, and Vietnam was one of the areas where the blocs were in conflict. However, there were some in Kennedy's circle who suggested that Ho Chi Minh and the North Vietnamese were not so much the tools of Moscow and Peking as an independent national force which resented all outside tutelage.

Ho was certainly supplying the rebel Viet Cong in South Vietnam with arms, training, tactical advice and, finally, men. Ngo Dinh Diem, the American-supported ruler of South Vietnam, was receiving an impressive amount of arms, training, tactical advice and men from the United States. He had not, however, implemented his promises to introduce economic and political reform into South Vietnam.

In the 1950s American aid to Diem had averaged about $300 million a year, most of it economic aid. But only a small amount went to the countryside where most South Vietnamese lived. This diversion of aid to the rich in the cities and to corrupt government officials was accompanied by military aid. The original officers and NCOs who administered this side of United States assistance were powerfully impressed by their experiences in Korea. They prepared the South Vietnamese forces for the sort of attack which North Korea had launched against the South in June 1950. At the same time they advised their superiors in Washington that all was going well. The South Vietnamese army was efficient and ready to take care of any military threat.

A few, a very few, officers took a different line. They held that the main threat was guerrilla war and that the South Vietnamese had shown no aptitude for that sort of conflict. By early 1961 there were about 15,000 Viet Cong operating in South Vietnam and they were making considerable strides in the countryside. In September 1961 the Viet Cong captured a provincial capital, and Saigon's morale sagged. It fell further with reports of Viet Cong successes in the Mekong river delta.

Kennedy sent General Maxwell Taylor and Walt W. Rostow, a trusted White House aide, to Vietnam to find out what could be done to retrieve the situation. Their report was mainly military. Taylor, a soldier of impeccable reputation, proposed that Americans take over certain tasks which appeared to be beyond Vietnamese capabilities.

These included air reconnaissance and an air lift. He also suggested that the United States send a task force of perhaps 10,000 men to be used to maintain security around the perimeters of airfields and other defensive missions and to provide an emergency reserve if the Vietnamese Army appeared to crumble in any situation.

As might be expected, the report also included proposals for political reforms that would bridge the gap between Diem and the people. Taylor and Rostow hoped that implementation of the two plans would help the South win a civil war that was expanding daily. Although the report appeared too ambitious to some, Kennedy, aware of the United States' prestige involved, decided to go ahead. In December he ordered the start of an American build-up in Vietnam with General Paul Harkins as the commander in Saigon. Diem and his associates were delighted. They themselves had done little to put into effect the reforms they had promised Washington.

At the outset the introduction of American troops appeared to be more successful. The American advisors flocked into Saigon and dispersed to the countryside, to instruct the Vietnamese army in the latest arcane devices of warfare. They were hampered by the fact that they were advisers, not commanders. Both Washington and Saigon wished to minimise their role and maximise that of the Vietnamese army for reasons of morale, but the first group of advisers did create a feeling of confidence, long absent, by their bravery and their willingness to listen to the peasants and do what they could to improve their conditions.

One immediate result was that Viet Cong activity in the countryside was reduced, temporarily at least. This produced from the Secretary of Defense, Robert McNamara, one of the first of the long series of optimistic forecasts about the war offered by American leaders. 'Every quantitative measurement we have,' he said, 'shows we are winning this war.' His optimism touched the President, who told Congress in his State of the Union message that 'The spearpoint of aggression has been blunted in South Vietnam'.

But there remained the problem of South Vietnam's internal politics, for which Kennedy appeared to have no clear answer. Diem was obviously failing to carry out the promised reforms. Henry Cabot Lodge Jr, the new American ambassador in Saigon, advocated heavy American pressure to induce Diem to carry out the reforms Americans considered necessary. Diem, under pressure from his generals, temporised. On 1 November 1963 he was murdered. His death was the moment for a serious rethinking of America's position. While Kennedy hesitated over the alternatives—of pulling out altogether or of stepping up America's commitment— he himself was struck down by Lee Harvey Oswald's bullets in Dallas, Texas, on that fateful afternoon of 23 November 1963. Thus it fell to his successor, Lyndon Baines Johnson, to bear the burden of decision in Vietnam.

The news of the President's assassination visibly distressed Nikita Khrushchev. In the whole course of the cold war no two men had stood closer to the abyss of a nuclear holocaust. Kennedy's death robbed the West of the fruits of that experience, but perhaps in some indefinable way the older man was affected by the clash with the young American and what he stood for. It is as though the duel of will and nerves over Cuba took the fight out of the Soviet leader. At all events, the last two years of Khrushchev's power were the most quiescent in Soviet history. In most places the Soviets reduced their activities or failed to take opportunities on offer. Although Kwame Nkrumah's Ghana provided a base for Soviet subversion in Africa— short-lived as it turned out—communism was not notably successful in winning converts in the newly independent states which were popping up all over the continent. There were indications that Khrushchev also wanted to end the Soviet involvement in Indo-China.

Similarly, Soviet reverses in the Congo (now Zaire) seemed to have left Khrushchev discouraged, as communists are not supposed to be. And there had been other reverses, for instance in Burma where the local strong man, General Ne Win, had hundreds of Burmese communists arrested in November 1963. To the South, where the Chinese had defeated the Indians in a short war in the Himalayan heights at about the same time as the Cuban missile crisis, the Soviets had sided with the Indians, and incurred further charges of revisionism from Peking.

Indeed, in some way, these charges were justified in ideological terms. For instance, in April 1964 Khrushchev had conferred the order of Hero of the Soviet Union and of Lenin on the Algerian leader Ben Bella. Then in May that year, on a visit to Egypt to inaugurate the Aswan dam built by the Soviets, he had also made Nasser a Hero of the Soviet Union. Such honours were normally reserved for communists and not given to the leaders of states which outlawed their communist parties, as did both Algeria and Egypt.

These eccentricities, on top of Khrushchev's record of international setbacks, worried and displeased his senior colleagues. In
their eyes he had made too many mistakes, attracting on occasion the
laughter and ridicule reserved for clowns, and they decided (behind
his back, of course) that he had to go. In a carefully organised and
bloodless confrontation on 14 and 15 October 1964 they stripped
him of all his offices. He was blamed for 'hasty decisions', the 'cult of
personality', 'phrase-mongering' and other heinous offences against
communist orthodoxy. His life was spared and the Soviet Tsar
became just another old-age pensioner.

In Moscow, as in Washington, new names and new faces appeared
on the cold war scene as it moved into its next phase.

PART 3
THE BREZHNEV YEARS:
'DÉTENTE'

9 Back onto the Offensive

Leonid Brezhnev, who stepped into Khrushchev's shoes in October 1964, was a very different kind of man. Such are the uncertainties of history in the top-secret state that it is not clear to this day whether Brezhnev actually took part in the palace *coup* that unseated Khrushchev: he was on an official visit to East Germany when the plot was being hatched. Nevertheless, he was everybody's choice for the key post of First Secretary of the Communist Party of the Soviet Union. As he was little-known to the outside world, many Kremlinologists made the mistake of dismissing him as a grey, colourless party functionary, the ultimate *apparatchik*, the compromise candidate without enemies.

It was true enough that he appears to have avoided making enemies, whereas Khrushchev had made too many. But when the world got to know him better—in the heady years of 'détente'—he turned out to be a personality in his own right, gallant to the ladies, fond of fast cars and a dab hand with anecdotes. When he took over in October 1964, however, with the frozen-faced Aleksei Kosygin as Prime Minister, the visible image of Brezhnev was of a dour, plodding, unimaginative party hack. Looking back, it can be seen that he had, in Soviet terms, an extraordinarily successful career—especially in foreign affairs. By the time of his death, in 1983, his reign had spanned nineteen years—about a quarter of the history of the Soviet Union. During this time, the size and power of the Soviet Empire had expanded enormously, and the goal of victory in the cold war was no longer a strain on the imagination.

Unlike Khrushchev, Brezhnev does not seem to have been involved in a struggle for power, even in his early years as party boss. Suave, self-composed and ruggedly handsome with his strong black eyebrows, he naturally assumed the authority of supreme power, and was received abroad with the honours of a head of state or of government before he bothered to assume the corresponding titles. In time, and almost as an afterthought, he took all possible titles to himself, and became not only party boss, but President of the USSR, Marshal of the Soviet Union and Commander-in-Chief of the Soviet Armed Forces.

The new leadership in Moscow lost no time in returning to the offensive after the lull that prevailed during Khrushchev's last two years in office. Three momentous decisions were taken:

(1) To provide North Vietnam with modern weapons.
(2) To overtake the United States in strategic weapons systems.
(3) To create a global navy.

Only the first of these was clearly detectable at the time, although the evidence for the other two decisions has since become overwhelming. But as the Vietnam war constitutes the major fact of the post-Khrushchev era we must deal with it first.

Vietnam

During Khrushchev's years of supreme power the Soviets had kept out of South Vietnam, contenting themselves with shouting encouragement from the sidelines. Ho Chi Minh's subversive apparatus had set up a political organisation in South Vietnam, calling itself the National Front for the Liberation of South Vietnam (NFLSV), the military arm of which was generally known as the Viet Cong, meaning simply Vietnamese communists, in Vietnamese. As with other revolutionary and terrorist organisations, the NFLSV attached a great deal of importance to diplomacy—that is, to winning friends and influencing people in as many countries as possible.

When Khrushchev fell, the Front had officers in Peking, Pyongyang (North Korea), Djarkarta (Indonesia), East Berlin, Cairo and Havana (Cuba). But they had knocked in vain on Moscow's door. Brezhnev and Kosygin lost no time in jettisoning this cautious policy. In November 1964, only a few weeks after Khrushchev had gone, Brezhnev invited the NFLSV to open an office in Moscow.

Looking at the Vietnam war from the comfortable distance of Moscow, the Soviet leaders had two considerations uppermost in their minds. One was the American interest and involvement in Vietnam. There were thousands of American advisers in South Vietnam, but not, at that time, combat troops. Under the unwritten rules of the cold war, the Soviets sought to extend their influence or domination everywhere, but avoided the risk of a direct confrontation with the Americans. Although Brezhnev and Kosygin had decided that Khrushchev had been too passive in the recent past, they were basically as cautious as he was in dealing with the United States. But anybody studying the situation in South Vietnam objectively towards the end of 1964 might well have concluded that the South could not hold out much longer.

Since the murder of President Diem a year earlier, there had been a succession of weak and short-lived military governments. None of them seemed capable of containing, let alone defeating, the Vietnamese communists. By inviting the NFLSV to open an office in Moscow, the new Soviet leaders signified two things: their formal approval and impending support for the Front, and their belief that they could now afford to involve themselves in South Vietnam without the risk of a clash with the United States.

The second consideration in their minds was the state of the world communist movement. The Sino–Soviet dispute was at its height. One of its most striking features was the struggle between the two communist giants for control over other communist parties, especially in South-East Asia, where Chinese communist influence was naturally at its greatest. During this period Chinese agents eliminated the pro-Moscow leadership of the communist parties in Burma and the Philippines. Peking already had a controlling influence over Malayan communist guerrillas, who operated from Thailand, and the Thai Communist Party.

But of all of the parties in South-east Asia, the most spectacularly active and successful was the Lao Dong Party in North Vietnam, with its offshoots in neighbouring countries. At that time, the Soviets were trying to organise an international communist conference in Moscow, with the aim of restoring their shaken authority over the international movement. It was important to them to detach the Lao Dong Party from the clutches of the Chinese, who were apparently succesfully supplanting the Russians in their dealings with Hanoi. The Russians calculated that by inviting the Lao Dong's extension in South Vietnam (in effect, its branch office) to set up shop in Moscow, they could resume their traditional place as the dominant influence over the party which the former Comintern agent, Ho Chi Minh, had created on their orders.

On 26 November 1964 the Soviets pledged that they would give North Vietnam all necessary help. Early in February 1965, the new Soviet Premier, Kosygin, led a powerful Soviet delegation to Hanoi. While the Russians were there, but without prior consultation, Viet Cong guerrillas struck at the American airfield and billet area at Pleiku in the central highlands. Seventy Americans were killed or wounded, and seventeen helicopters and three transport planes were destroyed. That afternoon, on 7 February 1965, American and South Vietnamese planes raided North Vietnamese targets in swift retaliation.

This turn of events undoubtedly caught the Soviets by surprise. They had not expected the Viet Cong to attack American installations, nor would they have expected an immediate American retaliation. They were apparently indignant and embarrassed; on their side, the Vietnamese communists were delighted. The Soviets had dropped hints about the usefulness of peace talks to end the war. But the communist leadership in Hanoi, intoxicated by its successes in South Vietnam, were not interested in peace talks. They smelled victory, and reckoned that by attacking the Americans, they would force the Soviet Union into the war on their side. As for the United States, the Vietnamese communists had listened to the Chinese stock phrase about the Americans being 'paper tigers' for so many years that they may have come to believe it. Almost certainly, they discounted the possibility of massive intervention from the Americans based in South Vietnam.

They were wrong about the Americans, and, initially at least, about the Soviets as well. At any rate, Kosygin and his delegation left Hanoi without any public commitment to help. A fortnight or so later, on 1 March 1965, the international communist conference took place as planned in Moscow; and the Lao Dong Party boycotted it.

After an abortive attempt to bring the Vietnamese communists to the conference table, President Lyndon B. Johnson decided in June 1965 to authorise the use of American combat troops in Vietnam. This was the start of the great escalation of the Vietnam war.

The Soviets now realised that a deepening American involvement in Vietnam would suit their purpose well. From their point of view, others were doing their fighting for them, as had been the case in Korea, and they risked little in shipping military supplies to Hanoi so long as the United States remained wedded to the fiction that American forces were in Vietnam only to support Saigon against communist rebels.

We should note a further strategic consideration. In Indonesia, the communist party staged a remarkable recovery after the defeat of the Moscow-sponsored rebellion in 1948, until in the early 1960s it could claim to be the largest communist party not actually in power, with some 3 million members. Its able leader, D. N. Aidit, tried hard to steer a middle course between Moscow and Peking, although the Chinese were gaining the upper hand, when, on 30 September 1965, the physical collapse of President Sukarno led the party into making what turned out to be a premature bid for power. The Army took over and an appalling massacre of communists and their families followed. Original estimates of up to 500,000 killed have since been scaled down to a probable 200,000. Some years earlier, the Soviets had sold $140 million of arms to Sukarno on credit—their usual method of creating a client-state. The downfall of the Sukarno regime and the collapse of the attempted communist take-over in Indonesia were serious blows to Moscow. Vietnam thus became the decisive arena of conflict in Asia.

By 1966 American forces in Vietnam had the plans and the strength to launch crippling attacks on the North. They did not do so because of political restraints. One reason was that the Administration of Lyndon B. Johnson, who succeeded Kennedy, was impressed by the fear of Chinese intervention. Although the absence of American diplomats in Peking may be some excuse, it does not excuse the overall misjudgement of the Johnson Administration of the turmoil that swept China during the great Cultural Revolution. At any rate, war was not declared. The American forces were burdened with a philosophy of 'war, no war' that in the end forced their withdrawal.

The United States was not committed to its involvement in Vietnam. Although there are detailed reports of isolated actions, ample documentation of the attack on Cambodia and the frustrated invasion of Laos, the war remains to most Americans a shapeless, incoherent affair. At the time, this encouraged confusion in the minds of the American public over the enemy. To military experts in the field or those in positions of responsibility in Washington, the real enemy was clearly North Vietnam, armed and equipped by the Soviets and the Chinese. But the public focus was on the Viet Cong, who in reality were a dangerous but secondary guerrilla subsidiary of the North Vietnamese army. The result of this confusion between official and public opinion can be seen in one notable incident.

This was the Têt Offensive, launched by the North Vietnamese and the Viet Cong, but principally the former, in January 1968. The attacks began in the northern and central provinces on 30 January and the main assault on other objectives opened on 31 January. The offensive was carried out with skill and daring. One quarter of the district capitals, 36 of the 44 provincial capitals and five of the six largest cities, were assailed. Communist forces penetrated the grounds of the American Embassy in Saigon, where they were routed by Marine guards and Army military police. The most significant political success was in the ancient imperial city of Hué, where the attackers stormed the citadel, and held on to it for 26 days.

But by ordinary military standards the offensive was a failure. The somewhat inflated figures issued by the Johnson Administration on the basis of reports from General William Westmoreland, the commander in Vietnam, were that about 45,000 of the 84,000 men involved in the offensive had been killed by the end of February. These are the figures quoted by President Johnson in his memoirs. Even if the toll was not that high, if the attackers had lost 25,000 men, the military cost was excessive. But the political consequences outweighed this, or indeed, even a higher cost.

The 'success' of the Têt Offensive seemed to signal to opponents of the war in the United States and among America's allies that the conflict could never be won. By then, American public opinion had solidified to the extent that it was probably too late to expect a united nation to respond to a declaration of war against North Vietnam, although it is evident from some reports on Moscow's reactions to the offensive that this is what the Soviets feared. They were by then deeply involved in the transfer of arms, ammunition and other military equipment to Vietnam on a scale far greater than anything the Soviets had offered their clients in the Middle East.

After Têt the military and political position of the United States steadily deteriorated. There were spasms of offensive actions such as the ill-conceived and ill-implemented descent into Cambodia under the Administration of Richard M. Nixon, who became President in January 1969. There were frequent bombing offensives, many of which fell just short of success largely because the Air Force's political masters in Washington misjudged the effect of the bombing on North Vietnam's willingness to negotiate a peace satisfactory to both sides.

The war against communism in South-east Asia dragged on. The policies and slogans of the previous decade became objects of mockery.

Who believed now in the domino theory?

Meanwhile, the global duel with the Soviet Union outside Vietnam continued apace. Its course was now directed from the American side by a pair as ill assorted as Eisenhower and Dulles. They were Richard Nixon, President of the United States, and Henry Kissinger, at first head of the National Security Council and later, to his great satisfaction, Secretary of State.

Vietnam was a legacy of the outgoing Democratic Administrations. It is evident, from what we know now, that both Nixon and Kissinger realised that the United States was in a 'no-win' situation in view of the stubborn resistance of the North Vietnamese and the Viet Cong and of the growing, often violent opposition to the war in the United States. They also realised that the United States could not successfully meet the global Soviet challenge so long as the Vietnam war continued.

In a series of secret negotiations involving President Thieu of South Vietnam and representatives of the Viet Cong, agreement was reached in Paris in January 1973 which brought the war to an end, at least as far as the United States was concerned. Nixon and Kissinger gave the impression to all but the American people that the United States would immediately intervene should Hanoi fail to abide by the agreements. As it turned out, the United States did nothing further to prevent the collapse of South Vietnam and its take-over by the North Vietnamese forces in 1975.

Thus for ten years and more after Kennedy's death, Vietnam became the major American preoccupation of the cold war. This was not, however, how the new men in Moscow saw things.

Strategic subversion

Looking at the world from Moscow at the end of 1964, with Khrushchev out of the way, the Soviet leaders saw much to cause dissatisfaction. The dispute with China was at its height, and the Chinese were having some success in setting up communist parties or groups in rivalry to the established Moscow-line parties. Their reach was long, indeed, and in distant Brazil, there was now a Communist Party of Brazil—small but effective—which took its directives from Peking, as distinct from the established Brazilian Communist Party, under the veteran Luiz Carlos Prestes.

In other ways, too, Brazil was a problem for Brezhnev and his colleagues. The Soviets had always been interested in this Latin American giant, with its enormous economic potential, and in 1958 Boris Ponomarev, the master-hand of subversion, had singled out Brazil and Chile as good examples of the united front technique, in which local communists were working with trade unionists and political groups for long-term objectives.

Under a left-leaning president, João Goulart, Brazil had been moving fast in a direction pleasing to Moscow. Then in March 1964, the armed forces under Marshal Castello Branco seized power in a bloodless and popular *coup d'état* and communist hopes were dashed.

Conceivably, what worried the Soviets most at this time were the freelance activities of the Cuban leader, Fidel Castro. Castro and his close collaborator, the Argentine Ernesto 'Ché' Guevara, subscribed to the school of 'instant' revolution, according to which, if you want a revolution, all you need to do is to start one with some appropriate act of violence, and the rest will follows.

Boris Ponomarev and his Politburo boss, the senior ideologist Suslov, could not give their approval to such adventurist revolutionary ideas. The world communist conference at the end of 1960 had given the label of 'national democracy' to Castro's regime, but they wanted him to go two steps further: by becoming a communist, and by agreeing to take orders from Moscow.

A year later, on 2 December 1961, Castro obligingly took half the first step by publicly declaring that he had been a Marxist for years. But he continued to foment revolutionary violence in Peru, Colombia, Venezuela and other places, totally outside Moscow's control. The Soviets made a determined attempt to bring such activities under their control by calling a conference of Latin American communist parties in Havana, Castro's capital, in November 1964. But the results were meagre.

In October 1965, after constant Soviet prompting, Castro merged various revolutionary groups into a single Communist Party of Cuba, thus taking the second half of the first step the Soviets expected of him. But still Moscow's hold was incomplete.

Repeated failures had no apparent effect on Castro, whose unbounded faith in his own revolutionary methods remained entire.

In the spring of 1965, he had a near-miss in the Dominican Republic when miscellaneous revolutionaries came close to taking power until President Johnson of the United States sent in the Marines and foiled them.

In January 1966, Castro convened a Tri-Continental Conference in Havana and set up an Afro–Asian–Latin American People's Solidarity Organisation with the ambitious aim of co-ordinating revolutionary activities in the Third World. The Russians sent a delegation to Havana and went along with the inflamatory resolutions that were passed, but were still unhappy in that it was Fidel Castro, not Brezhnev, who was calling the shots.

Another Castroite failure seemed to prove the Russians right in their critique of Fidel's methods. In October 1967, Ché Guevara, the incurably romantic hero of the Cuban revolution, was captured and killed in Bolivia after an abortive attempt to convert apathetic Andean peasants (whose language his group could not speak) to his views on revolution.

All this was bad enough, but Castro went beyond tolerable bounds in January 1968 when he purged the old guard, pro-Soviet wing of his new Communist Party, and gaoled its leader, Aníbal Escalante. Brezhnev and his colleagues now decided to bring Castro to heel by whatever means seemed appropriate. Early that year, the Soviets threatened to cut off all economic aid to Cuba unless Castro stopped his public attacks on Moscow and refrained from launching revolutions without Moscow's prior approval. They blockaded the island, reducing the flow of oil to a trickle and halting all supplies of industrial materials for several weeks. Suddenly Castro's resistance collapsed, and in August when the Soviet forces entered Czechoslovakia, he shocked his leftist followers in many countries by publicly supporting the Soviet action.

In July 1969, the Soviet Politburo sent one of its leading troubleshooters, Defence Minister Marshal Andrei Grechko, to Havana, and work began on a base for Soviet nuclear submarines at Cienfuegos. By mid-1970, Castro had taken the second step the Soviets expected of him and Cuba had ceased to be a client-state to become, in the full sense, a Soviet satellite.

It was at this point that the long-term strategic foresight of the Soviets paid off. More than ten years earlier a senior KGB officer, Aleksander Alekseyev, posing as a Tass correspondent, had gone to

Cuba in the wake of Castro's victory in his struggle against the Batista regime to set up a Cuban intelligence service. The outcome was the Dirección General de Inteligencia (DGI). In his long anti-Soviet phase, Castro packed the DGI with men of his choice, under the direction of an anti-Soviet chief, Manuel Piñeiro Losada, but in mid-1970, Piñeiro was fired, along with the rest of the anti-Soviet personnel, and the DGI became an unconditional instrument of Soviet policy.

Thus Cuba became the Soviet Union's first remote control satellite, as distinct from Stalin's East European satellites which were held in subjection by the presence of Soviet armies. It was a major Soviet victory in the cold war, and no less a victory for being accomplished by force, albeit of another kind. Any country which puts its economy and security services in the hands of the Soviet Union can expect similar treatment.

Having established complete control over Cuba, the Soviets were free to pursue subversion in the Caribbean and Central America in accordance with their long-term strategic planning, which has among its objectives the capacity to threaten two of the major sources of oil in the Western Hemisphere: Venezuela and Mexico.

In March 1971 Mexico indeed suffered from an attempt to stage a revolution by fifty guerrillas who styled themselves the 'Movement of Revolutionary Action' (MAR). It was crushed, thanks to the vigilance of the Mexican authorities, when it turned out that the guerrillas had been recruited by the KGB and trained, first in Moscow, and later in North Korea. The Soviet ambassador to Mexico was expelled in consequence, but there could be no guarantee that another attempt would not be made in the future.

By the end of the 1970s, indeed, the area was threatened by an accelerated pace of Cuban-backed strife. The overthrow of the Nicaraguan strong-man, General Anastasio Somoza, by the Sandinista National Liberation Front in July 1979 was masterminded in Havana, and indicated that another 'falling domino' principle was at work when strife of a similar origin and motivation broke out in El Salvador and Guatemala. No island or state in the region could now be counted safe from Cuban-backed subversion—and all this in the United States' back yard.

But the Soviets did not have it all their own way in Latin America, as was shown in September 1973, when the leftist regime of Salvador Allende in Chile was overthrown by the country's armed forces, after covert involvement by the American CIA.

Though not a communist, Allende was an extreme left-wing socialist. In the presidential elections of 1970, he attracted only 36 per cent of the votes but came to power because the other two candidates could not agree to form a coalition.

He himself formed a coalition with the communists and the extreme left MIR. The Chilean Communist Party, led by Luis Corvalán, was the strongest and best-disciplined in Latin America, and loyal to Moscow. In what has been called the 'Santiago model' it set out to gain complete power through its control of two of the economic ministries, Finance and Labour, and of the trade union movement, while the Economics ministry was in the hands of an independent Marxist who worked closely with the communists. The strategy was to drive the private sector out of business by harassment, taxes and strikes. By the time of Allende's downfall, inflation was running at *1,000 per cent* a year.

The MIR wanted to go much faster and trained for violence. So did the extreme left wing of Allende's Socialist Party, under Senator Altamirano. As is usual in such cases of demand, the supply was provided, in part, by the Soviet Union.

KGB instructors were flown out to provide training courses in terrorism for the MIR (whose violent methods were at that time being denounced by the communists). For Altamirano's candidates, the Soviets arranged to provide North Korean specialists. All this went on in the deep south of Chile.

During the Allende period, the capital, Santiago, became the headquarters for the subversive activities of the Cuban DGI (under tight KGB control) throughout Latin America. Previously, these activities had been co-ordinated through the Cuban embassy in distant Paris.

But tactical setbacks in the cold war, like those in Chile and Mexico, did not deter the Soviet Union from continuing with its long-term attempt to obtain client-states in important strategic areas. In February 1966, for example, when Kwame Nkrumah of Ghana was overthrown by a group of military officers, hundreds of Soviet and Chinese agents were sent out of the country; but, like birds looking for trees to roost in, there were many other trouble spots in that continent where these agents could settle—oil-rich Nigeria being an obvious alternative. The Leninist principle is 'two steps forward, one step back'.

So, in the Brezhnev years the process of 'satellisation' was continued remorselessly. Although the methods used varied, the phases might include: a period in which lavish deliveries of arms made a country dependent on the Soviet Union; the arrival of Soviet 'advisers' in large numbers; the signing of a 'friendship treaty'; a *coup d'état* to place a Soviet puppet in power; if necessary, armed intervention; and in certain cases, Soviet or East European assistance in setting up a secret security or intelligence organisation. Let us look at some examples.

Having put Egypt deeply in their debt with Khrushchev's arms deal of 1955, the Russians found in the continuing Arab–Israeli dispute an ideal pretext to build up their influence. After Egypt's catastrophic defeat by the Israelis in the Six-Day War of 1967, Nasser's need for Soviet arms and expertise was greater than ever. Soviet advisors poured into Egypt. In time, there were about 20,000 of them, to be found at all levels of the armed forces and even of the Civil Service. Egypt, already a client-state, was turning fast into a satellite.

After Nasser's death in 1970, his successor, Anwar al-Sadat, began to display signs of impatience with his Soviet protectors. In April 1971 he gaoled the well-known politician Ali Sabry and some lesser figures. Puzzled, the Soviets sent Boris Ponomarev and President Podgorny to Cairo, where Sadat was apparently talked into a further period of docility. In what was to become a model for many pacts of its kind, Egypt and the Soviet Union signed a fifteen-year Treaty of Friendship and Co-operation on 28 May 1971.

A clause in the treaty could be interpreted as justifying Soviet intervention in Egypt's domestic affairs in certain circumstances. Egypt, however, retained its residual sovereignty, and on 18 July 1972, in a spectacular gesture of self-assertion, President Sadat announced the expulsion of nearly all his Soviet advisors. It was another Soviet tactical defeat in the cold war and a bad one of its kind. Perhaps to Sadat's surprise, and certainly to his relief, they left quietly.

About a year earlier, in July 1971, the Soviets had suffered a serious reverse in the Sudan when the local Communist Party, the strongest in Africa, briefly seized power, with the connivance of the Soviet embassy. The Sudanese leader, General Nimeiry, however, ousted the communists, brought them to trial and executed them.

If the signature of a treaty of friendship with the Soviet Union is taken to denote client status, then the following countries have also qualified: *India* (1971), *Iraq* (1972), *Somalia* (1974), *Angola* (1976), *Ethiopia*, *Vietnam* and *Afghanistan* (all in 1978); and *Syria* (1980). Some of these cases call for further comment.

With their usual foresight, the Soviets saw the potential for subversion in Portugal's African territories in good time. Although 'people's revolutionary war' was an invention of the Chinese with Vietnamese refinements, the Soviets did not need to be taught that such wars are won or lost on the home front. In the Portuguese Communist Party they had an unconditional instrument of the Soviet will.

On Soviet instructions, the Portuguese communists set up a clandestine party in the most advanced of the African territories, *Angola*, as long ago as 1955. About a year later, the party spawned a front organisation, the Popular Movement for the Liberation of Angola (MPLA), which launched a rebellion against Portugal in 1959. Two years later, it was learned that, from the start, the Soviets had trained terrorists and guerrillas from Angola in camps in the USSR.

In Mozambique, on the eastern coast of southern Africa, a similar story unfolded. The Front for the Liberation of Mozambique (FRELIMO), set up in 1962, went into armed rebellion two years later. Arms, money and training were provided by the Soviets. In tiny Portuguese Guinea, the PAIGC (African Party for the Independence of Guinea and Cape Verde Islands) was the necessary fighting front.

The key, however, was in Portugal. The dour and able Portuguese dictator, Salazar, never wavered in his determination to hold on to Portugal's 'overseas provinces'. His successor, Caetano, also able, wielded less authority. The military budget exceeded 40 per cent of the income of this poor country. Dissatisfaction with the interminable war spread in the army, and a left-wing Armed Forces Movement was organised, with communist participation. On 25 April 1974 the Caetano regime was overthrown in a bloodless *coup*, and the Portuguese Communist Party boss, Alvaro Cunhal, went home to Lisbon and to a cabinet post after years of exile in Moscow and Prague.

In Mozambique and Guinea (or Guiné, as the revolutionaries called it). Moscow's men—Samora Machel and Amilcar Cabral—took over without much difficulty. The situation was more complex in Angola, where two anti-Marxist groups, FNLA in the north and UNITA in the south, held stretches of territory. The Soviets took the dramatic decision to step up deliveries of arms to the MPLA, and to fly out Cuban forces in large numbers. Within weeks, in 1976, 15,000 Cubans had been flown or shipped to Angola, together with hundreds of tanks. This massive use of surrogates was the pay-off for the Soviet Union's considerable investment in time and money in sustaining and controlling Fidel Castro's regime. (In passing, we should note that the Portuguese communists were less successful at home than in Africa. An attempted *coup* by the extreme left on 25 November 1975 was a failure. A commission of inquiry later found that the attempt was the outcome of a sustained campaign by the communists.)

The case of Somalia was somewhat different. The Soviets wooed that pastoral country's strong-man, General Siad Barre, assiduously. They helped him to set up a secret security organisation (as in Cuba) and provided arms and military training on a lavish scale (as in Egypt). The usual Friendship Treaty confirmed client status.

The Soviets ran into an unaccustomed dilemma, however, arising out of a long-standing territorial and ethnic dispute between Somalia and Ethiopia. But Ethiopia, too, was a candidate for client status and satellisation. Colonel Mengistu Haile Mariam had emerged as the strong-man in a bloody settling of accounts on 3 February 1977. A Moscow-line hard-liner, Mengistu was in receipt of Soviet arms in large quantities, and set about creating a Leninist regime.

Towards the end of 1977, Siad Barre of Somalia made the mistake of invading the territory of his larger and more powerful neighbour. The Soviets had to choose between the two rival clients. Without hesitation their choice fell on the larger. On 7 November Barre retaliated by imitating Sadat's example and expelling 7,000 Soviet advisors from Somalia. The Soviets launched a massive airlift of arms and Cubans to Ethiopia, and even sent a Soviet General, G.Barisov, to take over Ethiopia's forces as overall commander. The war ended on 14 March 1978 with the total defeat and retreat of the Somali invaders. If the loss of Somalia was a defeat for the Soviets, victory in Ethiopia more than made up for it.

In Angola, Guiné, Mozambique, and now Ethiopia, the Soviets had by 1978 succeeded in setting up Marxist–Leninist regimes responsive to their needs. Their value to the Soviet Union is obvious when seen in the context of a global strategy involving the potential denial of vital resources to the West. The ultimate Soviet target could only be South Africa, with its vast resources of uranium, gold and other metals. At the same time, in an actual war, the Soviets would be able to control the ocean lanes around the Cape of Good Hope, along which the big oil tankers pass from the Middle East to Europe and North America.

Similar strategic interests naturally dictated Soviet moves in the Middle East itself. Here the Soviets first scored a victory in South Yemen (Aden and its hinterland). The extremist regime there served as a base for a protracted guerrilla war against the Sultanate of Oman, which occupies a key position controlling the Strait of Hormuz, through which flows a high percentage of the non-communist world's shipments of oil. With British advisors and tough forces of his own, the Sultan defeated the guerrillas at the end of 1975.

By then, however, the Soviets and East Germans had established a dominant position in South Yemen, which styled itself the People's Democratic Republic of Yemen, or PDRY. The Yemeni leader, President Salem Rubaya Ali, was judged insufficiently pliant to Soviet requirements, and on 26 June 1978 the Soviets had him overthrown and executed by their own nominees; Soviet naval forces shelled Aden in support of the Marxists, and Cuban-piloted Soviet planes bombed pro-government forces. Earlier in the year, the East Germans had been given control over security (including the inevitable concentration camps), and it could be said that South Yemen had emerged as the Arab world's first Marxist–Leninist state.

A war machine needs oil, so does a vast economy like the Soviet Union's, even though private consumption is kept artificially low. And satellites are thirsty for it. A major reality of the cold war is that the USSR was beginning to run short of oil in the late 1970s. The old oilfields in the Caucasus were drying up. The Tyumen oilfields in Western Siberia were being successfully exploited but were insufficient for the needs of a vast country and its surrounding empire.

There was plenty of oil in the Soviet Far East, but climatic conditions and distances made exploitation almost prohibitively expensive. The views of the best Western specialists coincided: Siberian oil was possibly the most expensive in the world, on a par with Alaskan oil, the presence of enormous reserves of the cheapest oil in the world in Saudi Arabia was strategically tempting.

Soviet interest in Middle East oil was a perilous fact of life as the decade of the 1980s began. It was a dual interest: a positive need for it, for Soviet and satellite purposes; and a negative need to be in a position, if this proved necessary in a Third World War, to deny it to the Western powers and Japan. About 60 per cent of the oil imports of Western Europe, at least 85 per cent of Japan's and some 15 per cent of America's, came through the Strait of Hormuz. Control of the Strait would give the Soviet Union a stranglehold on the advanced countries of the non-communist world.

By the middle of 1978, as we have seen, the Soviets had consolidated their hold on Ethiopia and South Yemen, on either side of the Gulf of Aden. They had also, by masterminding a military *coup* in Kabul on 27 April that year, installed a Marxist government in Afghanistan under their nominee, Nur Mohammed Tarakki. This was the culmination of a protracted process of indoctrination of selected Afghan army officers undergoing military training courses in the USSR. The new regime accepted at least client status with the signature, on 5 December 1978, of the standard Friendship Treaty. Apart from United States power, which was demoralised by Vietnam, one major obstacle stood between the Soviet Union and its Middle East objectives: the heavily armed forces of the Shah of Iran. It became necessary, therefore, to remove him.

We must guard against oversimplifying a complex situation. In the course of his crash programme for the modernisation of his Iranian empire, the Shah had made enemies, and inevitably created social tensions. Rapid industrialisation brought many thousands of peasants into Teheran and other big cities, and agriculture slumped. There was inflation, and there was corruption, and both aroused resentment even though the standard of living rose rapidly. Above all, the Shah had alienated the Shi'ite Moslem clergy by redistributing church lands, and by driving the religious leader, Ayatollah Khomeiny, into exile.

There is no space to describe the Iranian revolution in detail. The point of interest in our context is that the KGB and the International Department played a leading role in destabilising the Shah's regime: through the Moscow-controlled Tudeh party, especially among the oil workers; by printing much of the anti-Shah propaganda; by coordinating a worldwide campaign against the Shah; and indirectly through the violent actions of PLO-backed and Libyan-backed terrorist organisations.

The theocratic regime which replaced the Shah's rule was not, of course, one which the Soviets would view with any sympathy, especially in the light of the USSR's own large Moslem population.

The main objective, however, was achieved. When the Shah went into exile on 16 January 1979 his armed forces, which had been personally loyal to him, virtually disintegrated.

Subsequent events in Afghanistan must be regarded as part of the same process of advancing Soviet positions in the Middle East. Moscow's instrument in the *coup* of April 1978 was the People's Democratic Party of Afghanistan, formed in 1965. It was not, however, an unconditional instrument, and was divided into a pro-Soviet faction (*Parcham*) and a more nationalistic one (*Khalq*).

The leaders of the pro-Soviet faction were Babrak Karmal and the new President, Tarakki; the nationalistic faction was led by Hafizullah Amin. In a bloody counter-*coup* in September 1979, Amin overthrew Tarakki, who was murdered. Popular resistance to the Soviet 'advisers' in Afghanistan grew rapidly. On Christmas Day, the Soviets began to invade Afghanistan, initially through a massive airlift of troops. Amin was deposed, and the reserve Soviet puppet, Babrak Karmal, who had been ambassador in Prague, was brought back to replace him. Shortly afterwards, Amin was executed. The Soviets had contrived to make the dead President believe that the object of the airlift was to help him put down the rebellion against his rule.

The invasion of Afghanistan had brought the Soviets to within a few hundred miles of the Strait of Hormuz. Any further trouble in the Gulf, like the war between Iraq and Iran which broke out in 1980, could only work to their long-term advantage.

In the Far East, the surrender of the South Vietnamese forces to the communist invaders on 30 April 1975 was the grand climax to the protracted struggle waged by Moscow's ex-agent, Ho Chi Minh, since the 1920s (although Ho himself did not live to see the victory of which he was the architect). The Vietnamese communists lost no time in uniting the two halves of the country; Saigon, capital of the south, was renamed Ho Chi Minh City. In accordance with Ho's plan of 1930, Laos was incorporated into the new greater Vietnam with little apparent difficulty. Cambodia was a problem of another order. Although the Cambodian communist organisation, Pracheachon, had been established by the Vietnamese, the communist organisation fell under the control of an extreme faction led by Pol Pot, who was anti-Vietnamese but maintained close links with the Chinese People's Republic.

The Pol Pot regime proceeded to carry out one of the most

horrifying massacres in modern history, exterminating not only all members of the pro-Western government, and Hanoi-trained communists, but virtually the entire middle and professional class. Although there are no absolutely reliable figures, it must be assumed that at least one-third of the total population of 7 million were killed.

At the beginning of 1979 the powerful army of the new Socialist Republic of Vietnam invaded Cambodia, occupying the capital, Pnom Penh, on 7 January. Although the forces of Pol Pot's Khmer Rouge (Red Khmers) organisation continued to resist, it could be said that Ho Chi Minh's dream of restoring the former French empire under Vietnamese communist rule had been fulfilled. In the preceding months, the New Vietnam had joined the Soviet Union's Comecon economic union, and Soviet advisers had moved in to take the place of the departing Chinese. Brezhnev could therefore claim to have achieved the Soviet ambition of establishing a remote control satellite, or at least a client-state, in the Far East and on China's borders.

The war between Vietnam and Cambodia was the first of its kind between communist states, and it was followed shortly afterwards by a limited Chinese incursion into Vietnamese territory, at the end of which both sides claimed victory.

This account of Soviet advances in the Brezhnev phase of the cold war makes melancholy reading, although we should not overlook the many significant setbacks suffered by the Kremlin in the same period. These setbacks alone should put us on our guard against thinking there is some kind of historical inevitability about the success of communism as a world force. A careful reckoning of what happened in the years following Khrushchev's fall shows that the contrary was the case. That is, Soviet communism has never appealed as a spontaneous popular force to overthrow long-established traditions of government. The popular movements of these years, as in Iran, all had different origins. But what the record does show is the versatility of the Soviet leaders in turning potential trouble-spots to their own advantage and their ruthlessness in imposing their regime, with brute force where necessary, whenever the opportunity to do so arose.

Nevertheless, the Brezhnev years saw spectacular advances by the Soviet Union in the military and psychological fronts of the cold war, fronts which directly concerned the United States and its Western allies. The West has generally accepted the term 'détente' to describe this process, a term which is as misleading as its predecessor, 'peaceful co-existence'. To understand the origins of 'détente' properly, we must once more return to the time of the palace revolution which removed Khrushchev from supreme power.

10   The Soviet Quandary

The new Soviet leaders very soon came up against a fundamental dilemma inherent in the nature of the Soviet system. In economic terms, the system was beginning to get bogged down in its own inefficiency. Despite the impressive achievements of Sputnik and intercontinental ballistic missiles, Soviet technology lagged behind that of the advanced Western countries and Japan. But the system could not be abandoned, or even modified beyond a certain point, without calling in question the monopoly of power of the Soviet Communist Party. As for technology, the Soviets needed access to the achievements of Japan and the Western countries, whose system the ruling party was pledged to destroy.

It was a double dilemma, and even a treble one, in that, in the name of Leninist ideology, they were bound to encourage revolution all over the world, to the detriment of the very governments whose help they needed. Yet they could not discard international subversion, even if they had so wished, without losing their revolutionary credentials and being outflanked on the left by China and the proliferating Trotskyist or fundamentalist groups, who were accusing the Soviet Union of having lost its revolutionary fervour to creeping bureaucracy.

In Stalin's day, economic performance had not been a comparable problem. With unlimited terror at his disposal, the dictator had expended millions of lives to collectivise agriculture. Indifferent to consumer needs, he had given the Soviet Union a powerful steel industry and a war economy. Khrushchev had seen the need for more consumer goods, but quantity and not quality was the determining principle. When presenting the Programme of the 22nd Soviet Party Congress he had made absurd predictions, one of which was that by 1970 the Soviet Union would surpass the United States in industrial production per head of the population.

His successors quietly buried these claims, as mountains of unsold goods accumulated in the shops. In September 1965 Premier Kosygin adopted reforms proposed by Professor Yevsei Liberman, who had dared to suggest that state enterprises should be made profitable and have the right to dismiss workers who were not efficient.

In 1966 Kosygin and his colleagues began shopping abroad in earnest. In April, for example, Foreign Minister Gromyko visited Italy and concluded an agreement for the construction of a Fiat automobile factory in Russia. Towards the end of June, President de Gaulle visited Moscow and discussed a programme for Franco–Soviet co-operation in the exploration of space and in general technological development. At the end of the year Kosygin made a follow-up visit to Paris. Two months later, he was in London, where the British Prime Minister, Harold Wilson, tried hard (but failed) to enlist Soviet support for attempts to bring peace to Vietnam. A Soviet–British trade treaty was signed, but not until June 1968.

Any further Soviet attempts to 'shop around' in the West were, however, halted in the wake of a major crisis—an attempt by the communist party boss of Czechoslovakia, Alexander Dubcek, to inaugurate a new kind of 'communism with a human face' for his country.

As in Hungary twelve years earlier, the pressures in favour of change seemed irresistible. Dubcek had taken over from President Novotny as party boss on 25 January 1968. On 6 April, General Ludvik Svoboda was elected President and Oldrich Cernik appointed Premier. Indeed, a new party programme was published, with pledges of freedom of speech, press, assembly and religion.

These measures aroused widespread enthusiasm, not only in Czechoslovakia but abroad, and European social democrats and visitors from the Americas and elsewhere arrived in Prague in great numbers to see for themselves what was going on. Brezhnev and his colleagues began to put pressure on Dubcek to check the liberalising tendencies of which they disapproved. Dubcek, however, declined invitations to attend conferences in Warsaw or Moscow in mid-July, although he did try to save his experiment by declaring, and repeating, that Czechoslovakia remained a faithful member of the Warsaw Pact (thus avoiding, as he hoped, a fatal error of Premier Nagy in Hungary in 1956). On 22 July Brezhnev took an unprecendented step when he flew to Prague accompanied by the entire Soviet Politburo. At the same time, he ordered Soviet forces to concentrate on the Czech borders, ostensibly for manoeuvres.

One man who followed these events anxiously, and almost with a proprietorial interest, was President Tito of Yugoslavia. Another was the Rumanian leader, Ceausescu, who was having some success in running an independent foreign policy while maintaining an absolutely rigid police state at home. (This, incidentally, was undoubtedly what saved the Ceausescu experiment. The one thing the Russians could not tolerate was any relaxation of the Communist Party's monopoly of power. Had they done so, the contagion would have spread throughout the Soviet empire, and things would rapidly have got out of control.)

In August, Tito and Ceausescu each went to Prague on separate visits, to demonstrate their support for Dubcek and to try, if possible, to forestall Soviet intervention.

On the night of 20 to 21 August, however, 200,000 Warsaw Pact troops invaded Czechoslovakia. The Rumanians ostentatiously stayed out of the invading force, which soon grew to 650,000 men.

This was naked Soviet imperialism of the most brutal kind. The KGB arrested Dubcek and took him in handcuffs to Moscow, where he was mercilessly grilled. Back in Prague on the 27th, he announced the repeal of several important reforms.

Early in September, the Soviet Deputy Foreign Minister, Kuznetsov, arrived in Prague, and Dubcek was forced to re-introduce preventive censorship and ban the political clubs that had been flourishing in the 'Prague spring'.

At the beginning of October, the Czech leaders were summoned to Moscow and forced to pledge that the reforms they had introduced would be abandoned. There was a further price to pay: they had to accept Soviet military occupation 'temporarily' (they were not to know that the occupation would still be in force a decade and more later).

The humiliation of Dubcek was gradual. He was removed from office in April 1969, ousted from the praesidium of the Central Committee at the end of September that year and finally expelled from the Communist Party on 26 June 1970. The unconditionally pro-Soviet regime of Dr Husak settled in for a long stay.

The Brezhnev Doctrine

The most ominous outcome of the occupation of Czechoslovakia, from the standpoint of the rest of the world, was the 'Brezhnev Doctrine'. It was a legalistic squaring of the circle. In a statement at the Fifth Congress of the Polish Communist Party in November 1968, as reported in *Pravda* of the 13th, the Soviet leader reaffirmed respect for sovereignty on the one hand, and on the other, claimed the right to intervene in a socialist country where 'socialism' was deemed to be threatened. On *sovereignty*, Brezhnev said:

> Socialist states stand for strict respect for the sovereignty of all countries. We are resolutely opposed to interference in the affairs of any states, to violation of their sovereignty.

On *intervention*, however, this is what Brezhnev had to say:

> When internal and external supporters hostile to socialism attempt to turn the development of any socialist country in the direction of the restoration of the capitalist system, when a threat arises to the cause of socialism in that country, a threat to the security of the socialist commonwealth as a whole—it already becomes not only a problem for the people of that country but also a general problem, the concern of all socialist countries.

In such circumstances, Brezhnev declared, armed intervention was justified. In other words, what he was saying was that once a country was 'socialist', and once the Soviet Union had accepted it as such, then it could *never* be permitted to change its political system, whatever the views of the majority of the people. Sovereignty, then, was re-interpreted to mean the inviolability of its socialist (communist) system.

Although spokesmen have denied from time to time that there was any such thing as a 'Brezhnev Doctrine', these principles have been reaffirmed on a number of occasions, and were to be invoked eleven years later, when the Soviet Union invaded Afghanistan.

As always in Soviet history, an act of aggression is followed by an attempt to reassure the world—in other words, by what the communists call a 'peace campaign', more accurately described by the contradictory term 'peace offensive'.

So it was after Czechoslovakia, as it had been after Hungary. The Soviets had calculated that the invasion and occupation of Czechoslovakia would set off an outcry in the West, but that they would run no risk of military retaliation. They also calculated that public interest in the question would gradually wane and that they could therefore, after a suitable interval, resume their proposals for 'peace'.

What they did, in 1969, was to resurrect the idea of a collective security pact, which Molotov had proposed in 1954. This time, they suggested a 'European Security Conference'. They kept coming back to the theme, and coupled it with suggestions that NATO and the Warsaw Pact should both be dissolved. These proposals were well designed to please the Left in Western countries, but also to please idealists and the gullible. From the point of view of Western defence, the danger was the flaw in the argument that if the two military blocs were dissolved it would mean the withdrawal of American troops from Europe, and therefore of the protective umbrella which the American presence cast over the Alliance. If the Americans did withdraw, they would be 3,000 miles and more away across the Atlantic, and unlikely to return in a hurry; whereas the Soviets would be where they had always been, with little in their way should they wish to overrun Western Europe.

It is important to note that by this time (1969), the Social Democrats (SPD) were in power for the first time in West Germany, with Willy Brandt as Chancellor.

Willy Brandt was determined to break with the rigid foreign policy he had inherited from the long line of Christian Democrat governments. Germany, he argued, was still a divided country twenty-four years after the end of the Second World War. There was a case in his eyes for an entirely new overture to the East, which he called his *Ostpolitik*.

At the Potsdam Conference in 1945 the Soviet Union, America and Britain had recognised the Oder–Neisse Line as the *de facto* eastern border of Germany, but it was held to be only a 'temporary boundary' pending a general settlement in Germany as a whole. Brezhnev wanted more than that: he wanted the Western Allies to recognise the post-war boundaries of Europe as permanent and *legitimate*; to recognise the German Democratic Republic (East Germany).

Brandt's *Ostpolitik* met the Soviets more than half-way. The West German government signed treaties with Moscow and with Warsaw, in August and December 1970, respectively. Under these treaties, the German Federal Republic recognised the borders of East Germany, and of Poland's Oder–Neisse frontier. There was also a Four-Power Agreement on Berlin, signed in September 1971, under which the Soviets were allowed to open a large mission in Bonn. These new installations gave the Soviets and their East German satellites fresh opportunities for espionage. Finally, West Germany formally recognised the communist regime in East Germany under the General Treaty between the two German governments signed in November 1972, which provided that both should seek admission to the United Nations.

In return, the West Germans and their allies secured a written Soviet undertaking to facilitate surface transit of traffic to West Berlin through East German territory. But West Berlin remained militarily vulnerable as before. The Berlin Wall stayed where it was and indeed, after the signature of the treaties, new electronic devices were installed to bring death automatically to any East Germans wishing to take refuge in West Berlin.

Meanwhile in January 1969 Richard Nixon had come to power in the United States. Despite an anti-communist past, the new President was in a mood for exploratory talks with the Kremlin as well as with Peking, a mood to which the elusiveness of military victory in Vietnam contributed.

Brezhnev knew that without the technology and easy credit terms he needed from the West and Japan the entire Soviet system would gradually collapse. In no domain was this more urgent than in agriculture, where productivity remained abysmally low after decades of collectivism.

In April 1971, therefore, addressing the 24th Congress of the Soviet Communist Party, Brezhnev launched his 'Peace Programme'. In ringing tones, he called for a conference on European security and for the dissolution of NATO and the Warsaw Pact.

It is now known that Brezhnev, surprising though it might seem, did not find an automatically favourable response to his proposals in the communist world, or among his own colleagues. Many were troubled about the long-term implications of a security pact in Europe, which might leave them unable to fall back on the military power of the Soviet armed forces if they got into trouble with the people of their own countries.

Moreover, some of them were worried that the search for 'détente' with the West might lead to a loss of credibility of the Soviet Union as the leader of world revolution. In 1973, two years after the Peace Programme had been launched, these critical voices were still being heard. To reassure and silence the critics, Brezhnev summoned East European communist leaders to a meeting in Prague. Each of the East European Party bosses was well aware that they would be thrown out of office if it were withdrawn.

Brezhnev asked for their trust. He explained the economic difficulties faced by the Soviet system, and in terms that almost amounted to a paraphase of Lenin's words in his famous memorandum of more than half a century earlier, he argued that détente would bring the Soviets the technology and easy credits they needed from the West. By 1985, he said, with Western help achieved through détente, a decisive shift in the correlation of forces would have taken place, to the advantage of the Soviet Union. And when that had happened, the Soviets could impose their will everywhere.

A full account of this crucial meeting reached Western intelligence through an informant who was present. Western governments, however, chose to ignore the information, which would have remained secret but for the Watergate affair in the United States, when much secret intelligence was leaked to the press and the media. The full story was in fact told by William Beecher, in an article in the *Boston Globe* of 11 February 1977. Beecher had been assistant secretary for Public Affairs in the Pentagon in 1973 and had had access to the intelligence report of the meeting.

It was at this stage of Brezhnev's career that he revealed his unsuspected gifts as a charmer and successful travelling salesman. As an integral part of 'Operation Détente', the party boss and Premier Kosygin—both of whom normally showed bored or impassive faces to the outside world—were shown wreathed in smiles as they made speeches about peace in various countries.

In Bonn, Brezhnev kissed Frau Brandt's hand with old-fashioned gallantry; in Hollywood, he roared with laughter as the giant American film actor, Chuck Conners, playfully lifted him off the ground.

The Soviet propaganda apparatus let it be known that the party boss was fond of fast and impressive cars. President Nixon presented him with a Lincoln, and President Pompidou of France gave him a special Citroen, while Chancellor Brandt came up with a top-of-the-range Mercedes. In June 1977, President Giscard d'Estaing gave him two more splendid cars.

By the spring of 1973, all this public relations and *bonhomie* was beginning to pay off for the Soviets. In May that year, Brezhnev visited Bonn, and concluded a ten-year agreement for co-operation in the economic, industrial, technological and cultural fields. The leave-taking at Cologne airport was protracted because of effusive handshakes, and take-off was delayed by thirty-five minutes.

In France the following month, Brezhnev had seven hours in *tête-à-tête* with President Pompidou. On 10 July, two ten-year programmes were signed by the two governments. Under the first, France was to invest between 5,000 and 7,000 million francs in the USSR. They were to build a cellulose factory at Ust Ilim in Siberia; repayment was to be in cellulose produced by the factory (that is, at the discretion of the Soviets). Under the other programme, the two countries were to co-operate in space exploration, atomic energy and colour television. French help would be provided for the development of Siberian gas fields; and again, payment was to be in kind.

Although Brezhnev did not visit London, Prime Minister Harold Wilson went to Moscow in February 1975, and announced on returning that his government would provide the Soviet Union with credits up to nearly £1,000 million.

Important though Brezhnev's Bonn and Paris summits were, the decisive exercises in 'détente' summitry were with the American presidents. There were three Brezhnev–Nixon summits, and one with Gerald Ford.

As with the European summits, the Soviet–American ones concerned trade and credits, but unlike the European ones, they also dealt with arms control as between the two superpowers, through the Strategic Arms Limitation Talks (better known as SALT).

The Americans had been pressing the Soviets for these talks, but initially the Soviets dragged their feet. In 1965–6 they had made a start with the enormously expensive installation of an Anti-Ballistic Missile (ABM) site—that is, the construction and deployment of missile capable of detecting incoming missiles high in the sky and destroying them before they hit the ground.

The Americans, reluctant to tie up so much capital in an ABM system of their own, did not commit themselves until a Senate vote on 24 June 1968. This triggered an immediate Soviet response. Within three days Foreign Minister Gromyko announced that his government was now ready to discuss Strategic Arms Limitation.

Interestingly, the Soviet ABM protected Moscow, whereas the American one, at Grand Forks, North Dakota, protected mainly itself.

The first Nixon–Brezhnev summit, held in Moscow in May 1972, resulted in a treaty limiting the Soviet Union and America to two defensive missile sites (ABMs) each; and an agreement to freeze land- and sea-based missiles at their existing levels.

For the second summit, Nixon and Brezhnev began their meeting in Washington, then moved to the President's Pacific coast home at San Clemente, California. On 25 June 1973 the two men signed a final communiqué which was hailed in both camps as a great contribution to world peace. For the first time, the Americans accepted a position of slight strategic inferiority to the Soviets.

As always, the Soviets refused any inspection on the spot. This meant that each side had to content itself with 'inspection' by spy-in-the-sky satellites and other technical means. Taken together, these agreements constitute SALT 1.

Between the first and second Nixon–Brezhnev summits, a start had been made on a European security conference (officially known as the CSCE, or Conference on Security and Co-operation in Europe.) In preparatory talks, the Soviets had tried to confine the conference to European powers alone, which would have left the West Europeans virtually at the mercy of the Soviet giant by excluding the Americans. They soon gave in on this point, however, and the formal preparatory talks took place in Helsinki in November 1972, and lasted until June the following year.

Stage 1 of the actual conference brought the foreign ministers together in Geneva for a meeting lasting only five days (3–7 July 1973). Stage 2 was much tougher. Diplomats and other high officials assembled in Geneva on 18 September 1973 to fill in the details left unclear by the foreign ministers. They had hoped to complete their work in time for Stage 3 (the final stage) due to begin in the summer of 1974. But the talks dragged on and on, with the Soviets contesting all points every inch of the way, so that the last stage was not reached until July 1975.

Why were these negotiations so protracted? It must be remembered that these were dealings between the representatives of two fundamentally dissimilar systems: the collectivist and totalitarian one, bent on imposing its will on the rest of the world, preferably without war; and the pluralist and open systems of the West, which were merely trying to defend themselves while safeguarding 'peace'.

The work was divided among four committees, each considering a 'basket' of proposals.

Basket 1 dealt with such matters as prior notification of major military manoeuvres or troop movements, under the heading of 'confidence-building measures'.

Basket 2 dealt with trade and economics.

Basket 3—the most important to the West—considered human rights, cultural exchanges, freedom of information and related matters of public communication.

Basket 4 concerned follow-up measures, to ensure that whatever set of agreements was reached would be observed after the conference was over.

The wrangling was perhaps less intense over Basket 1 (confidence-building) than over the other 'baskets'. No real progress was made in Basket 2, the Soviets insisting on 'most-favoured nation' treatment from the Western countries and access to the European Common Market, while maintaining the Soviet bloc as a sealed economic system under centralised control.

The debates were at their most time-consuming in Basket 3. The Western negotiators maintained that a true defence implied unrestricted movement of people from the Soviet Union and Eastern Europe to the West, and vice versa. They wanted Soviet citizens to be able to read Western newspapers freely, and not just communist papers, such as the French *L'Humanité* or the British *Morning Star*. But the Soviets contested each proposal, point by point, in the end conceding little of substance.

It was in the Basket 4 committee that the Soviets made their most determined effort to cut out American (and Canadian) participation in the follow-up process. They proposed the creation of an All-European Commission to ensure observance of the recommendations of the conference. Fortunately, the West Europeans supported the United States' contention that this was an inadmissible procedure.

While the discussions were inching forward, Nixon and Brezhnev had their third summit, this time in Moscow in June 1974. By then, the American President was in serious trouble over the so-called 'Watergate affair', after the uncovering of a plot, with White House approval, to break into Democratic Party headquarters in the Watergate apartment building in Washington.

Watergate possibly made Nixon more ready than he would have otherwise been to make concessions for the sake of popularity at home. Brezhnev, in contrast, was far less vulnerable. He had already succeeded beyond reasonable expectations in proving to the sceptics of the communist world that 'détente' would bring access to Western technology. Between March 1973 and March 1974 alone, the United States' government had granted the USSR credits totalling $400 million at the low rate of 6 per cent interest.

The actual money had been provided by such private banks as the Chase Manhattan and Bankers Trust. As Lenin had forecast in 1921, and Brezhnev himself more recently, the capitalists had proved eager to help a regime intent on their destruction.

Shopping for grain after a disastrous harvest in 1972–3, the Soviets had bought 750 million dollars' worth of American wheat at artificially low prices, leaving the Americans short on their home market and contributing to inflation. Moreover, during the eighteen months or so of 'détente' preceding the third Nixon–Brezhnev summit, the Soviets had added a further 1,500 tanks to their weaponry on the European front, outnumbering NATO by three to one.

The summit yielded a treaty limiting underground nuclear tests to 150 kilotons (compared with the Hiroshima bomb of 20 kilotons), and a protocol to the 1972 ABM agreement limiting the Soviets and the Americans to one defensive missile site each, instead of two; neither country, in fact, had showns signs of wishing to build more than one.

Other decisions were: a call for an early final stage to the security conference; a mutual declaration of non-interference in internal affairs; a further agreement on industrial, economic and technical co-operation; and the opening of consulates-general in Kiev (American) and in New York (Soviet).

Because of the gulf between the two systems, these agreements were less even-handed than they looked. For instance, the agreement to refrain from intervening in each other's internal affairs was meaningless in that America, as an open society, was wide open to Soviet subversion, whereas Soviet society was almost hermetically sealed. Indeed, the Soviets made it clear that they considered even the broadcasts of the Voice of America and of the American-funded Radio Liberty in Munich, beamed on the USSR, as 'interference'.

For the same reasons, the opening of a Soviet consulate-general in New York gave the Soviets infinitely more opportunities for espionage in the United States than the United States gained through its proposed consulate-general in Kiev.

Another point to note about this third summit is that the treaty limiting testing was not to come into force until 31 March 1976. The Soviets would, therefore, have all the time they needed to fix six independently targetable warheads on to each of their awesome SS-9 and SS-18 missiles. The Americans, too, would gain time, but there was no comparison between the 'throw-weight' capacity of the two sides' missiles. Each Soviet warhead delivered 500 kilotons, and each missile could carry six warheads. On the American side, the Minuteman could take no more than three warheads, and the warheads delivered only 200 kilotons each. The treaty therefore guaranteed, in practice, a massive Soviet superiority in total throw-weight by the spring of 1976.

President Nixon was forced into retirement by Watergate before the fourth in this series of summits, and his place was taken by President Ford who, accompanied by Secretary of State Kissinger, went to Vladivostok, in the Soviet Far East, to meet Brezhnev, in November 1974. This new summit confirmed the advantage the Soviets had extracted from Nixon, giving them time to catch up with the Americans on the deployment of MIRVed missiles. (In strategic jargon, MIRVs are Multiple Independently Targeted Re-entry Vehicles; that is, a single warhead containing a number, sometimes as high as nine, of single nuclear missiles which can attack individual targets when they reach enemy country.)

At the time of the Vladivostok meeting the Americans already had 918 MIRVs on deployment and the Soviets had none. But the agreement placed no limits on either throw-weight or qualitative improvement. The Soviets were thus allowed to introduce MIRVs and arm them with their much heavier and more numerous warheads per missile, and with a good chance of overtaking the American technological lead in accuracy of delivery.

The final stage of the security conference took the form of a summit of all the participants at Helsinki in July 1975. It was, in effect, the ritual coronation ceremony of 'détente'.

The end-result of the lengthy process was a massive document styled the Final Act, and embodying in language of some imprecision the many points covered in the foregoing discussions and negotiations.

What did the Soviets get out of Operation Détente? Certainly, the technology and trade on easy terms had been forthcoming, as Brezhnev had calculated, although there had been two setbacks. One was a move by Senator Henry ('Scoop') Jackson towards the end of

1974 to tie any major extension of US–Soviet trade to an easing of Soviet restrictions on emigration from the USSR. This so infuriated Brezhnev that, at the end of the year, he denounced the 1972 Soviet–American trade agreement.

The other setback came at about the same time, when the Congress decided to limit credit to the USSR at low interest to $300 million, thus dashing Soviet hopes that the United States would play a major part in developing Siberian natural gas reserves.

Against this, the Americans committed themselves in October 1975 to selling the Soviets at least 6 million metric tons of grain between 1 October 1976 and 30 September 1981—an astonishing admission on the Soviet side that its collectivist agriculture was incapable of feeding the Soviet people after sixty years of communism.

With special reference to the Helsinki negotiations and the security conference as a whole, the Soviets could reasonably claim a partial, but not a complete victory. We have mentioned their objectives, both stated and unstated. The final tally worked out as follows:

Stated objectives
The dissolution of NATO and the Warsaw Pact: not achieved.
The immutability of frontiers in Europe (in other words, Western recognition of the permanence of Stalin's European empire): partially achieved. Willy Brandt's *Ostpolitik* had given the Soviets formal recognition of the frontiers of Poland and East Germany.

But recognition of the 'immutability' of frontiers eluded them at Helsinki. Instead, Western negotiators insisted on 'inviolability'. The difference is subtle but important. 'Immutability' would have meant Western recognition of the permanence of the ideological or systematic division of Europe. 'Inviolability' ruled out the use of military force to alter existing boundaries, but would not exclude, say, the merging of the two German states by agreement.

Thus the West recognised only the fact that the three Baltic Republics of Latvia, Estonia and Lithuania were under Soviet rule. These nations had been independent sovereign states between the two world wars. In Britain and the United States, Latvia still maintains an independent diplomatic presence dating back to that brief period of freedom.

A final document with the force of a peace treaty: not achieved, in that the Final Act was not binding in international law.

Unstated objectives
Withdrawal of American forces from Europe: not achieved.
Progress in the psychological, political and military disarmament of the West; considerable success, from the Soviet standpoint. Before the end of 1975, for instance, both the American and British governments announced large cuts in defence spending.
The Finlandisation* of Western Europe: notable progress.
For example, President Giscard d'Estaing of France in a press conference on 21 May 1975 rejected any discussion of a common European defence structure, on the ground that the Soviets were against it. Again, the ruling Social Democrats (SPD) in West Germany campaigned for election in 1976 on the line that a victory for the Christian Democrats would be a 'security risk' in that they were less welcome to the Soviets. Another example: American and British invitations to Boris Ponomarev in 1975 and 1976, respectively, were truly 'Finlandistic' or appeasement-like in that he was the man in charge of the global strategy of subversion against the West.

The harnessing of Western technology to Soviet needs:
Brilliantly achieved, as we have seen.

Perhaps the most significant aspect of the whole process, however, was the fact that the concessions were almost entirely one-sided. Some marginal gains were made on the Western side, such as transit rights and easier family visits to and from East Germany. The Western negotiating teams at Geneva and Helsinki congratulated themselves on having refused 'immutability' in respect of the boundaries of the Soviet bloc, and on having obliged the Russians, for the first time, to discuss their own performance in human rights.

But these were minor satisfactions in comparison with what the West had given away: the major West German concessions; the provision of massive credits, amounting to a kind of Marshall Plan in reverse, and transfers of technology, much of which was of military application; and above all, the readiness of Western governments to

---

*The term 'Finlandisation', though naturally offensive to a brave and independent people, describes the situation whereby Finland, while enjoying autonomy in domestic affairs, feels compelled to 'clear' any foreign initiatives with its giant neighbour, and refrains from joining international alliances.

accept the concept of 'détente' at face value.

In the eyes of the Soviets, meanwhile, nothing had changed. They went on waging the cold war in Ethiopia, in Angola, in South Yemen and elsewhere, completely unrestrained by the Final Act at Helsinki. The 'concessions' on human rights and freedom of information which the Western governments thought they had won turned out to be illusory.

One Western statesman who had occasion to discover for himself that little had changed was President Giscard. On a visit to Moscow in October 1975, he publicly interpreted 'détente' as implying a relaxation of ideological tensions. In retaliation , Brezhnev snubbed him by cancelling part of the agreed programme without notice.

In December 1976, a writer in the Moscow review *International Affairs* gave this Soviet definition of détente: 'Détente serves as a basis for peaceful competition between socialism and capitalism on a world-wide scale, and is a specific form of the struggle between them.' He added, as a matter of course; 'The final victory of socialism over capitalism in this competition is objectively inevitable.'

An important Soviet defector, Stanislav Levchenko, who had served the KGB in Japan, was present when a leading member of the Central Committee of the Soviet Communist Party (CPSU) made a speech to the Tokyo embassy staff after the signing of the Helsinki Agreements. His apparently clear and precise recollection of what his colleague had said is quoted in John Barron's book *KGB Today : The Hidden Hand* (Reader's Digest Press, New York, 1983):

By inducing NATO nations, including the Main Enemy, to sign the Helsinki Agreements, the Soviet Union achieved one of the greatest triumphs since World War II. The Soviet strategy was so ingenious that Western leaders thought they had triumphed. The fools even were eager to sign. Poor Fools! They did not understand that they were caught like stupid birds in our trap. They dream now of disintegrating our monolithic society by exploiting the principles of the Helsinki Agreements—free exchange of information, freedom of travel, of immigration, human rights and other bourgeois absurdities.

Poor fools! It will take years for them to understand. We will sell their books, magazines and newspapers to foreigners in hotels reserved for foreigners, and we will burn the rest. Western countries think that now rotten dissident organisations will grow like mushrooms in our land. Ha, Ha, Ha! Let them hope. Our glorious Chekists [the KGB] know their business. In the next few years, we will rid ourselves of dissidents once and for all. We will put them all in prisons and labour camps and reform them by force into productive members of society. Meanwhile, we shall exploit the principles of the Helsinki Agreements to undermine capitalism from within.

By all overt and covert means, we shall manipulate public opinion in Western countries as we like, and drown out criticisms of our military build-up. We have the resources to create dozens of new organisations in the West and to reinforce existing front-line organisations. Our glorious intelligence services will seize all the new opportunities to operate on a much higher and wider scale, taking advantage of the friendlier attitude towards the USSR.

We shall turn public opinion in the West, particularly in Western Europe, against the USA. Everywhere we shall plant seeds of distrust against the Main Enemy. The Helsinki Agreements offer us historic opportunities to weaken our enemies, and we shall grasp all.

Thus, from the Soviet viewpoint, the cold war went on, and détente was just another battle tactic in it. We must now consider the response of successive American administrations to this tactic: The policy of the Reagan Administration, however, is dealt with in Chapter 12.

11 Settling for Number Two

The Vietnam war and the Watergate scandal were terrible shocks to the American national psyche. President Nixon's involvement in the latter created such a crisis of confidence in the institutions of government as to make outsiders wonder if all Americans had taken leave of their senses. Here was the greatest upholder of democracy in the world abandoning itself to the tyranny of self-exposure and public humiliation. To these same outsiders, it seemed as if the American communications media had become so obsessed with commercial reward and their own power as to represent a far greater threat to the workings of democracy than the unhappy occupant of the White House was alleged to be. In cold war terms, the damage was incalculable. The CIA, to take one example, was an obvious target. Old controversies, like the Bay of Pigs fiasco, and new ones, like Allende's downfall in Chile, were given such a working-over as virtually to destroy the effectiveness of the West's principal defence against the offensive acts of terrorism and subversion practised non-stop by the Soviet KGB.

Coinciding as Watergate did with the end of the Vietnam War, the sentiment in the United States was overwhelming: no more wars, no more interventions. The draft, which had been in effect since before the Second World War, was abandoned and the fighting services were told to find their men and women through recruitment. The turbulent years that had begun with the Berlin blockade appeared to die in a welter of national self-abasement and a poorly concealed thirst for peace at almost any price. Only one section of opinion in America was able to keep its head above water and even make progress against the tide, and this was the pro-Israeli lobby. Even this powerful force might have been unable to influence events but for an unusual Soviet challenge which came early in Nixon's second term.

In October 1973 Egyptian and Syrian forces launched heavy attacks upon the Israeli positions holding the Suez Canal and the Golan Heights, which faced Syria in the north-east. The Arab forces were initially successful. Israel, caught by surprise, largely due to the unwillingness of senior commanders and eminent politicians to accept the estimates of junior intelligence officers, fought back with bravery and enterprise. The war might have passed into history as a local encounter won in the end by Israel had it not been for a curious Soviet move.

The Soviets, like every other leading power, had joined in the universal cry for a ceasefire. When this failed to develop as quickly as they had wished and their Syrian clients appeared to be in danger of losing not only the war but Damascus, their capital, Soviet airborne units began to concentrate in Hungary. The evidence of concentration was there, attested by satellites and from information passed on by agents on the ground. Soviet intentions to this day are less clear: they were probably smarting from their expulsion from Egypt and looking for a come-back. But the assumption in Washington was that they would be used against the Israeli forces to enforce a ceasefire. There was, therefore, a strong possibility of the October War expanding into a major conflict.

The Nixon Administration's reaction was to order an alert of all United States forces including the triad of nuclear weaponry; ICBMs, bombers and submarines armed with ballistic missiles. Just as had happened in the Cuban missile crisis, this concentration of force sufficed to quieten the Soviets. The threat of Soviet intervention receded. But in the planning offices of the Pentagon it was noted that the Soviet military establishment of 1973 was a great deal more formidable than that of 1962. Nor were there any signs of a slowdown in the continuing struggle to establish the Soviet Union as a military power equal to the United States.

The first moves in the strange, arcane process that became SALT 1 had already been born in the fertile brain of Kissinger. Since his own writings are manifestly self-serving it is difficult to ascertain the motives that drove him. There is the implication in some of his conversations with men like Admiral Elmo Zumwalt, then Chief of Naval Operations, that he believed that the Soviets were inevitably going to become the stronger of the two superpowers and that

Strategic Arms Limitation Talks would slow this process. There is also the view, held by many, that Kissinger and Nixon believed that a successful conclusion of SALT 1 could be linked to Soviet restraint in other fields, notably in the Third World.

But Nixon's views, although forcefully argued in his book *The Real War*, inevitably appear, like Kissinger's to be self-serving and the work of hindsight. The fact of the matter is that the United States entered the summit negotiations with a sizeable lead in nuclear weapons, in numbers, and in vehicles of attack over the Soviet Union. The 1970s ended with this situation reversed.

Both sides, however, pressed ahead with improvements to their nuclear weaponry and the pace of these improvements has been impressive. The United States, warned by Pentagon experts and a chorus of civilian specialists that the silos for the Minuteman III ICBMs would be vulnerable to Soviet missile attack by the middle of the 1980s, turned to the mobile MX missile, which would carry as many as ten nuclear warheads.

The submarine force was to be revitalised by the introduction of the Trident boats, each carrying twenty-four Trident missiles with a range of 4,000 miles. These missiles would also be fitted into some of the Poseidon submarines already in service. Development began on a second generation of Trident missiles with a range of 6,000 miles.

Such improvements, if expedited, should have maintained America's lead in nuclear weapons. But they were not expedited. Experts within the Pentagon and Congressional leaders disputed the proper launching system for the MX. Construction of the Trident submarines lagged. Meanwhile the third leg of the triad, the term applied to the three American strategic forces, showed signs of age. This was the B-52 bomber, an aircraft designed in the 1950s for service in the 1960s. By 1979 some of the aircraft were older than the pilots who flew them. Fortunately the basic design of the B-52 was a triumph of aeronautic engineering. The elderly aircraft could be and were subjected to improvement without seriously damaging their operational capability. But by the end of the 1970s it was apparent that most of the older aircraft would be useful in war only as carriers of air-launched cruise missiles. Their role as a penetration bomber was over.

The United States Air Force had believed that its new bomber, the expensive and sophisticated B-1 would replace the B-52 as the major

American air weapon. But President Jimmy Carter, who entered office in January 1977, ended development of the aircraft. The cruise missile, a derivative and improvement of the German V-1 weapon of the Second World War, was put forward as a substitute.

The cruise missile, which could be launched by sea, from the air or the ground, was hailed at the outset as the panacea for America's problems in the strategic nuclear race. It was cheap, it was mobile, and it could be produced by the tens of thousands. Economy-minded Senators and Congressmen were full of praise for it. The acclaim was extraordinary for a weapon that had not been fully tested and which, even its supporters agreed, would be vulnerable to hostile interceptors if they could see it. There is no shortage of Soviet aircraft assigned to the defence of the Soviet Union, which has about 2,600 interceptors backed by some 10,000 surface-to-air missile launchers. America's decision to move ahead with the cruise missile provoked an extensive expansion of Soviet radar systems, including some new devices capable of detecting the low-flying cruise missiles.

American emphasis on defence was more than matched by an impressive Soviet modernisation of their strategic nuclear weaponry, all of which went to show: first, that limitations on the numbers of launchers does not really affect the ability of either side to deliver a lethal nuclear blow, and second, that restraint on America's part in strategic nuclear weapons development and production is unlikely to promote a similar restraint in the Kremlin. The ultimate result was that, by early 1980, General Richard F. Ellis, head of the Strategic Air Command, admitted to an audience in New York City that the Soviet Union now had the edge, he hoped only temporarily, in strategic nuclear power. Secretary of Defense Brown's response was that there was still a nuclear equivalence although, he conceded, one side or the other might draw ahead for a time.

By 1976 the Ford Administration and, belatedly, the people of the United States began to realise that détente had a different meaning for the Soviet Union. The improvement in Russian strategic nuclear weapons, it now became apparent, was being matched by the modernisation and expansion of conventional forces. Two aspects were important. Under Admiral Sergei G. Gorshkov the Soviet Navy attained a capability for overseas intervention it had never known in the past. Russian warships became as familiar on the west coast of Africa, in Indo-Chinese ports or off the Horn of Africa as their fishing fleets.

Two helicopter carriers were followed by the deployment of *Kiev* and *Minsk*, authentic aircraft carriers although smaller than their giant American counterparts. The essential change was not lost on the smaller countries of the Third World. The Soviet Union now had the means to project its power across the world.

The second important development within the overall modernisation and expansion of the Russian forces occurred in its transport air command. This was an area where the United States had long been dominant. But as early as the late 1960s the Soviets were demonstrating their ability to move large forces by transport aircraft. New, larger transports rolled onto the runways. Aeroflot, the civil air fleet, was marked for reinforcement. The final demonstration of the Soviet Union's new military mobility came in the last week of December 1979 when, without apparent strain, three divisions were flown into Kabul to assist in the invasion of Afghanistan.

These developments took place during the period when the Carter Administration was accepting, without protest, the reduced production of a new tank and the MX missiles, deciding not to build the B-1 bomber and rejecting production of the enhanced radiation weapon, better known as the neutron bomb.

Although successive defence budgets promised new aircraft, helicopters, armoured personnel carriers and tanks to the services, they were arriving in the vital overseas stations, West Germany and South Korea, in minute quantities. A programme of unilateral disarmament was taking place. And to the American people, certainly as far as America's intellectual leadership was concerned, it did not seem to matter.

By the last years of the 1970s it was clear even to some of Carter's advisers that the flow of international events was running against the United States. The President had extracted a promise from the NATO allies in 1977 to increase defence budgets by 3 per cent. A programme to enhance the readiness of Alliance forces and to improve reinforcement was put in hand.

The problems, however, were not in Europe but elsewhere, in southern Africa, in South-east Asia and in the Middle East. By the terms of the original treaty, NATO's geography was limited on the south by the Tropic of Cancer and in the east by the Turkish–Soviet frontier.

Nixon and Kissinger had made the first gesture toward restoring relations with the People's Republic of China. Carter took the final step. He announced in 1978 the resumption of full diplomatic relations, which meant, among other things, the abandonment of America's difficult, but on the whole, loyal allies in Nationalist China, the Republic of China on Taiwan. He had played the China card.

The PRCs relations with the Soviet Union had been deteriorating ever since the late 1950s. By 1978 the communist Chinese, fearful of the growing strength of the Soviet forces in east Asia were building diplomatic relations with the Americans, the British, the French and, indeed, any industrial power whose resources might be tapped for the modernisation of the People's Liberation Army.

The PLA, as Western experts saw at first hand in 1976, was in sorry shape. Its men, soldiers, sailors and airmen, were vigorous, motivated and intelligent, but it lacked almost all the requisites of a modern army. Its tanks and artillery, obtained from the Soviets or built on Soviet blueprints, were twenty years out of date. The command and communications system ante-dated the Second World War. The devoted and eager pilots of the air force would have been shot down by the Russians. The navy, the third largest in the world in numbers, was tied to the shore because of a lack of tactical aircraft to provide cover once it ventured beyond coastal waters.

Mao Tse-tung died in 1976. Relations of a sort had already been established between Peking and Washington, but the assumption of real power by Deng Xiaopeng brought a fresh and pragmatic mind to the top of the Chinese party and government. Deng realised that the PLA reflected Mao's estimate of military strength; a nuclear force at one end and a mass army at the other. Deng understood that war with the Soviet Union would not be, inevitably, a nuclear war.

China had no modern, conventional forces that could make the slightest dent on a Soviet force that was poised to overrun Manchuria, China's most important industrial area. At the same time Peking looked with fear at the growing Soviet influence in Vietnam. China was in the process of being outflanked from the south.

In these circumstances *rapprochement* with the United States was almost inevitable. The Chinese did not abandon, nor could they, their basic opposition to Western 'imperialism' as exemplified by the United States. But co-operation with that imperialism appeared in 1978 to be the safest counter-balance to the 'hegemony' represented by 45 Soviet divisions and 3,000 aircraft in Asia, to say nothing of a vastly superior Pacific fleet, arrayed against the PLA.

The United States, although by no means as inferior to the Soviets as the PRC, also had strong reasons for establishing closer relations with Peking. The Administration knew, although it did not admit it publicly, that American military strength had ebbed since 1975. This was not solely the reluctance of successive administrations to call for the sacrifices required to repair American defences or to the dwindling of the defence industry that had once made the country the 'arsenal of democracy'. It owed something too, to the belated perception that the Soviet challenge was no longer confined to NATO's central front in Europe, that it was strengthening in places like the Red Sea, the Persian Gulf, South Yemen and eastern Siberia.

To balance this the China card had to be played. The military consequence was not and could not be an all-out American effort to re-arm the PRC. That was beyond American industry or, for that matter, the combined industries of the principal Western powers. The Soviets knew this, but they could not be sure. They have a healthier respect for American industrial prowess than many Americans. The United States might not be shipping vast numbers of aircraft, tanks and guns to China, but the possibility existed, and it was that possibility that worried Moscow.

The political consequence was that the Soviet Union recognised that the PRC with its vast resources of manpower, its potential wealth in oil and other resources, was now on terms of co-operation, if not friendship, with the one Western power that, given time, could direct that manpower and exploit those resources to arm the 'yellow hordes'. Lenin had said, 'China is a sleeping giant, let her sleep'. The Americans were now on hand to arm the awakening giant.

The recognition of the PRC and the resumption of normal diplomatic relations came after thirty years' hostility, a war in Korea in which Chinese fought Americans and another war in Vietnam in which the Chinese helped America's enemies with supplies and labour.

Understandably the move surprised the world. Some rejoiced, some deplored but, today, it appears almost inevitable.

The interests of China and the United States converged on one salient issue; the possibility of Soviet aggressive expansionism. It was in the deepest interests of both countries to prevent such expansionism if possible and, if it were not, to contain it.

But playing the China card hurt America's position in several countries hitherto confident that their ties with the United States would survive any strain. Taiwan was the main casualty. The American switch from Taipeh to Peking was seen by many as an abandonment of an old and faithful ally. This was noted in Tehran and half a dozen other capitals that enjoyed close diplomatic, economic and military links with Washington. The China card was played, it should be remembered, less than four years after the United States had failed to intervene militarily on behalf of its protégé in South Vietnam during the final North Vietnamese offensive in 1975 that destroyed the Saigon regime. This failure had aroused earlier doubts about the durability under other pressures of American commitments. The move toward Peking set the alarm bells ringing in many capitals.

Was this venture into *realpolitik* justified by events? It did not obviously prevent the Soviets from moving into Afghanistan. Indeed, some experts believe it accelerated it. It probably accelerated the flow of Russian economic and military aid to Vietnam. This was running at a rate of $3,000,000 a day in mid-1980. It probably strengthened among Soviets the old, deep fear of the yellow peril in the east; a fear that had no basis in military fact. The leaders of the Soviet Union could and did exploit the American move toward China as yet another sign of imperialist encirclement and called for redoubled efforts by the defence industry and the armed forces.

Despite all these factors, it is most probable that the move complicated Soviet planning. The Kremlin could not ignore the possibility that the United States might decide to provide considerable economic and military aid to China, the effect of which could only be to increase China's power, relatively to that of the Soviet Union.

Inevitably, there was an ambiguity about Washington's relations with Peking, after the long years of recognition of Taiwan as the 'Republic of China'. President Carter's decision to recognise the PRC and the termination of the Mutual Defence Treaty with Taiwan, from 1 January 1979, were much criticised in Congress, especially among Republicans.

During his election campaign, Ronald Reagan was sharply critical of these measures. As a result, relations with the PRC were severely strained during the first few months of President Reagan's Administration. In June 1981, however, the President sent his new Secretary of State, Alexander Haig, to Peking, where he declared that the US was ready, in principle, to supply arms to China. The

Chinese communists, however, turned down the offer, unless the Americans stopped supplying Taiwan with weapons. This, the Americans were not prepared to do.

Meanwhile, Soviet–Chinese talks continued on a desultory basis. If, as has been reported, the Soviets feared that the United States might turn the PRC into a true superpower, the prospect seemed unlikely in mid-1983. Although it was to America's interest to modernise China's ageing military equipment, it seemed out of the question that even the US could spare the vast resources that would be needed to bring the People's Republic to superpower standards, either economically or militarily, even assuming the will to do so, which was conspicuously lacking.

In any case, the ultimate answer to the questions raised by the cold war does not lie in the new Peking–Washington link. It lies with the people of the United States. That answer need not be nuclear war; in fact, nuclear war appears the least likely contingency. The real answer is whether the American people have the will to continue to fight the long duel with the Soviet Union. 'To fight' does not mean to hurl rockets across the world. It is most likely to mean full support of the national effort in proxy wars across the world.

Until now, the United States, in Angola, Eritrea and Afghanistan, has refused to become directly involved. But should Soviet expansionism touch the sources of American economic life, the oil of the Persian Gulf, the metals of southern Africa, the choice will be between involvement and the abdication of global power. If the first is chosen, Americans and their allies will be pitted against the Soviets and their allies in the Middle East, southern Africa, the Caribbean and North-east Asia. The wars are unlikely to reach the intensity or duration of the Vietnam war. In some areas there will be no more than long drawn-out skirmishes in which politicians, not the general staffs, will call the tune.

To prepare for these and other contingencies the Congress in 1980 passed a record budget. Billions upon billions of dollars were to be lavished on nuclear and conventional services. Allies in Europe and Asia took heart, although their encouragement was adulterated by deeply seated doubts about the abilities of President Carter to lead a united and strengthened America, and their ignorance of the real policies which Ronald Reagan, his successor, might follow.

Thus the 1980s dawned in uncertainty, an uncertainty made all the worse by a realisation by the Americans and their allies that the balance of power had shifted slowly to the Soviet Union and the Warsaw Pact. The significant victories of the cold war were in the past, an increasingly distant past. The breaking of the Berlin blockade, the successful defiance of Khrushchev over Berlin, the triumph over the Cuban missile crisis, all of these had proved, if they had proved anything, that progress in the cold war depended on, at the very least, equality in military power. That had disappeared. Now, belatedly, the United States was seeking to regain that edge. The primary question was—and is—time. Would there be time to build the long-range transport aircraft that will ensure that an American intervention force can be flown to some isolated oasis? Would there be time to construct the ships to carry the Marine Corps' arms and equipment to distant seas? Would there be time to develop the new fighter aircraft that would more than match the three new Soviet fighter and attack aircraft now under development? Above all, would there be time to awaken the American people to the realities of a war that would be less than the two great world conflagrations of this century but in its impact on America's overseas requirements equally deadly? Only time will tell, and to the worried planners in the Pentagon, the prime question was, would we be given the time?

12   The Quandary Deepens

To look at the continuing cold war from the Soviet standpoint is always a salutory exercise. Not being politically at risk every few years through free elections, the Soviet Union has the enormous advantage of continuity of leadership. The only basis for the 'legitimacy' of its rule is the ideology of Marxism–Leninism. In foreign policy, the ultimate objective has never wavered: to extend Soviet-style communism to all countries of the world without exception. This objective is regarded not only as a right but as a *duty*.

Significantly, this duty was spelt out in the fourth Constitution of the USSR, promulgated in 1977 and immediately dubbed the 'Brezhnev Constitution'. Thus, Article 28 deals with Soviet Foreign policy which' . . . is aimed at ensuring international conditions favourable for building communism in the USSR, safeguarding the state's interests for the Soviet Union, consolidating the positions of socialism world-wide, supporting the struggles of peoples for national liberation'.

As always with communist texts, the full meaning emerges only if the political semantics are grasped. Thus 'socialism' means Soviet-style communism, the official view being that the USSR has achieved 'socialism', with 'communism' still in the unspecified future. The reference to the 'socialist commonwealth' under the Brezhnev Doctrine of 1968 illustrates the Soviet meaning of socialism (see Chapter 9). 'National liberation' means Soviet-backed guerrillas or terrorists. Elsewhere in the 1977 Constitution, 'national liberation' is interpreted as a step towards 'socialism'.

Article 69 imposes on every citizen ' . . . the international duty . . . to help maintain and strengthen world peace'. Again, semantic definition is needed: 'Peace' does not mean the absence of war. It refers to the state that will prevail when Soviet-style communism has been extended all over the world. Or, as Lenin himself put it: *'It is only when we have vanquished and completely destroyed the bourgeoisie throughout the world that wars will become futile'* (*Complete Works*, 3rd edition, Vol. 23, p. 67).

In the light of this philosophy, the Soviet leaders look upon any unilateral Western concessions as cheap victories. They will take whatever is on offer, without feeling the need to make reciprocal concessions on their side. Negotiations being a form of 'struggle' or a continuation of war by other means, the only 'concessions' they will be prepared to make will be one of two kinds. Khrushchev, for instance, was prepared to make the 'concession' of withdrawing Soviet missiles from Cuba in 1962. In other words, having overstepped the mark, the Soviets will sometimes retreat part of the way if faced with determination on the other side. Even then, Khrushchev extracted concessions from President Kennedy, such as the withdrawal of American missiles from Turkey, and the President's undertaking not to make a further attempt to overthrow the Castro regime.

The other kind of 'concession' the Soviets will make will be in the shape of purely formal undertakings, in the Final Act at Helsinki—in other words, making promises which they have no intention of keeping.

In the light of these realities, there is an instructive parallel between the experiences of Jimmy Carter and Neville Chamberlain. The lesson which Chamberlain learned so painfully at Hitler's hands in the 1930s was that appeasement does not pay. So it was with the unilateral concessions of the Carter period.

Not long after his inauguration, President Carter, in a speech at Notre Dame on 22 May 1977, sent an unmistakable signal to Leonid Brezhnev, when he called upon the nation to abandon its 'inordinate fear of communism'. If Brezhnev himself had written Carter's speech, he could not have served Soviet interests better by disarming the American people psychologically. The phrase is worth requoting in context:

Being confident of our own future, we are now free of that inordinate fear of communism which once led us to embrace any dictator who joined us in that fear. I am glad that that is being changed.

We hope to persuade the Soviet Union that one country cannot impose its system of society upon another, either through direct military intervention or through the use of a client-state's military forces, as was the case with Cuban intervention in Angola.

To the Soviet leadership, the second of these paragraphs, in particular, could mean only one thing: that the Soviets could go ahead and project their power, either directly or through their surrogates, anywhere in the world, without fear of a confrontation with the United States—that is, with complete impunity.

It is in this light that some of the events already covered in preceding chapters should be looked at again. Over the years there had been a number of specific signals, affecting one area or another. Thus in the wake of the Watergate scandal, the United States Congress had blocked supplies of ammunition to the South Vietnamese forces after the Americans had withdrawn their own forces under the Paris Agreements of January 1973. This meant that the Soviet Union's Vietnamese protégés could go ahead with the 'final offensive' when they felt ready. The demoralised South Vietnamese defenders collapsed, and the communists overran Saigon on 30 April 1975.

Late that year, the Senate turned down a request from Henry Kissinger, the then Secretary of State, for authority to help the anti-communist guerrillas in the former Portuguese territory of Angola, in Southern Africa. The refusal was enshrined in what became known as the Clark Amendment, after Senator Dick Clark who happened to be Chairman of the Senate's Foreign Relations Sub-Committee on African Affairs. The Clark Amendment specifically prohibited the use of allocated funds, 'for any activities involving Angola other than intelligence gathering'. President Kennedy's guarantee to Castro in 1962 was an important earlier signal to the Soviet leaders. Protected by this 'guarantee', the Soviets could consolidate their hold over the island regime, and in time use the Cuban armed forces as their principal surrogates overseas.

Similarly, with Carter's reassuring blanket endorsement of 'persuasion' (as against force or the threat of it), Brezhnev knew he had the green light for a further wave of expansion. It was not by accident that 1978 was a bonus year for the Soviets, with the airlift of Cuban troops to Africa (reaching a total of 40,000), the initial *coup* in Afghanistan, the similar *coups* in South Yemen and Ethiopia and the fall of the Shah in Iran.

As with territorial and political expansion, so with negotiations. Anxious for agreement in the second round of the Strategic Arms Limitation Talks (SALT II) Carter made unilateral concessions: he suspended production of the enhanced radiation/diminished blast warhead (misleadingly known as the 'neutron bomb'), scrapped plans for the B-1 supersonic bomber, and voluntarily limited the range of the cruise missile, so that it could not reach Soviet territory from West European bases. Far from producing corresponding concessions on the Soviet side, these further signals were interpreted as so many signs of weakness on the American side. The Soviets went ahead with their own supersonic bomber, the Backfire, and used SALT II to build up a margin of superiority over the United States. Carter got his agreement, but the Senate voted to reject the SALT II Treaty.

By then, even Carter had had to shed some of his illusions. When, on Christmas Day 1979, the Soviet armed forces began their invasion of Afghanistan, he publicly confided that he had learned more about the true nature of the Soviet regime that day than in his previous years in office. In January 1980 President Carter imposed an embargo on United States grain deliveries to the Soviet Union, along with an embargo on the sale of phosphates and other fertilisers. Later that year, Carter proclaimed a boycott of the Olympic Games, in which he was supported by the government of Mrs Margaret Thatcher in Britain.

Safe in the knowledge that they were in no danger of a military confrontation with the United States, the Soviets simply pressed on with their invasion and occupation of Afghanistan, against unexpectedly tough local resistance. The grain embargo, although a significant indication of a change of attitude in Washington, was no more than an inconvenience. The Soviets merely placed their orders with alternative suppliers—most notably, Argentina. And the Olympic Games went ahead, despite the boycott.

The lowest point ever in American prestige in the world was reached when a complex operation to rescue some fifty diplomats and staff from the American embassy in Tehran, who had been seized as hostages by Iranian revolutionaries, aborted in April 1980.

In the face of such evidences of American weakness, the Soviets continued to probe for promising openings and to take advantage of any opportunities that presented themselves, during the last two years of the Carter presidency. It may be useful to illustrate their strategy (in effect, the practical application of the provisions of the 1977 Constitution) in Africa, Latin America, Western Europe and the United States.

Africa
A large, though ambiguous, part has been played in Soviet strategy by Colonel Khadaffi of Libya. The ambiguity lies in his own unpredictability and impulsive ambition. When he first seized power in a military *coup* in 1969, he professed to wish to create a purely Islamic regime that would be equally opposed to communism and capitalism. His natural taste for violence, and his hobby of dispensing aid to terrorists all over the (non-communist) world made him, however, an easy target for the Soviet Union. If you help terrorists engaged in 'struggling' against 'imperialism' and 'capitalism'—that is, terrorists who are also receiving Soviet help—you are, *ipso facto*, on the Soviet side in the 'war called peace'. The territories of the Soviet empire being, by definition and totalitarian control, out of bounds to terrorists, the terrorist war is conducted exclusively (or very nearly) in what might be called the Target Area of Soviet expansionism. Understanding this, the Soviets decided to help Khadaffi help the terrorists.

They therefore concluded with Khadaffi, on 23 May 1976, what still stands as the biggest single arms deal in history, undertaken to provide Libya's tiny armed forces of 37,000 men with enormous quantities of military hardware. Although no overall figure was published, the late President Sadat of Egypt's estimate of $12 billion as the total of the deal is probably close to the mark. By then, Khadaffi had discovered that his Islamic ideology was elastic enough to abandon its initial attitude of 'a plague on both your houses'; the attacks on capitalism continued, those on communism had ceased.

The arms deal made Libya a client-State of the USSR, though not in the fullest sense a satellite. The Soviets enormously enhanced Khadaffi's nuisance power, and could help him win his battles, but they could scarcely claim to control him. The most they could do was to encourage him to fulfil his ambitions in ways that were helpful to the Soviet grand design. It became clear early in 1980 that Khadaffi's main ambition was to build a Saharan empire, stretching from the Atlantic ocean to the Red Sea. As he envisaged it, the empire would incorporate the Western Sahara, formerly Spanish, the Saharan areas under Tunisian and Algerian rule, the northern regions of Mali, Niger, Chad and Nigeria; the Sudan; and perhaps southern Egypt.

In March 1980, the Libyan information service published a map showing as Libyan territory some 134,000 km² of Chad, Niger and Algeria and containing large deposits of iron, phosphates and uranium. But this was, as the expression has it, 'just for starters'.

As part of his scheme, Khadaffi supported a heterogeneous band of guerrillas known as the POLISARIO (Peoples' Front for the Liberation of Saguiat el Hamra and Rio de Oro), who tried to wrest control of the ex-Spanish Sahara from Morocco. He also stirred up armed rebels against the moderate President Bourguiba of Tunisia early in 1980. Later that year, and this time with full and explicit Soviet support, Khadaffi decided to make a military bid for the former French colony of Chad. On 28 September 1980 he declared: 'Chad belongs to Libya's vital space.' His timing was immaculate. For years, Chad had been wracked by insurgency. By mid-1980, there were at least four main rival armed groups, including those of the official government, under President Goukouni Oueddei. The French, who, under President Giscard d'Estaing, were normally ready to defend a Francophone government threatened with aggression, were paralysed by this fragmentation of power.

In October, Khadaffi took up residence near the Chad border. There in November, the Soviet ambassador to Libya and several high-ranking officers of the Soviet armed forces came to confer with him and put the finishing touches to the offensive plan. The technique of Soviet strategic and tactical planning, at the disposal of a client—as successfully tried out in Ethiopia in 1978—was being used again.

Reconnaissance flights of Libyan-Soviet TU-22s, piloted by North Korean surrogates, pinned down the forces of the main rebel groups due for elimination (those of the former Defence Minister, Hissène Habré). Then a massive Soviet airlift started. Armoured vehicles, Soviet helicopter gunships and plastic fuel-containers went in, along with Ilyushin-76s, capable of carrying 80-ton loads over a range of 5,000 kilometres. The final arsenal at Khadaffi's disposal included 200 Soviet tanks, automatic machine-guns of French manufacture and Soviet missiles-launchers. Libya's regular army then moved in, rapidly conquering the whole of northern Chad up to the capital, N'Djamena. On 7 January 1981 Khadaffi announced a 'merger' between Libya and Chad. In Moscow, the Soviet leaders would undoubtedly chalk this up as another victory in 'this war called peace'.

As it happened, this particular 'victory' was short-lived. Under intense pressure from France and from various African countries, Colonal Khadaffi withdrew his forces from Chad in November 1981; and in June 1982, Hissène Habré's forces fought their way back into the capital, with Oueddei and his men in flight. The Soviets had been ready to help Khadaffi to invade and occupy Chad, but not to defy the collective opinion of the African states by enabling him to stay there.

In 'Black' Africa (south of the Sahara) the Soviets are more continuously active than in the northern areas of the continent. In Mali, for instance, they quietly built up an impressive military and 'cultural' presence. Some 5,000 Malian students, returning from the USSR in batches over twenty years, filled their country's civil service, while many of Mali's military officers were trained and indoctrinated in the Soviet Union.

Some 200 Soviet military advisers were training Malian officers in the use of Soviet arms and equipment, and a landing strip 3,200 metres long was built at Mopti, with another planned at Gao.

Having achieved the satellisation of the former Portuguese territories of Angola and Mozambique, the Soviets looked to the ultimate prize of South Africa. The Soviet interests in that country go right back to the early days of the Bolshevik Revolution, and the Communist Party of South Africa was set up by Lenin's Comintern as long ago as 1921. The main dissident political organisation of black South Africans, the African National Congress or ANC, now banned, has long been under complete communist control and is therefore an instrument of Soviet policy in the special circumstances of South Africa. (In the words of the Chairman of the Party, Dr. Yusef Dadoo, the party 'has become completely integrated with the ANC').

This fact gave special interest to the claim, on 2 June 1980, by the London office of the ANC that it was responsible for a daring act of sabotage of South African Sasol (oil from coal) installations that had been in the headlines. This show of force did not mean that the ANC, even with Soviet help, was capable of mounting a long-term and sustained terrorist campaign that might destabilise the South African system. South Africa's black population, deprived of voting rights under the apartheid policy, and subject to many forms of petty harassment or discrimination, have genuine political grievances. However, the country's security system was highly organised, and apparently well able to keep violence under control. The time for full-scale use of the ANC would come much later, with the regime isolated and demoralised. As always, the Soviets used violence as only one, and not necessarily the most important, of many techniques in the armoury of subversion. In the case of South Africa, the Soviet strategy has been to gain control of neighbouring countries that could be used as bases for operations against that country; to mobilise African and world opinion against South Africa, while making it politically or psychologically impossible for Western countries to support the Afrikaaner regime, or even in the long term to trade with South Africa.

Although final success (if it ever comes) was a long way off as these lines were written, Soviet policy has had some impressive successes. It is, of course, relatively easy to mobilise independent black African States against a white-controlled regime which discriminates against its black population. By automatically siding with the Third World countries in the United Nations, the Soviet bloc acquires merit on the cheap. One of the more concrete successes of this policy was the decision of the UN General Assembly to recognise the Namibian terrorist organisation, SWAPO, as the sole representative of the people of Namibia, thus overriding in advance the outcome of possible general elections in that territory.

SWAPO stands for South-West African People's Organisation. It is a terrorist organisation which, under its leader Sam Nujoma, turned to violence in 1966 when the International Court of Justice in the Hague rejected a charge that South Africa was abusing the mandate (initially granted by the defunct League of Nations) under which it administers this former colony of the Kaiser's Germany. Marxist–Leninist in ideology, it gets most of its arms, money and training from two of the Soviet Union's surrogates, Cuba and East Germany, using Angola as a base.

With UN backing and its own ethnic roots in the majority Ovambo tribes which straddle the border with Angola, it stood a pretty good chance of succeeding the South Africans as the ruling force in Namibia—if allowed to do so. If this happened, the Soviets would gain yet another Marxist–Leninist satellite in Africa, control over some important mineral resources, a base with which to mount operations against South Africa, and—not least—a hinterland to South Africa's sovereign port of Walvis Bay—a superb harbour which, if it fell into Soviet hands, would give Admiral Gorshkov, the

Soviet Naval Commander-in-Chief, a key point from which to dominate the sea lanes of the South Atlantic (the changed outlook for Southern Africa after the advent of the Reagan Administration in the United States is considered in later passages in this chapter).

South Africa's other neighbour, Zimbabwe, to the north-east, is a still more important strategic objective for the USSR. For years, the Soviets armed, financed and trained the terrorist/guerrilla force of Joshua Nkomo's Zimbabwe African People's Union (ZAPU), on the assumption that Nkomo was bound to come out on top in the long drawn-out struggle of the blacks against White Rhodesia. This assumption was mistaken. Unexpectedly—to the departing British as well as to the Russians—the leader of the rival ZANU (Zimbabwe African National Union), Robert Mugabe, swept into power in the elections that followed the Constitutional settlement in December 1979 negotiated at Lancaster House in London.

Although Mugabe was a self-professed Marxist–Leninist, he had turned to China, not Russia, for help during the fighting phase, and initially showed little desire even to open diplomatic relations with Moscow (although he later relented). As always, however, the Soviets looked to the longer term. In the event, they did not have long to wait. Mugabe himself signalled a change of course in mid-October 1981, when he declared that Zimbabwe was ready for a maximum development of its relations with the USSR. 'As a Socialist country, Zimbabwe regards the USSR as an ideological ally,' he said. Some months earlier, he had imported 150 North Korean instructors to train an elite brigade. At about this time, the Soviets transferred their operational centre for intelligence, political action, subversion and the provision of arms for Southern Africa, from Lusaka, the Zambian capital, to Harare (as Salisbury, the capital of Rhodesia, was now known).

The only counter-force of any importance in the area was the well-trained and well-equipped military machine of the Republic of South Africa, which from time to time staged armed incursions across the borders of Angola, Zimbabwe or Mozambique. The most spectacular of these raids was against Angola in October 1981. Some 4,500 South African troops, with heavy air support, drove deep into Southern Angola. They killed hundreds of SWAPO 'guerrillas' who had been raiding Namibia from Angolan bases. More significantly, they seized more than 3,000 tons of Soviet equipment, killed four Soviet military personnel and captured a fifth.

In addition to such demonstrations of strength, the South Africans discreetly provide material aid and advice to anti-communist guerrilla groups in Angola, Zimbabwe and Mozambique.

Central America

There was a passing reference to the fall of the Somoza regime in Nicaragua in Chapter 9. We now look at this situation in greater detail.

On 19 July 1979 armed units of the so-called 'Sandinista revolutionary movement' entered Managua, capital of the Central American republic of Nicaragua. Earlier, the local strong-man, President Anastasio Somoza, who had inherited his dictatorship from his father, had fled the country. Later, Sandinista agents were to murder him in Paraguay, where he had taken refuge.

Who were the Sandinistas and why did they drive Somoza into exile before having him assassinated? Certainly they had no reason to love him. The organisation was named after General Augusto C. Sandino, who had opposed the United States' occupation of Nicaragua in the late 1920s and early 1930s, and had been assassinated on the orders of Somoza's father.

More relevantly, the full name of the organisation was Frente Sandinista de Liberación Nacional. Although professing to be a broad democratic front grouping various tendencies, the Frente Sandinista was firmly in the grip of Marxist–Leninists and under the ultimate control of the Cubans (and therefore of the Soviets, who had 'satellised' Fidel Castro's regime by the late 1960s (see Chapter 9).

As is customary, however, the Sandinistas were presented through the media (especially in those well-known organs of East Coast liberalism, the *New York Times* and the *Washington Post*) throughout their bloody struggle for Nicaragua as just a rather nice bunch of liberals fighting for justice and to rescue their country from a cruel dictatorship.

This skilful exercise in image-building was unfortunately helped by the fact that Somoza did indeed run a rather nasty dictatorship; but the Sandinistas lost little time, once in power, in demonstrating that their respect for democracy was merely a wartime expedient designed to whip up public support for their cause, especially in the United States.

Even before the Sandinista victory, the United States was in possession of detailed evidence (which President Carter kept unpublished) that the final offensive of the Sandinistas had been planned in minute detail by the Cuban general staff. In overall charge was the Cuban General Zenen Casals, whose previous battle experience had included a spell in Cuba's semi-colony, Angola. Moreover, the arms used by the Sandinistas were shipped by Fidel Castro's regime. In the London *Daily Telegraph* of 6 August 1970, the well-known columnist Robert Moss quoted from a CIA report dated 2 May and classified 'Secret : No Foreign Dissemination', which had come into his possession and which described Cuban plans to use Nicaragua as the model for similar revolutionary uprisings in Guatemala, El Salvador and other countries of the area.

Not surprisingly, Nicaragua's new government early in 1980 secretly sent a delegation to Moscow, where close party-to-party links were formally established between the Frente Sandinista and the Communist Party of the Soviet Union.

Appropriately, the Frente Sandinista was invited to send its own delegates to the 26th Congress of the CPSU in February–March 1981; needless to say, no Nicaraguan party outside the Frente Sandinista was represented. By mid-1981, indeed, the Sandinistas had almost completed their totalitarian grip on Nicaragua. All nine members of the National Directorate were Marxist–Leninists trained in Cuba, and Nicaragua was fulfilling its preordained role as a base for training and assistance to revolutionaries in Guatemala and El Salvador.

With the enormous propaganda apparatus of the Soviet Union at its disposal, the international Left has an insatiable appetite for Causes with which to stimulate indignation and produce resolutions in all countries not already under dictatorships of the Left (and a few of the Right). In its day, the Spanish Civil War was the great Cause. In the 1960s, it was Vietnam. When Allende was overthrown, it was Chile. When the military government started hitting the left-wing terrorists hard, it was Argentina. Iran was a long-running Cause under the Shah.

But even such bubbling causes can run out of steam. The Vietnam war ceased to be a Cause when the communists won their victory. Chile was less interesting when the initial excesses of the Pinochet regime were toned down. Argentina was a hardy perennial, but the Left was not much interested in the excesses of the mullahs in Iran once the much milder regime of the Shah had collapsed.

Then came El Salvador. Having located it on the map, the propagandists found with glee that it had all the right ingredients: a traditional economy of absentee landlords and oppressed peasants, a ruthless military junta, right-wing death squads, left-wing terrorists/guerrillas who could be represented as spearheading a popular uprising; and, in the background, Uncle Sam with Teddy Roosevelt's big stick and the disguised colonialism of the United Fruit Company. In the United States, Britain, France, Germany and the rest, committees sprang up like magic to support the people of El Salvador.

During the last phase of the Carter presidency, in particular, the anti-American line of the propaganda was really rather unfair. The American Administration, in fact, was bending over backwards to avoid supporting the junta and to be seen to be supporting the aspirations of the 'people of Salvador'. The United States Ambassador to San Salvador, Robert E. White, was one of the principal liberals in the State Department (he did not last long when the Reagan Administration came in).

The Carter team's concern with the social injustices of El Salvador (and Guatemala) was doubtless sincere and perhaps commendable—as it had been when the people of Nicaragua were thought to be groaning under the yoke of the Somoza dictatorship. Nicaragua had already shown, however, as Cuba and so many other places had shown before, that the way to cure social injustices and institute respect for human rights does not lie in handing a country over to Marxist totalitarians. The real problem, in terms of 'this war called peace', was that the social conditions in El Salvador, Guatemala and elsewhere were merely the pretext for Soviet intervention by proxy.

After all, from the Soviet standpoint, the exploitation of such causes and the provision of aid to communist guerrillas of one kind or another merely amounted to a strict observance of the provisions of the 1977 Constitution.

The Advent of Reagan

Elected by the American people on the crest of the wave of revulsion against the Washington establishment, and on the promise of honest government, President Carter was the victim of a change in the national mood which his own policies did much to accelerate. The mood that had brought him to power was one of disgust, self-doubt and self-criticism. the mood that unseated him was one of patriotic revival and the renewal of the pioneering spirit that had made America great.

The hopes of 'Middle America', of the 'silent majority', of the great mass of ordinary Americans who wanted their country to remain Number One and could see for themselves that in terms of power it had been relegated to second place by the USSR—of all those who longed for the restoration of initiative and private enterprise—were centred on the former Governor of California, Ronald Reagan.

They had their way, by a landslide, in the presidential election of November 1980. The new incumbent, who was seventy when he took office in January 1981, had attracted to his entourage on the way to the White House a brilliant team of advisers, many of whom, though not all, were subsequently nominated to responsible office. (In time, however, his inability to fill all key posts with trusted 'Reaganites' would prove a source of weakness in dealing with the manifold aspects of the Soviet threat.)

Although not a specialist on foreign affairs, President Reagan had learned the hard way, during his Hollywood years as President of the Screen Actors' Guild, the true character of communism and of communist subversion. He came to power well briefed on the nature of the Soviet threat in all its aspects and convinced of the absolute necessity for rebuilding America's strength, by which he specifically meant the CIA as well as the Pentagon and all its weaponry.

For the Soviet leadership, President Reagan presented an almost unprecedented problem. Unlike all his predecessors from Franklin Delano Roosevelt on, he seemed quite impervious to the attractions of East–West summitry, though willing enough to meet with Allied heads of state or government. He was in no particular hurry to renew arms negotiations with the Soviets, and (although much derided in the Western press as a 'cowboy' and 'trigger-happy') was soon to show himself capable of taking tough decisions and sticking to them, even if the pace of his Administration seemed at times infuriatingly slow.

Unable to influence him by direct contact, as his predecessors had been, the Soviets concentrated their vast resources of propaganda and disinformation to smear him as a 'warmonger'. to aggravate tensions within the Western Alliance and to undermine the basis of popular support upon which any President of the United States must necessarily rely for the pursuance of his policies.

The aspects of foreign affairs that most concern us in that context are: arms control and the 'peace' campaigns; the Siberian gas pipeline project and transfers of technology to the Soviet bloc; in general the state of the Alliance; Central America; Southern Africa; and the Middle East, with special reference to 'Palestine' and the Arab–Israeli dispute. Each calls for concise analysis.

Arms and 'Peace'

In 1977, during the Carter Presidency, the Soviet Union started deploying a new line in medium-range ballistic missiles, known as the SS-20s. Western strategists, alerted by satellite intelligence, were quick to grasp the fact that these weapons constituted a new kind of threat. Highly accurate, with a sophisticated guidance system, they are capable of hitting targets up to 3,100 miles away. Each SS-20 is equipped with three, separately targetable nuclear warheads. Highly mobile as well, they are far less vulnerable to counter-attack than the older S-4 and S-5 missiles.

Deployed in western Russia, the SS-20s were thus capable, in one devastating blow, of annihilating all NATO's military installations. Theoretically, they were capable of delivering warheads of up to 150 kilotons in yield. However, as the distinguished French strategist, Air Force General Pierre-Marie Gallois, and others, pointed out, they could achieve the same objective of destroying NATO's military potential if equipped with small warheads with a yield of no more than 3 kilotons, without massive nuclear fall-out, and indeed virtually without damaging the environment.

Ironically (as we shall see), it was Chancellor Helmut Schmidt of the German Federal Republic who first drew the attention of President Carter and the European Allies to the danger of the SS-20s. The response came at the end of 1979. Specifically, on 12 December 1979 the Foreign and Defence Ministers of NATO met in Brussels and passed a crucially important Resolution, which has become known as NATO's 'two-track decision'. Why 'two-track'? Because the Allies agreed (a) to start deploying the new generation of American medium-range nuclear weapons before the end of 1983, but only if (b) by that time there had been no substantial progress in arms control talks between the United States and the USSR.

The Soviets must have had advance information about the

outcome of the NATO meeting, for even before it took place they had launched yet another of their periodical 'peace' campaigns, with communist-sponsored demonstrations in Holland and Belgium.

An earlier campaign, specifically against the so-called 'neutron bomb', well organised in several countries, had been markedly successful, and had culminated in an announcement by President Carter on 7 April 1978 that production of this weapon would be indefinitely deferred. (The term 'neutron bomb', widely disseminated by the Soviet propaganda apparatus, was deliberately misleading. Not a bomb but a warheard, the weapon had the single purpose of stopping an enemy tank offensive, literally in its tracks, by killing the tank crews, but without civilian casualties or destruction of buildings or the environment. The neutron warhead was thus a purely defensive and in the nuclear age, a remarkably humane, weapon which would damage only the aggressors. Nevertheless, Soviet propaganda has presented it as a particularly 'foul', 'capitalist' weapon, designed to kill people and preserve property—a grotesque distortion of the truth.)

Shortly after he came to power, President Reagan lifted his predecessor's embargo on production of the nuclear warhead. Once again, the Soviet leaders noted that they were now up against a leader who could see through their manoeuvres. Their response was to step up their propaganda campaign. A new world-wide campaign against the 'neutron bomb' was launched simultaneously on 5 February 1981 with an article in the Soviet daily *Pravda* and an announcement from Romesh Chandra, the Indian communist who is President of the Soviet-controlled World Peace Council (WPC).

The campaign against the 'neutron bomb', however, soon yielded to a more massive and sustained campaign against the deployment of the new American weapons—Pershing II and the cruise missiles—in certain West European countries. Specifically, 464 cruise missiles and 108 Pershing II ballistic missiles were to be shared out between Britain, West Germany, Holland, Belgium and Italy. Naturally these were the countries that bore the brunt of the Soviet-backed campaign. Throughout 1981 and 1982, anti-nuclear, unilateral disarmament groups stepped up the demonstrations, the pamphlets and the posters calling on the respective governments to refuse to deploy the new weapons and to set the example by renouncing nuclear weapons.

In all these countries, communist activists played a leading role in the campaign, although (in accordance with Lenin's precepts) the great majority of participants consisted of essentially non-political people motivated simply by an understandable horror of nuclear war. In each country, however, the local branch of the Soviet-controlled WPC was mobilised to spearhead the attack.

The maximum impact was made in Holland, West Germany and Britain. A special focus of attention were the American military bases in Britain and Germany. In both countries, the main left-wing parties (the Labour Party in Britain and the Social Democratic party or SPD in Germany) were much affected by the campaign. In Britain, the Labour Party committed itself officially to one-sided nuclear disarmament and to the closing down of the American bases, while professing a desire for Britain to stay within NATO. In the Federal Republic, the situation was more complex. Pacifist sentiment was strong in a country which had suffered defeat in two world wars, which had emerged from the trauma of Hitler and Nazi rule, and which was divided into two areas, communist in the East and democratic in the West.

Paradoxically, although it was the Social Democratic Chancellor, Helmut Schmidt, who had initially called for a response to the Soviet SS-20s, it was his party that was most rapidly affected by pacifist and neutralist ideas. The situation, however, changed with the departure of the SPD's coalition partners (the Liberals or FDP) in the autumn of 1982, and the victory of the Christian Democrats under Chancellor Helmut Kohl in the general election of 6 March 1983.

In Britain, the Labour Party was overwhelmingly defeated in the election of 9 June 1983, and with it the unilateralist cause represented principally by the Campaign for Nuclear Disarmament (CND) which had identified itself with that party.

The Conservative Party, under the Prime Minister, Mrs Margaret Thatcher, was returned to power with a greatly increased majority and was unambiguously committed to maintaining the British deterrent and deploying the new American missiles.

In the United States, a parallel but not identical 'peace' campaign was launched in the second half of 1981, considerably later than in Western Europe. Having won, then lost, the campaign against the neutron warhead, the Soviets had no further incentive to concentrate upon this weapon, intended for use, eventually, in Western Europe against a possible Soviet tank offensive. Nor did it make sense to emphasise the new American medium-range missiles which were the main issue in Europe, where the thrust of the campaign was to make it psychologically and politically impossible for Allied governments to go ahead with their deployment.

In the United States, in contrast, the key word was 'freeze', the objective being to frustrate the Reagan Administration's plan to close the 'window of vulnerability' which, as the President had said, had opened up during the Carter presidency. Within months, the United States Congress was flooded with letters and appeals to the Administration to commit itself to a freeze on all nuclear weapons testing, development and production. A number of public figures identified themselves with the freeze, including Senator Edward M.Kennedy, brother of the late president, Averell Harriman, former ambassador to Moscow and negotiator of the Test Ban Treaty of 1963, and Paul Warnke, President Carter's Director of the Arms Control and Disarmament Agency. The most specific target of the co-ordinating organisation, the National Clearing House for the Nuclear Freeze Campaign, was the proposed MX missile system, designed to close the 'window of vulnerability' because of its capacity to destroy 'hardened' Soviet nuclear sites and thus prevent a Soviet second strike in the event of a nuclear exchange.

In his book, *KGB Today* (from which we have already quoted in Chapter 10), John Barron gives specific details of Soviet involvement in the American freeze movement and in similar movements in European countries. In the United States, the main Soviet specialists involved were Oleg Bogdanov, an International Department expert on what the Soviets call 'Special Measures'; and Yuri Kapralov of the KGB.

It should be remembered, of course, that the 'peace' movement, whether in the United States or in Europe, was necessarily one-sided. In the Soviet Union itself, only anti-American and anti-Western 'peace' propaganda is allowed and the only permitted groups are those sponsored by the authorities. No campaign in favour of reciprocal disarmament measures is tolerated. A small group of dissidents attempted an appeal for multilateral disarmament in June 1982, but was immediately harassed by the KGB.

While the 'peace' movement was gathering speed in the affected countries, United States–Soviet negotiations were in progress in Geneva, where they began on 30 November 1981, about a year after the presidential election that put Ronald Reagan in the White House. Progress, if any, was indeed agonisingly slow. The main point at issue was the deployment of the Soviet SS-20s. The American side argued that the advent of these weapons had tilted the previous more or less even balance of 'theatre' nuclear weapons (as distinct from the 'strategic' intercontinental ones) in favour of the USSR. The Soviets countered with the view that the SS-20s merely restored the balance, and supported their argument by counting the British and French nuclear weapons along with those deployed by NATO.

The American starting-point was the so-called 'zero option', meaning that the United States and its allies would scrap plans to deploy Pershing II and the cruise missiles if the Soviets dismantled the existing SS-20s already deployed (which by May 1983 had reached 350). The Soviets, however, rejected this proposal out of hand, and on 30 March 1983 President Reagan modified his original plan by offering to deploy only a limited number of the new missiles in Europe, if the Soviets would reduce the number of SS-20s on deployment to the same figure.

This, too, the Soviets rejected. All they were prepared to do was to reduce the number of SS-20s deployed if the Western side agreed not to deploy any of the new missiles. This was, of course, unacceptable to the Americans, who pointed out that *any* significant number of SS-20s would still leave the Soviets with a dangerous advantage, unless a corresponding number of the new American missiles were also deployed. A further point was that even if the full complement of American missiles were deployed—572 in all—and the Soviets completed their programme of 500 SS-20s, the Soviet side would still have a decided advantage, since the American weapons have only one warhead each, whereas each SS-20 carries three.

There seemed no easy way out of this contradictory position, and in the early months of 1983 the Soviets resorted increasingly to threats of 'automatic nuclear response' if the new American weapons were deployed in Europe.

We now turn to the impact of the Reagan Administration in specific regions.

Africa

Under President Carter the United States maintained a front of cold hostility towards the South African government, declined to receive leaders of anti-communist groups in southern Africa, such as Jonas Savimbi of Angola, and pressed hard for the independence of

Namibia (South-west Africa) from South African control. The United States was a member of the Group of Five entrusted by the United Nations to try to persuade the South Africans to accelerate the pace of independence through general elections under UN supervision; the others were Britain, France, West Germany and Canada.

It was soon clear that the Reagan Administration, unlike its predecessor, was ready to consult the South African authorities and take due note of Pretoria's security requirements in respect of Namibia. The assistant Secretary of State for African Affairs, Chester Crocker, although criticised by the Reaganites as an alleged 'liberal', was charged with sounding out the South Africans on these lines, while in Washington, Secretary of State Alexander Haig held secret talks with the South African Prime Minister, P.W.Botha.

Encouraged by this more understanding American attitude, the South African government ruled out any further negotiations on the independence of Namibia, unless three prior conditions were met:

(1)   The departure of the Cuban forces, estimated at around 20,000, from Angola.

(2)   Firm guarantees for the security of the white minority in Namibia.

(3)   Restoration of peace and order in Namibia (implying the defeat of the SWAPO terrorists).

The UN endorsement of SWAPO as sole representatives of the Namibian people was, of course, totally unacceptable in Pretoria. By and large, these conditions were acceptable to Washington.

The American attitude thus represented a new and disturbing element in Soviet calculations. With Carter in power, they could count on mounting American pressure on South Africa to confer independence on Namibia, in other words, to hand over the territory to Moscow's nominees. Now they no longer enjoyed this advantage.

In one important sense, however, the Russians retained the initiative. Despite much optimistic talk about the agreement 'in principle' from the Angolan government that there should be a withdrawal of Cuban troops, as part of a package involving the independence of Namibia, the determining fact was that there was no reason to believe that the Soviet Union would agree to allow the Cubans to go.

It was the Soviets who had put them there in the first place and, ultimately, the decision was in their hands.

The situation could, however, change if the Marxist government in Luanda, the Angolan capital, broke with Moscow and expelled the Cubans (just as, in other circumstances, the Egyptian and Somalian governments had expelled Soviet personnel). The question was unresolved when these lines were written. Early in 1983, however, the hard core of pro-Moscow people in the ruling People's Movement for the Liberation of Angola (MPLA) were being removed in a party purge. The possibility of a break with Moscow could therefore not be entirely discounted.

Latin America

It was not until February 1981, some weeks after Ronald Reagan's inauguration as President of the United States, that the United States Administration decided to release the evidence about Soviet bloc involvement in El Salvador which President Carter had wanted to keep quiet about. On 16 February the new Secretary of State, Alexander Haig, sent one of his top professional assistants, Lawrence Eagleburger, on a round of European capitals, with a boxful of evidence.

The most striking item was a captured document reporting on a visit by a Salvadoran leader (thought to be the secretary-general of El Salvador's Communist Party, Shafik Handal) to North Vietnam in June 1980. The Vietnamese leaders had agreed to supply 60 tons of arms and ammunition—mainly weapons abandoned by the departing Americans and their South Vietnamese allies. Among the items were 1,620 M-16 automatic rifles, 198 machine-guns, 48 mortars, 12 anti-tank rocket-launchers, 1.5 million rounds of ammunition and 11,000 mortar rounds. On a visit to Ethiopia, the local Marxist dictator, Colonel Mengistu, had pledged 150 submachine-guns, 1,500 M-1 rifles and more than 600,000 rounds of ammunition.

Wherever Handal (if he was the man) went, he met the top people and came away laden with gifts or promises. In East Berlin, for instance, the party boss, Erich Honecker, personally promised $1 million worth of aid. Other visits, to Bulgaria, Czechoslovakia and Hungary were proportionately productive. The Mecca of the communist world, Moscow, was likewise on the itinerary. There,

Handal (or whoever it was) saw Ponomarev's deputy on the International Department, Karen Brutents, and the man in charge of Soviet relations with Latin America, Mikhail Kudachin. By then, the Salvadoran war-chest was full, and the remaining problem was transport; which the Soviets solved, using the Cuba–Nicaragua route.

These details and others were incorporated into a State Department White Paper. Nevertheless, a full year was to elapse before the Reagan Administration followed up with action, in the shape of a group of military advisers to help the beleaguered Salvadoran government against the communist guerrillas. In March 1982 the people of El Salvador defied threats and actual violence from the terrorists to vote in general elections that were boycotted by left-wing parties. The military threat to El Salvador continued to grow, despite this undeniable success for the democratic process.

President Reagan and some of his closest advisers, including the National Security Adviser, Judge William Clark, were determined to prevent a communist take-over in El Salvador. Any further such defeat in America's 'backyard' would lead to a widespread loss of credibility for the United States as an ally. It was an open secret that the CIA, under William Casey, was involved in a substantial piece of 'covert action' by helping to arm and train Nicaraguan dissidents operating from neighbouring Honduras.

This firmness in the face of communist aggression nevertheless ran into determined opposition both in the media and in the Congress. Directly in line with propaganda from Havana and other communist capitals, a number of well-known journalists and television commentators played their part in working up public opinion in the United States against President Reagan's policy in Central America on the ground that America was 'heading for another Vietnam' in El Salvador. Early in December 1982, Representative Edward P.Boland sponsored an amendment prohibiting the CIA or the Defense Department from using public funds 'for the purpose of overthrowing the government of Nicaragua or provoking a military exchange between Nicaragua and Honduras'. Astonishingly, the amendment was adopted by 411 votes to 0.

The Boland Amendment thus took its place alongside the Clark Amendment of 1976 (mentioned earlier) prohibiting American assistance to the anti-Marxist guerrillas in Angola. The wording of the Amendment allowed the Administration some latitude, but was a reminder of the power of the House of Representatives, in which the opposition Democrats held a majority, to frustrate the policy of a president elected by a landslide majority.

The Falklands War of 1982 does not directly concern us here, but it is worth mentioning one point. When it broke out, with the Argentine invasion on 2 April, the Americans had persuaded the Argentine government to send a fighting force to El Salvador to help the government in its fight against the communists. The war itself, and the decision of the United States to side with Britain in the dispute after the failure of the mediation attempt by Secretary of State Haig, killed this project.

The Middle East

Soviet attempts to use Arab countries and movements for their own purposes have never been consistently successful, as the expulsion of the Soviet advisers from Egypt in 1971 demonstrated. Whether because of the advancing age and incapacity of the Soviet leader, Leonid Brezhnev, or for other reasons, the Soviet Union played a singularly passive role in the protracted crisis which began with Israel's invasion of Lebanon in June 1982.

The explicit object of the Israeli invasion was to eliminate the military presence of the PLO in Lebanon. As mentioned in an earlier chapter, the Soviets adopted the cause of the Palestinian organisation in 1974, and might therefore have been expected to help the PLO in their hour of need. Beyond verbal denunciations of the Israelis, however, there is no evidence that the Soviets provided any such help: a fact which undoubtedly caused them to lose face in Arab eyes.

There was a further reason for Soviet involvement in the fact of the close relations between the USSR and the Baathist regime in Syria. On 8 October 1980 the two countries had signed a Treaty of Friendship and Co-operation, one of a number of similar treaties, the prototype for which was the treaty with Egypt in 1971. The Soviet–Syrian Treaty, however, went further than the rest—and even further than the Soviet–Iraqi Treaty of 1972—in that it amounted virtually to a military alliance between the two countries. Both before and after the signature of the treaty, the Soviet Union supplied Syria with huge quantities of modern weapons. At the time of the Lebanon crisis, there were at least 5,000 Soviet personnel in Syria.

Although the Israelis, during the crisis, bombed Syrian forces in occupation of the Bekaa Valley in northern Lebanon, there was again no sign of activity on the part of the Soviets. It was not until the early weeks of 1983, some months after Brezhnev had died and been succeeded by Yuri Andropov, that the Soviets intervened on Syria's behalf. As a result of the patient shuttle diplomacy of the President Reagan's special envoy, Philip Habib, and of the new United States Secretary of State, George Shultz, the Israelis had conditionally agreed to evacuate their forces from southern Lebanon. The condition was that the Syrians should do likewise in the north.

At that point, in January, the Soviets delivered an advanced version of their SA-5 ground-to-air missiles to Syria. As soon as the Syrians knew they were to receive the SA-5, their negotiations with the Israelis took on a different, and harder, tone. The effect of this belated Soviet move was thus to prolong the foreign occupation of Lebanon and delay any serious attempt to bring back stability to the area.

Empire in Crisis

In the view of a number of experienced observers, the Soviet system and empire entered a profound crisis in the late 1970s. For the first time since the failure of the Archangel expedition in 1919 it became possible, in all seriousness, to envisage their collapse.

The paradox of the crisis was that it coincided with the apex of the Soviet Union's military power. Its nature could be summarised as follows:

Failure of the economic system.
Heavy foreign indebtedness.
Endemic corruption at all levels.
General popular rejection of the official ideology.
Dramatic increase in mortality, both infantile and adult.
Heavy increase in fatal heart diseases.
Soaring alcoholism.
Declining standard of medical care.
Increasing unrest in the East European 'provinces' of the empire, especially Poland.

All recent high-level Soviet defectors, such as Vladimir Kusichkin in Britain and Stanislav Levchenko in America, have testified along those lines. So, too, have non-political dissidents, including, of course, the great writer Aleksandr Solzhenitsyn and the less well known but patently honest Aleksandr Zinoviev, in his remarkably objective books, *Homo Sovieticus* and *Communism as Reality*. (These essential works have been published in Russian and French; English translations have been prepared and were due for publication in 1983 or 1984.)

Detailed analyses have been made by American scholars, on the basis of official Soviet statistics and other data, by American scholars in both the private and the public sectors. These include Murray Feshbach of the Center for Population Research at Georgetown University, Washington, DC; Christopher Davis, a demographer; Dr William A.Knaus of the George Washington University Medical Center; and George Baldwin of the Foreign Demographic Analysis branch of the United States Census Bureau. (For ease of reference, all are quoted in John Barron's *KGB Today*.) The following significant facts or trends emerge.

Mortality. The mortality rate in the Soviet Union increased from 6.9 to 10.3 deaths per 1,000 people annually, between 1964 and 1980, mainly because of 'sharp increases in death rates for infants and males aged 22–40' (Feshbach). Between 1971 and 1979, infant mortality rose sharply from 22.0 deaths to 35/36 deaths per 1,000 births (Feshbach and Davis). These trends are the reverse of those in advanced Western countries. In the United States, for instance, the infant mortality rate fell from 12.9 in 1979 to 11.7 in 1981.

Medical care. In a speech on 23 February 1981 Brezhnev himself admitted deficiencies in medical care. Medical equipment is often obsolescent and in short supply, especially in rural areas. Paid 'black market' surgical operations are common (Feshbach).

Heart disease. Soviet deaths from all cardiovascular diseases increased from 247 deaths for every 100,000 citizens in 1960 to more than 500 in 1978—the reverse of American trends (Klaus).

Alcoholism. Drunkenness has long been rife in the Soviet Union. What is significant is the current trend upward. Alcoholism is a major cause of increased adult mortality, and is spreading among women and young people. According to Feshbach, the average Soviet family now spends nearly as high a proportion of its income on alcohol as the average American family does on ordinary foodstuffs.

The economy. The Liberman experiment, described in Chapter 10, was not conducted on a sufficient scale to solve the crisis of unsold

stockpiles of unwanted goods. Nor could it. The rigid and bureaucratic system of centralised planning worked, up to a point, for heavy
industry (such as coal and steel) and electrification. It is hopelessly
inefficient for the consumer market. As always, agriculture remains
the black spot. The Soviet system, after nearly seventy-five years of
communist rule, cannot feed its citizens.

Corruption. Some forms of corruption, especially the black market
in spare parts and raw materials, are essential to the system, in that
factories cannot fulfil their quotas without it (even though 'economic
crimes' carry the death penalty as a maximum deterrent). But corruption is now prevalent at all levels, including the militia and the
police.

The Soviet Union is not, of course, alone in any or all of the social
ills mentioned above. What makes the Soviet case significant is the
fact that for many years (see Chapter 10), the Soviet leaders boasted
that the USSR would catch up with and overtake advanced
'capitalist' countries, while Lenin used to boast that his revolution
would create a new type of man, *Homo Sovieticus*, with all the virtues
and none of the vices that disfigure humanity elsewhere. Communism, or abundance for all, was supposed to be on the way.
Instead, the trend is downward and the boasts are no longer being
made. As a result, cynicism in high places has become the norm.

In recent years, members of the ruling elite of the USSR (the
'Nomenklatura') have at times been brutally frank in conversatrion
with former compatriots whom they encounter on trade or other
missions abroad. The shortcomings of the system are readily
recognised, but the ruling elite are confident that the West will
always bail them out. Meanwhile, whatever the Soviets have (including, for instance, Poland and Afghanistan), they will hold on to.

It is this aspect of the system which Western observers, especially
among liberals (in the American sense of an abused term) find particularly hard to understand. *The system cannot reform itself without the
risk of collapse, since ideology remains its only source of legitimacy and justification.* At best, only superficial improvements are possible.

If such fundamental problems were purely internal, the outside
world could breathe more easily, but they are not: the ideology commands expansionism abroad. If it did not, 'this war called peace'
would not be a reality. Soviet society is now profoundly militarised,
at all levels from primary school upwards. The needs of the armed
forces have top priority, and the armed forces have an unquenchable

thirst for high technology, much of which is either stolen from the West and Japan through industrial espionage, or is provided openly from the same sources, usually on credit. In other words, the suppliers provide not only the technology but the money to pay for it. We shall return to this aspect of the Soviet problem. At this point, however, some comments on the great Polish crisis are needed.

Poland

A major wave of industrial unrest in Poland in 1980 culminated in strikes in the Baltic port of Gdansk (Danzig). The officially sponsored 'trade unions' virtually ceased to exist towards the end of the year, and were replaced by an unofficial general trade union known as Solidarnosc ('Solidarity') whose leader, Lech Walesa, rapidly became famous internationally. A volatile political situation developed.

The First Secretary of the ruling United Workers' Party (Communist), Edward Gierek, was forced to step down and was replaced by Stanislaw Kania, who had been running the secret police. In one year, from February 1980 till February 1981, three successive prime ministers were appointed, the last being General Wojciech Jaruzelski, a political general who had risen to be Commander-in-Chief of the Polish Armed Forces.

From the Soviet standpoint, the events in Poland presented a major problem and a specific dilemma. The essence of the problem was that the Soviet regime could not tolerate the emergence of Solidarity as an independent source of workers' power in a workers' state. If tolerated and allowed to function over a long term, it would have been an inadmissible challenge to the Leninist basis of all Soviet-controlled states, including the USSR itself. The dilemma facing the Soviet leaders was whether or not to intervene directly with military force, as in Hungary in 1956, in Czechoslovakia in 1968 and Afghanistan in 1979–80.

In March 1981, shortly before the attempted assassination of President Reagan on the 30th, precise intelligence is believed to have reached the White House to the effect that the Soviet armed forces, with the support of East German troops, were preparing to invade Poland. The Administration issued a solemn warning to the Soviets about the consequences of an invasion. Whether in response to the warning or for other reasons, the Soviets decided not to invade.

The Soviet quandary was absolute. It appeared to be about as dangerous to intervene militarily as not to intervene. Had the Soviet forces invaded Poland, there were good reasons for supposing that the Polish forces would resist. Prolonged resistance would increase the danger of contagion in East Germany, Hungary and elsewhere. Moreover, any heavy loss of life in Poland would possibly provide the psychological shock, especially with a determined Administration in Washington, to produce at least near-unanimity within the Alliance, to halt all transfers of technology to the USSR, and possibly even to impose a general trade ban.

Through 1981 the Soviets tried every possible device except direct military intervention: police provocation of Solidarity, alternations of promises and bullying and the systematic round-up of potential resisters. In the end, they hit upon the ingenious idea of a sponsored military take-over by the Polish armed forces. On 11 December 1981 Jaruzelski proclaimed martial law.

Although ostensibly it was the Polish Army, not the Soviet, that had taken over, the reality behind martial law was Soviet power. In a press conference on 23 December President Reagan revealed that the proclamation had been drafted and even printed in Moscow as early as the preceding September. The Polish Army, moreover, was under indirect Soviet control under the Warsaw Pact organisation, based in Warsaw, and under the command of the C-in-C, the Soviet Marshal V.G.Kulikov. In addition, the USSR maintained two tank divisions in Poland. The fiction of a purely Polish armed intervention enabled the Soviet leaders to claim that they were not intervening in what was still described as an internal matter for the Poles to settle among themselves.

The Western responses to these momentous events were mostly feeble. President Reagan set an example, first by halting American shipments of grain to Poland and imposing restrictions on Polish shipping in United States' waters, then by banning exports of computers to the USSR; but grain shipments to Russia continued. It was a sign of the inroads of 'Finlandisation' in Western Europe that other governments showed no inclination to follow Reagan's lead.

In France, President Mitterrand's socialist–communist government strongly condemned Soviet and Polish official behaviour, but took no action. The worst record was that of the German Federal Republic. Chancellor Schmidt chose the moment of Poland's agony to hold his first private meeting for eleven years with the East German leader, Erich Honecker and to have it on East German soil, still under Soviet occupation thirty-six years after the end of the Second World War. The Foreign Minister, Hans-Dietrich Genscher, publicly opposed American sanctions and declared that West Germany would continue to send food to Poland.

The Siberian Pipeline

A related and still more glaring example of Allied disunity concerned the Soviet project for the building of a major natural gas pipeline running from Siberia to West Germany. On 18 June 1982 President Reagan announced an extension of the ban of December 1981 on the export of oil and gas technology to the USSR. Henceforth the ban would apply not only to American companies, but also to foreign subsidiaries of such companies. The ban ran into united Allied opposition in Europe. Even the British government under Margaret Thatcher joined in the chorus of criticism of the President's proposal, on the ground that contracts had already been signed and had to be honoured.

The President had weakened his case by ending the previous ban on the export of American grain to the USSR—a decision which the Americans defended with the argument that the Soviets paid hard cash for the grain while they used Western money on credit for the pipeline scheme. In time, European objections prevailed, and the President rescinded his embargo on participation by European subsidiaries of American multinationals.

These dissensions within the Alliance and a growing feeling in the United States that the European countries were failing to make a full contribution to NATO's defences contributed to a rebirth of isolationist sentiment in the United States. The West, meanwhile, had fallen into what some observers labelled the 'credit trap', of their own making. By mid-1982 the total indebtedness of the Soviet bloc to Western banks had reached $80.7 billion, of which Poland's quite disproportionate share was $24 billion. The 'credit trap' is best described as the situation in which debts are periodically rescheduled (in other words, are not repaid) and in which the lending banks are compelled to lend borrowers more money so that the *interest*, though not the principal, of previous loans may at least be paid.

This situation, amounting in practice though not in name to a massive Allied aid programme to the Soviet Union and its European empire, developed at a time when the Western banking system was already in deep trouble over similar rescheduled debts contracted by such countries as Mexico, Brazil, Venezuela and Argentina.

To put the matter in perspective, the mountain of debt continued to grow during 1982 at a time when the Soviet Union was disbursing gigantic sums to pay for its foreign adventures: thus, Cuba, which had furnished a major expeditionary force for the Soviet empire's colonial wars in Africa, was costing the Soviet people and State a staggering $10 billion a year; while Afghanistan and Vietnam accounted for a further $1 million *a day*.

The Advent of Andropov

In November 1982 Brezhnev died, and was succeeded as General Secretary of the Communist Party of the Soviet Union (CPSU) by Yuri Andropov, who for the past sixteen years had been Chairman of the dreaded KGB. His advent to the top office in the USSR was accompanied by a spate of 'revelations', presumably inspired by himself and disseminated by the Disinformation Department of the KGB, to the effect that he was a liberal at heart, spoke excellent English and was a man of culture.

More relevantly, it was Andropov who introduced a peculiarly nasty punishment—the psychiatric treatment and incarceration of political dissidents. It was he, too, who, early in his KGB career, created a new Chief Directorate of that organisation, the Fifth, to deal exclusively with internal dissent. Again it was Andropov, in his role as Soviet Ambassador to Budapest at the time of the Hungarian uprising in 1956, who lured the Hungarian military leader, General Pal Maleter, and others to their deaths on the pretext of inviting them to negotiations at the embassy.

Among 'inspired' stories reproduced in the Western media when Andropov took over as party boss was the notion that now was the time for President Reagan to 'seize the opportunity' for meaningful negotiations with the Soviet leadership.

When Konstantin Chernenko, a Siberian *apparatchik*, became party boss upon the death of Andropov in February 1984, nothing in the Soviet Union had changed. The ideology was the same, and so was the Constitution. The threat continued, undiminished.

13   1984 and Beyond

Once upon a time, one of Stalin's henchmen objected to the proposed show trial of a leading Old Bolshevik on the grounds that it might make an unfavourable impression on public opinion in the West. 'Never mind, they'll swallow it,' Stalin retorted. Experience had shown him that so-called opinion-makers seldom express their own independently arrived-at views or report what is as plain as the noses in front of their faces; most often, they only repeat what they believe is acceptable in their own intellectual milieu. They follow the conventional wisdom of the time. Thus, as we have had occasion to point out time and time again, Western liberalism has never freed itself from the delusion that communism—that is, fascism of the left—has a virtuous goal which ultimately justifies the means it employs. The result has been that from the moment of Lenin's seizure of power in 1917 every communist atrocity has been explained away as justice executed in the name of this goal. Whatever the reality of Soviet practice, the West has managed, in the end, to swallow it.

So it happened that at the Yalta conference in February 1945, although the crimes of Lenin and his associates, the terrible purges of the 1930s, even the Nazi–Soviet Pact and its consequences, were all on the debit side of the account, the leaders of the Western democracies were prepared to write them off and extend unlimited credit to Stalin. And Stalin naturally took full advantage of the situation in which he found himself.

Whenever Roosevelt and Churchill raised the problem they faced of satisfying their own public opinion, Stalin invariably replied that what they needed to do was more 'propaganda work'. As far as he was concerned, Roosevelt and Churchill brought up the subject of public opinion only to justify their own positions, and he used to boast at their meetings that he 'kept his press in order'. On at least one occasion Churchill is on record as saying that he wished he had the same control over the British press as Stalin had over the Soviet press.

What use, one wonders, would Churchill have made of it? While Stalin steadily moved his troops forward into the Balkans and Eastern Europe, the Western leaders did no more than ask that a 'free press' be allowed to monitor what went on in these territories. But what use would this 'free press' have been against Soviet tanks and bayonets? And why did Churchill wait so long—indeed, wait until he was no longer in power—to come out in public with the iron curtain image?

When he actually had the power, he used it to suppress the truth about what was really happening in Europe, especially as far as the Cossacks and other Russians were concerned, who had chosen to fight against the Soviet regime. So Stalin succeeded in making Roosevelt and Churchill his accomplices. By meeting with him—at Teheran, at Yalta, at Potsdam—the Western leaders were doing Stalin's propaganda work for him.

For ten years after the Potsdam conference, the West was left to digest what had taken place at these wartime summit meetings while the other war which had been raging since 1917, the 'war called peace', dominated the international scene. In these ten years, summit meetings went out of fashion, so blatant was the Soviet power-drive, although Churchill in and out of office clamoured for them, more, it seems, from nostalgia for the heady days of the fight against Hitler than from sober assessment of their worth in the fight against communism. But Potsdam, code-name 'Terminal', was not destined to be the last by any manner of means.

In 1955 came the meeting in Geneva between Eisenhower, Khrushchev, Eden and Faure, when the West resumed its wishful thinking that Lenin's heirs really had abandoned his long-term objective of 'world revolution'. So committed was the West to its wishful thinking that not even the abortive meeting in Paris in 1960 could kill off the idea of summits. Instead, Kennedy agreed to meet Khrushchev in Vienna in 1961, and since then summit meetings of one kind or another have become a regular feature of Soviet policy, culminating in the series which accompanied Brezhnev's 'peace offensive'. Meanwhile European and Chinese leaders have entered the ring with various forms of summits of their own, so popular have they become as a media-oriented road-show.

Yet as the narrative of this book makes clear, none of these summits produced any positive gain to the West or to the values for which the West stands. The contrary, in fact, has been the case. After Yalta and Potsdam came the extinction of political life in Eastern Europe, culminating in the communist *coup d'état* in Czechoslovakia in 1948. In 1953, Soviet tanks and bayonets had to be called in to enforce communist dictatorship in East Germany. A year after the 1955 meeting in Geneva came the brutal crushing of the Hungarian bid for freedom. After Vienna 1961 came the Berlin Wall and the Cuban missile crisis, as though Khrushchev were deliberately giving the young Kennedy a slap on the face.

With Brezhnev's détente came the invasion of Czechoslovakia, crueller measures against Soviet dissidents and an ever-widening spread of subversion and terrorism. And so, at each stage, the story repeats itself. Soviet deeds have directly contradicted Soviet words. Instead of peace, there has been the constant promotion of strife, leading to an actual war in Korea to the bloody upheavals in the Middle East of the 1950s, to the long-drawn-out misery of the peoples of Indochina, to the invasion of Afghanistan, to near civil war in El Salvador, and, no doubt, to new adventures already in preparation.

What, then, do these summit meetings signify? They provide an image of power which pleases the eye, and Western man has come to worship this image when his reason, if not his faith, should tell him otherwise. When the reality strikes him, he is shocked, but his shock is short-lived unless he himself is the victim of it, by which time it is too late. For just as total war involves total propaganda, so power in these circumstances acknowledges no distinction between right and wrong, truth and falsehood, but only between victors and vanquished. 'History', or 'the people', or whatever fiction men choose to live by, justifies those who come out on top and 'public opinion' will applaud their success with the offer of Caesar's laurel crown. At every step taken by the Soviets Stalin's voice may be heard echoing softly round the Kremlin: 'Never mind, they'll swallow it.'

So it is that today, televised images of power in the shape of tanks and guns, of rockets and marching men, when projected into the living-rooms of the West, subdue the will of the viewer and bring his mind to a state where he will believe anything he is told. A Hungary, a Czechoslovakia, an Afghanistan, speaks to him not of the wickedness of the Soviet regime but of its strength; the pictures he sees are not contradicted by words, since the words are written as commentary to the pictures: war is peace, invasion is liberation, enslavement is freedom. the picture is all that matters and the event itself passes into nothingness once the picture changes.

The English writer George Orwell foresaw this development in his prophetic novel *1984*, which was published in 1949 and immediately became one of the most famous literary documents of the cold war. The image of 'Big Brother', alias Stalin, then glowered down on all Europe; the torture-chambers of Orwell's 'Ministry of Love' were then working overtime in Stalin's Gulag Archipelago.

Orwell took the title of his novel, which now seems all too appropriate, by transposing the last two digits of the year in which he wrote it, 1948. But the idea for it had come to him five years previously during the war, when Roosevelt, Churchill and Stalin had first come together at Teheran to divide the world up between them. Teheran, Yalta, Potsdam—in Orwell's eyes, these wartime summits offered a spectacle of power before which mankind was prostrating himself.

In writing *1984* Orwell was not, as is commonly supposed, joining in the cold war argument—he took the evils of Soviet communism for granted, having experienced them himself in the Spanish Civil War and realising that they were inherent in Lenin's seizure of power in 1917. 'The seeds of evil were there from the start,' Orwell wrote. His book, *Homage to Catalonia*, is generally regarded as one of the best eye-witness accounts of the Spanish tragedy. *Animal Farm*, a brilliant satire on Stalinism and his literary masterpiece, appeared in 1945. Nor was Orwell primarily concerned with exposing the utopian ideals of humanists, as others in the same genre had done; Zamyatin's novel *WE*, for example, was an obvious source and Orwell freely acknowledged his debt to it. Orwell himself still believed in the British Labour Party, in power during the years he was writing *1984*, and he regularly contributed to the left-wing periodical, *Tribune*.

In *1984* Orwell was primarily concerned with the collapse of the intelligentsia in the face of power. 'I believe,' he wrote in answer to criticism that *1984* was a cold war diatribe, 'that totalitarian ideas have taken root everywhere, and I have tried to draw these ideas out to their logical consequences.' The scene of *1984* was laid in Britain as a warning 'that totalitarianism, *if not fought against*, could triumph anywhere'. Orwell's model for his Ministry of Truth was not, as most people believed at the time the book appeared, the Kremlin. It was, in fact, the British Broadcasting Corporation, which had become during the war the main propaganda arm of the British government. In the same way that, in the closing months of the war, Goebbels' Ministry of Propaganda represented the main source of strength in the dying Nazi order in Germany, so the BBC represented the shadow of British power in the new world-order brought about by the war and the collapse of Britain's imperial role.

It is from the roof of the BBC's headquarters in London that those other government buildings can be seen which are described in *1984* as being the four pillars of the state. In the BBC's nearby studios in Oxford Street, where Orwell himself worked, are the corridors and sinister underground rooms where Big Brother's work is done. And the point of the novel is not the love-affair between Winston Smith and Julia, but the way language had become abused to serve the interests of power rather than of truth.

Orwell's most valuable contribution to the cold war was his brilliant analysis of what he called in another essay, 'The Prevention of Literature'. In *1984* he introduced a whole terminology to describe what was happening to words—and so to thoughts—because of the needs of power. 'Newspeak', 'double-think', Big Brother himself, 'unperson'—a perversion of language which became necessary once the free world began to have dealings with the communist one, began, indeed, to accept the Leninist view of history which led, in the end, to the summits of Teheran and Yalta which first gave Orwell the idea for *1984*.

Now, with the year 1984 past us, Orwell's insights into the way public opinion operates appear all too accurate. He himself belonged to that generation of intellectuals many of whom felt compelled to become political activists during the 1930s and who may therefore be regarded as reliable eye-witnesses of the period. Yet they themselves have contributed to the creation of a new conventional wisdom about the 1930s. Thanks largely to them, images of Hitler and the specifically German form of totalitarian power are still held to constitute the principal threat to mankind, while the much more dangerous form of totalitarian power which communism represents is given the benefit of the doubt. And their influence over succeeding generations has continued, despite the disavowals most of them have made of their communist past.

The fact must be faced, however, that the activities of these Western intellectuals, for all their skill with words and ideas, had not the slightest influence on events. Despite all attempts to explain it away, it is the case that Hitler came to power legally in Germany and he retained the support of the German people until the very end.

In Spain, Franco, like Hitler, turned the communist threat to his own propaganda advantage and succeeded in keeping his position until his death forty years after his victory in the Spanish Civil War. One might add that the Munich agreement in 1938 was possible only because of the immense popular backing Chamberlain and Daladier received in Britain and France.

What, then do we really mean when we speak of 'public opinion'? If we are to judge by events, certainly not the mass of the people, or majority opinion. Nor even that mysterious force known as the *Zeitgeist*, or spirit of the age.

In his autobiography, *The Invisible Writing*, Arthur Koestler described his time as an undercover communist writer working under the direction of Willy Muenzenberg, the Comintern's versatile propaganda expert in the West. They were lurid times, and the communist Agitprop *Apparat* called for lurid methods, which caused Koestler and others to view their activities with a certain ambiguity. On the one hand, they recognised clearly enough 'the cynical insincerity behind the facade' of communism, and yet they were also persuaded to serve that totalitarian power system because of the 'fervent *mystique* of a genuine mass movement'.

The ambiguity Koestler described gives a clue to understanding the nature of 'public opinion'. For what he called 'the fervent *mystique* of a genuine mass movement' is, after all, no more than a *mystique*; it is a hoax, a fiction, an intellectual illusion. In politics no such thing as 'a genuine mass movement' exists apart from ordinary human passions organised through society; that is, the hopes, fears, hates and desires of individuals brought together in groups, in mobs, in demonstrations, in assemblies.

What the intelligentsia describes as public opinion is in reality no more than the opinion of like-minded people who need each other's reassurance that they are not alone in their views.

This, then, is how the so-called consensus comes into being. It mistakes its own intellectual conformity for mass opinion, and its propensity for doing so is increased in direct proportion to the increase in the means of communication at its disposal. For as the means of communication increase, so do the numbers of would-be communicators who swell the ranks of the intelligentsia and so persuade themselves that they are indeed participating in 'a genuine mass movement'.

Further, we should note that this conventional wisdom, or consensus, is in effect a form of death-wish. Why else should intellectuals seek to submerge themselves in 'a genuine mass movement' if not to serve mass power, or totalitarian power? As Orwell put it: 'The direct, conscious attack on intellectual decency comes from the intellectuals themselves;' and 'On a long view, the weakening of the desire for liberty among the intellectuals themselves is the most serious symptom'. The history of this war called peace has shown that the real threat to the West does not come from outside, from the Soviet Union or Maoist China, but from within, from the way this consensus operates in an ever-expanding media-dominated society.

Shortly before *1984* appeared in England, an event of similar importance on the ideological front of the cold war took place in France. On 1 April 1944 a senior official in the Soviet Purchasing Commission in Washington, called Victor Kravchenko, sought political asylum in the United States. Three days later, the *New York Times* carried an article in which Kravchenko explained why he wanted to leave the Soviet Union. Goebbels, of course, made what he could out of the story, but it does not seem that Kravchenko's defection created any stir in American government circles. It so happened that in the same year of 1944 two senior members of the American Administration visited the Soviet Union, and among the places they were taken to see was the Kolyma gold mining region in the Arctic, where the forced labour camps were at their most terrible. They were as much death camps as were Auschwitz, Treblinka, Dachau and the rest organised by the Nazis. Of course, special arrangements were made for the visit of the two Americans. One of them was no less a person than Roosevelt's Vice-President, Henry Wallace; the other was a Professor Lattimore, who then represented the Office of War Information and was an influential figure in deciding America's policy in the Far East. Both men gave glowing accounts of what they saw in the Soviet Union, and America remained firmly committed to Roosevelt's policy of appeasing Stalin.

Kravchenko went on to write a book, *I Chose Freedom*, which was published in 1946 and which described life in the Soviet Union for a communist party member like himself. He had been an engineer who managed to survive Stalin's pre-war purges, and he had witnessed the famine brought on by Stalin's economic policy and the chaos which followed the Soviet governments flight in panic after Hitler's invasion of Russia. In 1944, when Kravchenko defected,

Soviet Russia under Stalin had to be presented to the American public as America's natural ally, and the deficiencies which Kravchenko described and which would tarnish this image could not be admitted. But in 1946, the year of Churchill's 'iron curtain' speech. American public opinion had to be re-educated to accept the new ideological battle-lines of the cold war, and Kravchenko's book became a best-seller.

In consequence, Kravchenko and his book were treated to the full repertoire of communist defamation, a technique known as 'disinformation'—a thoroughly Orwellian term—which is still part of the regular Soviet armoury, meriting its own specialist department within the KGB, only today it is practised in more refined ways than the crude smears of these early cold war days. In France, attacks on Kravchenko reached a peak of virulence in a series of articles in a French communist periodical, *Les Lettres Françaises*, which appeared at various times between November 1947 and April 1948. The worst of the articles appeared over the name of a Sim Thomas, who was said to have been an American journalist, but who never identified himself.

The articles alleged that Kravchenko's book was a fake and Kravchenko himself a thoroughly disreputable figure who was known in the Soviet Union to be a drunkard, a cheat and an embezzler, and in the United States had shown himself to be a fraud, a liar and an agent of American intelligence. How such a man could find himself in high Soviet employment was a complication the communists did not bother to explain. After all, the top leadership of the Revolution had also been found, during the pre-war show trials, to be enemies of the people, imperialist spies, capitalist lackeys, fascist hyenas and so on.

Kravchenko took up the communist challenge and sued the French paper for libel, thus carrying the war into territory where the Soviet Union had many supporters, especially among members of the intelligentsia. The case came up in Paris in January 1949 and lasted through twenty-five sittings spread over ten weeks. It was a *cause célèbre* of the early cold war years, a microcosm of the ideological battle which Lenin initiated in 1917.

On one side was a system of thought which was totally subservient to Soviet power and which therefore had no objective standards of right and wrong, truth or falsehood; and on the other side were ordinary men and women who had the will to resist Stalin's lies and the courage to speak out. One by one, Moscow's witnesses tried to discredit Kravchenko's character and applaud Stalin's leadership; and one by one Kravchenko's witnesses testified to the accuracy of his account of Stalin's workers' paradise, some of them even saying that the horrors were worse than Kravchenko had described. It was here that the widow of the German communist leader, Margarete Buber-Neumann, described the infamous hand-over by the KGB of Jewish communists and others wanted by Hitler's Gestapo at the bridge of Brest-Litovsk, mentioned in an earlier chapter. Another of Kravchenko's witnesses described the terrible famine in Russia, brought on by Stalin, and how on his way to work one morning he had given a piece of bread to an emaciated peasant. When he returned in the evening, the peasant was still there holding the crust of bread, but he was dead. One of Moscow's witnesses had made light of the purges. Kravchenko answered: 'To me the purge means ten million victims, pulled-out teeth, sleepless nights in NKVD [KGB] prisons; it means torture and suffering. We are on different sides, you and I.' Another had praised Stalin's leadership in the war, and Kravchenko replied: 'It is the Russian people who won it, thanks to their efforts, their sorrow, their tears, their sufferings, their patriotism and their spirit of sacrifice.'

In another exchange, Kravchenko attacked a Soviet witness, called Kolybalov, finding in a Western courtroom a freedom of language no-one in Russia had known for half a century:

Kravchenko: All he knows how to do is to make rousing syndicalist speeches, which do nothing at all to increase the production of a factory . . . It is one thing to repeat resounding formulas in honour of the 'beloved chief Stalin'—
Kolybalov (angrily): You will please not mention in this place the name of my beloved leader Stalin! (Jeers, catcalls and roars of laughter from the spectators.)
Kravchenko: and it is another thing to manufacture pipes. I can speak of your beloved leader because I am in free France. I spit on your beloved leader! I have been waiting for this moment all my life.

Anyone unaffected by the images of power which had been projected in the West by the summits at Yalta and Potsdam would see at once that the rival witnesses were not speaking the same language. Moscow's was the language of the Leninist *coup d'état*, or 'newspeak', almost exactly as Orwell had described it in *1984*. 'So long as men like Kravchenko exist, so long there will be free men to answer them.' 'Whoever attacked Russia sided with Hitler.' 'I say that the only war with which we are threatened is an anti-Soviet war.' 'History has taught us that whoever styles himself anti-Russian becomes, by the virtue of that very fact, anti-French.' In support of this 'newspeak' the communists produced a parade, which was to become all too familiar over the years ahead, of Soviet stooges and fellow-travellers, some brought specially from Moscow, some from the United States and Britain, and some recruited locally in France, among the last being the French atomic scientist, Joliot-Curie. From Britain came two leading lights in this leftist galaxy, Zilliacus, the Labour Member of Parliament, and the Dean of Canterbury, the Very Reverend Hewlett Johnson, renowned for sermons in which he praised the loving humanity of Stalin. No-one really expected the mythical Sim Thomas to put in an appearance, but neither did his absence embarrass Moscow's defenders.

There were, after all, any number of Sim Thomases in the West waiting their turn to speak up for Marx, Lenin, Stalin and anyone else the party might nominate. Outside the courtroom, too, famous intellectuals like J.P.Sartre could always be relied on to take the same line, writers who would be looked up to by future generations of students long after Kravchenko's name had passed out of the headlines.

Nevertheless, on 4 April 1949 judgement was given for Kravchenko. The Soviet witnesses had found themselves out of their depth in Paris, taken aback by the judicial detachment of the French presiding judge, so unlike one of their own show trials, and by the masterly tactics of Kravchenko's counsel, Maître Izard, a hero of the French resistance. It was a victory not for regimes or parties or causes, not even for one system of government over another, but for truth itself, and therefore it was as important a victory as any of the cold war. But it is part of the moral of this book to point out that the West forgets too easily the lessons of the past. It allows a victory such as Kravchenko's to disappear too quickly in the shifting sands of the consensus. The intelligentsia, momentarily aroused by a sensation in a courtroom in Paris, soon turns back to its wishful thinking and listens anew to the siren voices of Moscow's apologists as they take up their familiar refrains.

In his book, Kravchenko had written that what he had found most striking about the West was 'the profound ignorance among alleged "experts on Soviet Russia" about the nature and organisation of power in the USSR'. He realised, he went on, 'that I must expect to be denounced and ridiculed by precisely those warm-hearted and high-minded foreigners on whose understanding and support I had counted'. Many an ex-communist like Arthur Koestler had experienced the same hatred from the West's liberal consensus. 'In the public eye,' wrote Koestler, 'the ex-communist remains an informer and war-monger.' Like many others who looked to the West for more than material freedom, Kravchenko eventually fell into despair. In February 1966, at the age of sixty-one, he took his own life in New York.

The publication in Britain of Orwell's *1984* and Kravchenko's libel suit in Paris, though attracting wide publicity in intellectual circles, hardly touched the basic attitudes of the British and French people towards the cold war. In both countries at that time there was a healthy awareness of the reality of the Soviet threat to Europe. What had become evident was that in the Western democracies sudden changes in national policy could take place as easily as in Stalin's Russia, the intellectual consensus performing in the former the same role as party propaganda did in the latter.

In the United States, however, the debate was more open and the question of how American opinion would respond to the demands of the cold war came to a head in 1946, the central figure being Henry Wallace, who was Vice-President for Roosevelt's third term but was bitterly disappointed not to be renominated in 1944. What the political currents were which bore Wallace out of the running and Truman into it do not concern us here, except to remind us that the whole history of the cold war might have been quite different—and from the West's point of view, disastrously so—had these currents not been present when Roosevelt came to choose his running-mate in 1944.

Wallace was the archetypal American fellow-traveller who was easily deceived by standard KGB tricks when he visited the Soviet Union with Owen Lattimore during the war. In Truman's Administration, he was Secretary of Commerce, the last of the original New Dealers in the cabinet. In 1946, no doubt from idealistic motives, Wallace felt he had to intervene in the public debate about the cold war. His views ran directly counter to the new, tougher line which Truman's Administration was adopting towards the Soviet Union.

Caught unawares, Truman himself momentarily gave the impression of not knowing his own mind, although privately he had formed an accurate enough picture of what Wallace stood for. In his diary, Truman called Wallace 'a pacifist 100 per cent'. He went on:

> He wants us to disband our armed forces, give Russia our atomic secrets and trust a bunch of adventurers in the Kremlin Politburo. I do not understand a 'dreamer' like that . . . The Reds, phonies and 'parlour pinks' seem to be banded together and are becoming a national danger. I am afraid they are a sabotage front for Uncle Joe Stalin. They can see no wrong in Russia's four and one-half million armed force, in Russia's loot of Poland, Austria, Hungary, Rumania and Manchuria. They can see no wrong in Russia's living off the occupied countries to support the military occupation. But when we help our friends who fought on our side in China it is terrible. When Russia loots the industrial plant of those same friends it is all right. When Russia occupies Persia for oil that is heavenly although Persia was Russia's ally in the terrible German War.

In September 1946 the division of opinion within the Administration came to a head, and Truman had to fire Wallace, who immediately became a focus for just the kind of opinion which Truman had summarised in his diary note. On instructions from Moscow, the Communist Party in America supported Wallace in everything, and they succeeded in largely taking over the platform from which Wallace had originally made his views known.

As things turned out, however, this was a miscalculation. The Democrats lost heavily in the 1946 elections and control of Congress passed to the Republicans, a fact which increased Truman's domestic difficulties but which also gave him a target when it came to the presidential campaign in 1948. In a spectacular razzle-dazzle whistle-stop campaign, Truman lambasted the Republican Congress, making it the scapegoat for all the country's discontents. Wallace meanwhile had entered the presidential campaign as a third candidate, but by this time both liberal opinion and labour had moved behind Truman. Wallace was therefore isolated, and forced to rely increasingly on the support of communists and fellow-travellers. The result favoured Truman, since with Wallace in the field the Republicans were unable to use the anti-communist argument against the official Democratic candidate. Truman's surprising victory against all the odds over

Dewey in 1948 may have caused the Kremlin to reconsider its tactics of 'disinformation' as far as internal American politics were concerned. Opportunities for a different approach altogether were soon to arise.

Historians have long recognised that during the 1930s communists established themselves in almost every significant branch of the American government. These were not, as is often supposed, individuals who happened to hold the left-wing views which were fashionable in the New Deal era and who discarded them as they matured in government service. On the contrary, they were recruited and organised by Moscow-directed underground agents. Americans have mostly been reluctant to discuss these facts openly for fear of being accused of bigotry; for fear, that is, of offending the liberal consensus and so being tainted with what came to be known as McCarthyism.

In 1948 and 1949 most of the facts about this penetration of government became public knowledge during testimony before Congress's House Committee on Un-American Activities, in which the young Richard Nixon, then an obscure member of the House of Representatives from Whittier, California, took a prominent part. The drama of these hearings centred round two men, Whittaker Chambers and Alger Hiss. At that time Chambers was a senior editor of *Time* magazine, but in the 1930s he had been a communist agent called Carl. He was a short, pudgy man, unkempt in appearance, with a tortured conscience and emotionally complex. His family were first-generation Americans.

Alger Hiss, on the other hand, was tall, handsome and urbane, a Harvard graduate with excellent connections, a distinguished member of America's east coast establishment. Because of their personal backgrounds, their appearances and their careers, Chambers and Hiss became symbols of a drama which at times rose to the heights of Greek tragedy. The best account is *Perjury* by Allen Weinstein, published in 1978, a painstaking and absorbing book which raises disturbing questions about American society and government.

In 1938 detailed information about Soviet espionage in Western Europe and America had been provided by a leading agent of Soviet Military Intelligence, General Walter Krivitsky. Krivitsky in turn persuaded Chambers, who by then had become disillusioned with Soviet policy, to tell all he knew to the government. The two men became friends and both went in fear for their lives, knowing the methods of Soviet intelligence. Chambers for a time slept with a pistol under his pillow, and he continued to be secretive in his ways, hiding material which would later incriminate Hiss as a kind of insurance policy. In 1941, however, Krivitsky was found dying of gunshot wounds in a Washington hotel shortly after returning from Britain, where he had helped uncover a Soviet agent working in the British cabinet code-room.

In 1939 Chambers tried to give his information to Roosevelt personally, but he had to content himself with a long private interview with Adolf Berle, an Assistant Secretary of State who was Roosevelt's right-hand man in charge of internal government security. Among the names mentioned by Chambers of men who were active members of communist cells were those of Harry Dexter White and Alger Hiss, both high in government service.

Roosevelt, however, took no action and, as we have seen, White went on to play a key role in determining America's monetary policy towards Britain after the war, while Alger Hiss was one of the senior State Department officials at Yalta and became largely responsible for American policy in the formation of the United Nations. According to Chambers' later testimony, Hiss was 'a devoted and at that time a rather romantic Communist', whose role was not so much espionage as exerting influence on American foreign policy, ultimately in line with Stalin's wishes.

Before the outbreak of the European war, it was alleged that Hiss had passed on secret information about Japanese moves in China and German moves in central Europe, both matters of great interest to Moscow, while as late as 1945 and 1946 it was also alleged that he was interesting himself in affairs outside his departmental responsibilities, including atomic research. From Igor Gouzenko in Canada came further information which pointed a finger at Hiss. Then in 1945, the FBI received additional information on Hiss from an Elizabeth Bentley who, like Chambers, had been active as an underground courier for the communists in the 1930s.

By now, the evidence on Hiss which had steadily accumulated on his State Department Personal File could no longer be ignored. He was interviewed by the FBI but satisfied them with his answers, and, to avoid a public scandal, he was eased out of government service by the end of 1946. He was then appointed head of the Carnegie Endowment, the chairman of whose Board of Trustees was John Foster Dulles.

Here matters might have rested. By the end of 1947, most of the communists in the government had been identified and moved out of harm's way, and their effectiveness in any case had been offset by the way the cold war had actually developed. By 1948 the Truman Doctrine and Marshall Aid, two of the most important initiatives of Truman's Administration, had passed through Congress and in that year support was forthcoming for the government's response to the Berlin blockade and the *coup d'état* in Czechoslovakia which led eventually to the formation of NATO.

By this time, therefore, with the exception of Wallace there was no serious political challenge to Truman's foreign policy. Its bipartisan quality was indeed its strength, as no-one in the Democratic or Republican parties doubted the reality of Soviet threats or Stalin's untrustworthiness. American public was united as seldom before or since on this issue.

Why, then, did the Chambers–Hiss drama cause such a tremendous stir in America? The usual explanation is that the Republicans on the House Committee on Un-American Activities exploited the case for publicity reasons at a time when they were desperately trying to break the long Democratic occupancy of the White House, 1948 being an election year.

In the light of all that has happened since 1948 it is necessary to be, cautious about accepting this explanation. The major part of Hiss's defence was to accuse Chambers of being politically motivated; that in attacking Hiss, Chambers was attacking Roosevelt and the New Deal. By association, therefore, every American liberal was identified with Hiss.

Along with this defence went an attack on Chambers' character, in which he was accused of being a homosexual and of taking a slighted lover's revenge on someone who had once shown him friendship. This defence and the methods by which it was promoted bore a striking resemblance to the smear campaign resorted to by Kravchenko's detractors. The appearance of Richard Nixon as one of the *dramatis personae* has further complicated the matter. It is said that Nixon and his colleagues manipulated the hearings in order to secure maximum headline coverage, the implication being that they were wrong to do so, or that they were doing so from motives of personal advancement only, or that the public were in some way being taken for a ride, or that the press reporters who provided the headlines were being taken for a ride.

None of these explanations seems convincing, and the idea that the media themselves might be responsible is unwelcome to liberal opinion in America, which prides itself on the openness of society and the freedom of the press. Whatever the underlying cause may have been for the sudden upsurge of public interest, the fact is that in search of sensations the media devoured the story, and in the course of it made victims of both Chambers and Hiss, their personal fate becoming secondary to the wider drama unfolding.

In Allen Weinstein's book the reader can follow all the ramifications of this absorbing story. Here, we can only give a brief rundown of the main events in it, with the reminder that inside America public opinion would tend to treat these events as of equal, if not greater, importance as the events then taking place in Europe, the Middle East and China, which would shape the world for the next quarter of a century.

On 3 August 1948 Chambers first gave evidence before the Un-American Affairs Committee. Through leaks and later open testimony the public gradually became aware of the names involved. Truman regarded the Committee as a political stunt of the Republicans, and he planned to terminate its activities if the elections restored the Democrats to control in Congress. But the Committee kept up its investigations throughout August, sometimes in open session, sometimes in closed executive session in which Nixon played the part of chief interrogator. On 5 August Hiss appeared for the first time. He denied all the allegations Chambers had made and said he did not even know who Chambers was. On 13 August Harry Dexter White was questioned and three days later he was found dead, apparently of a heart attack. But it may have been suicide, and it may have been murder.

On 16 August Hiss was questioned a second time, when he repeated his denials. Next day, Chambers and Hiss faced each other in closed session; on 25 August they confronted each other again in public, and on this occasion television cameras were present. On 27 August Chambers repeated his charges on a television show, *Meet the Press*, where he was unprotected by Congressional privilege. After waiting for a month, Hiss filed suit for slander, but his case disappeared when Hiss himself was indicted for perjury by a Grand Jury in New York. His trial came up on 31 May 1949 and ended on 7 July with an eight-to-four vote for conviction. A second trial was ordered which began on 17 November 1949 and lasted until January 1950. Convicted of perjury, Hiss was given a five-year sentence, which he served between March 1951 and November 1954, his appeal being rejected by the Supreme Court.

Everything about the case could have come from an American television soap-opera; indeed, it was, in its way, the prototype of all such soap-operas—a story which touched the highest figures in the nation, the ramifications of which seemed endless; Chambers in a tortured frame of mind, contemplating suicide, and other men struck down with heart attacks; a Catholic priest with access to FBI files; accusations of forgery by typewriter requiring careful sleuthing and minute analysis, and microfilm hidden in a hollowed-out pumpkin, a prothonotary warbler observed down by the Potomac, an old Ford car with windscreen-wipers worked by hand, and bad teeth. No script-writer could improve on these things; the press headlines, the photographs, the newsreels were better than any strip cartoon. And new material was forthcoming for further episodes.

On 7 January 1950, two weeks before the verdict of 'guilty' was pronounced on Alger Hiss, four politically-minded Roman Catholics met for dinner in a Washington restaurant. Two of them were academics, one was an attorney and the fourth was a Republican Senator called Joseph McCarthy. They discussed issues for the 1952 campaign, as McCarthy felt vulnerable in his state of Wisconsin, where his record as a public servant was not all that it might have been.

Pensions for the elderly and the St Lawrence Seaway were suggested as possible causes for McCarthy to champion, but neither of them fired his imagination. Then, someone brought up the subject of communism, a secular religion which has many things in common with Roman Catholicism. The idea seemed a good one, and after dinner the Wisconsin Senator asked his Senate Republican Campaign Committee to arrange speaking engagements for him over the Lincoln's Birthday weekend. This was duly done, the first one being scheduled for Wheeling, West Virginia, on 9 February 1950, before a Women's Republican Club. From Wheeling, he would go on to Salt Lake City and Reno.

On 9 February McCarthy arrived in Wheeling, West Virginia, having made no serious preparation for his speech. The communists-in-government issue and abusing opponents as 'pinkos' were part of the stock-in-trade of small-time politicians and newspaper-men, and McCarthy hoped for no more than to win some credit in Wisconsin for appearing to be active in national politics. He kept no record of his speech and it received little coverage in the media at the time. A portion of it was reported in the local press, the Wheeling *Intelligencer*, in which McCarthy was quoted as saying:

> While I cannot take the time to name all of the men in the State Department who have been named as members of the Communist Party and members of a spy ring, I have here in my hand a list of two hundred and five that were known to the Secretary of State as being members of the Communist Party and who nevertheless are still working and shaping the policy of the State Department.

These words launched McCarthy into a career which for more than four years made him one of the most powerful figures in American politics, a man whose name still sends shivers down the spines of American liberals and is regarded by them as synonymous with intolerance, witch-hunting and evil. In America, McCarthy himself is now generally forgotten, but McCarthyism has become a code-word which Americans use, like Watergate and Vietnam, to describe something about themselves which they would like to unthink, as Orwell would say.

Yet McCarthy's background was typically American. He was half-Irish and half-German, born in 1908, the fifth of nine children. His father was an impoverished farmer in Outagamie County, 100 miles north of Milwaukie in Wisconsin. Moderately competent at school, the young McCarthy went in for a short spell of chicken-farming and then took up law, paying for his studies by taking jobs as a dish-washer, petrol pump-attendant and road-construction worker. He became a small-town lawyer who at first supported the Democrats in local politics and then switched to the Republicans. In 1939 he won a local judgeship. In June 1942 he enlisted in the Marines as a first lieutenant, which later enabled him to adopt the nickname of 'tail-gunner Joe'. although he never saw active service in this capacity. In February 1945 he resigned from the Marines and was re-elected Judge.

In 1946, he entered the Senate, beating Robert La Follette, who had served as a Progressive for twenty years and who had earned the reputation of being a stalwart upholder of civil liberties and high standards in government.

McCarthy's was an impressive achievement for the son of poor parents from the backwoods of the Middle West, and although his methods were unsavoury, they were no more so, we may be sure, than those which secured advancement for many an aspirant to high office and even the presidency.

In Washington McCarthy made his way in the somewhat seedy world of lobby politics. He sponsored causes connected with real estate and sugar, the latter on behalf of Pepsi-Cola, in return for cheques which helped to pay for his gambling debts, and he engaged in other minor malpractices not uncommon on Capitol Hill.

After his weekend of speeches which began at Wheeling, on 9 February 1950, McCarthy found himself asked to explain his allegations, something he had never expected but which enabled him to develop his theme while continually altering the ground of his attack. The Senate instructed its Foreign Relations Committee to investigate the communists-in-government charge, and this body in turn delegated the task to a sub-committee under Senator Millard Tydings, the Democrats then being in power. The Tydings Committee provided McCarthy with a new platform which suited him admirably. Protected by Congressional privilege he could make all kinds of accusations, name any number of names, produce any document he liked from the bulging briefcase which he invariably carried about, but he never allowed himself to be pinned down on details or facts.

One of the names McCarthy brought up was that of Owen Lattimore, a Deputy Director of the Office of War Information under Roosevelt, whose name has already appeared in these pages. Lattimore always denied being a communist, but his views invariably coincided with Moscow's, and many of his associates were in a similar situation. Before McCarthy got hold of his name he had been an influential figure in American policy-making, especially in the Far East. McCarthy could not prove that he was a traitor; only that he was a fellow-traveller. In a society which prides itself on open government and public debate, how could the influence of such a man be countered, if not curbed? How could the Administration be sure of the loyalty of any official or scientist who had once had communist sympathies or connections? In other words, whether McCarthy himself believed it or not, there was substance behind his charges.

Events still unfolding in the cold war cast a lurid glow on

McCarthy's statements—after Hiss, there was Fuchs, the nuclear physicist who admitted handing over secrets to the Soviets; in June 1950 came the outbreak of the Korean War and the conflict between General MacArthur and the Administration which culminated in the General's dismissal in April 1951.

In June 1951 McCarthy took the floor of the Senate to deliver a lengthy and powerfully composed attack on the whole of Roosevelt's policy of appeasement towards the Soviets, the high point of which was a strong attack on General Marshall himself, then Secretary of Defense and one of the most respected figures in American public life. The speech had been written for McCarthy by reputable specialists in foreign affairs and for the most part was in a quite different style from his usual diatribes. But as a result of it, Marshall retired from public life.

Initially, his fellow-Republicans kept themselves aloof from McCarthy. Whittaker Chambers would have nothing to do with him. But the Republicans were embittered by Truman's surprise victory in 1948, which meant they would be kept from the White House for another four years, making twenty in all. When they realised that McCarthy's popular following was growing they began to support him. In Congressional elections in 1950, Senator Tydings was defeated in Maryland, largely at McCarthy's instigation and by the use of the most unscrupulous methods. In the same elections, Richard Nixon entered the Senate to become the vice-presidential candidate two years later.

In 1952 McCarthy was the sensation at the Republican Convention at which General Eisenhower was nominated to lead his party at last to victory. In the ensuing campaign, McCarthy was sponsored to appear on television, where he made a resounding attack on Adlai Stevenson. Needing every Republican seat he could muster in the Senate, Eisenhower toured Wisconsin alongside McCarthy and refrained from defending George Marshall, although Marshall had made Eisenhower and there was probably no one Eisenhower admired more. In the event, the Republicans won control of the Senate by a margin of a single seat, and it was thought that eight of the new Senators were beholden to McCarthy for their election.

In January 1953, with the Republicans now in command of Congress, McCarthy was nominated by them as Chairman of the Committee on Government Operations. If McCarthyism had been no more than a political stunt, it would have ended here. Certainly, Republican leaders expected his new position would divert McCarthy from his communist-in-government crusade. But McCarthy was not to be stopped just because his party was in power. He diverted the Committee's Permanent Sub-committee to his own investigative purposes and terrorised the State Department (now under John Foster Dulles). Two aides appointed by McCarthy, Cohn and Shine, made a hurried tour of American embassies in Europe causing hilarity wherever they went, but at the same time giving America's allies reason to think that the United States had fallen into a pit of madness. This weird pair wreaked havoc in the *Voice of America* and emboldened the Senator to attack the Army. In the resulting widely publicised hearings senior military men grovelled before McCarthy, while the new President ground his teeth in rage and did nothing.

And then, as suddenly as he had erupted onto the political scene in February 1950, McCarthy faded from it. In attacking the Army many people felt he had gone too far. Perhaps Eisenhower's presence at last made itself felt. In August 1954, some vestige of civic courage began to stir in his Senate colleagues. By December they roused themselves sufficiently to pass by 67 votes to 22 a motion of censure on him. It was only the fourth occasion in 167 years that the Senate took such action against one of his members. McCarthyism was over and soon McCarthy himself disappeared. He was not to be seen at the Republican Convention in 1956 and on 2 May 1957 he died alone in hospital from a liver complaint, probably brought on by over-drinking.

What are we to make of the phenomenon of Senator McCarthy? In appearance, he was burly and unattractive; in manner, he was coarse; in character, he was a liar, a fraud and a common crook. He went about unshaved and with his clothes in a mess; he belched and leered in public, his language was of the gutter. Most of his active supporters were to be found among manual workers. 'McCarthyism is America with its sleeves rolled,' McCarthy told a Wisconsin audience; and a radio commentator once said approvingly, 'To many Americans, McCarthyism is Americanism'. A public opinion poll taken in January 1954 showed that McCarthy enjoyed the support of a majority of his fellow-countrymen.

This brand of Americanism was aggressive, intolerant, anti-authoritarian, irrational. It preferred slogans to reasoned argument.

A favourite chant set up by supporters at a McCarthyite meeting was 'Who promoted Peres?'—a reference to a ludicrous wrangle in committee over an army dentist. When he was questioned about his own alleged bribery, tax-evasion and violation of banking laws, McCarthy's answer was 'I don't answer charges, I make them'. Pressed once about his facts, he replied 'Let's stop playing this silly numbers game'.

It can be seen that these characteristics had nothing to do with the cause McCarthy was championing. The average Detroit car-worker cared nothing for the fate of Chiang Kai-shek. Nor, for that matter, did McCarthy himself. He was quite capable of attacking Truman over the Korean War on the grounds that this was a ruse to deceive people from 'the mess in Washington'—another slogan favoured by McCarthy's supporters.

The McCarthy years made a lasting impression on American intellectual opinion. As a result, American conservatives, from Barry Goldwater to Ronald Reagan, have had to fight the extremist image of them promoted by the consensus. In the media bonanza which accompanied the Watergate affair, it became evident that in the eyes of the consensus since Richard Nixon was now the number-one bad guy, perhaps the old roles needed revising also. Anyone whom Nixon had crossed must be good. Hiss then emerged from obscurity, and with the help of friends went a long way towards retrieving his reputation. Proclaiming his innocence, as he had always done, he had his pension rights restored to him in 1972 and in 1975 he was re-admitted to the Massachusetts Bar.

McCarthyism also profoundly affected the ideological climate of the cold war. Liberal opinion was shocked and the old fellow-travelling arguments became respectable again. A good example of this appeared in Britain, where Orwell came under attack on the grounds that 1984 had closed men's minds against the possibility of seeing any good in Stalinist Russia. In an article entitled 'The Mysticism of Cruelty', published in December 1954, the veteran Marxist writer Isaac Deutscher accused Orwell of contributing to 'the waves of panic and hate that run through the world and obfuscate innocent minds'. Deutscher's contributions at this time to British periodicals were scholarly and plausible, and they anticipated Khrushchev's attempt to detach Stalinist excesses from the liberal image of Lenin and the Revolution. Tarnishing Orwell with McCarthyism was a necessary preliminary to preparing Western intelligentsia with the idea that with Stalin's death there could be a 'break with the Stalin era' and the way open to 'peaceful co-existence'.

It is by the constant repetition of such ideas in every available media outlet by men like Deutscher that communist manipulation of the consensus gradually takes effect. The soil is turned over and fertilised in readiness for another crop. After Stalin, how eagerly the West responded to the comedy team of Bulganin and Khrushchev! After Khrushchev, with his tub-thumping and missile threats, how welcome was the suave Leonid Brezhnev! And as Brezhnev lingered on in office, stumbling about the place and seeming on the point of expiring before the photographers' eyes, with what anticipation the media awaited his successor!

Commentators have described McCarthy as a demagogue, and certainly few men in American public life have displayed such effortless mastery of the techniques of attracting publicity. McCarthy was on target every time with the writers of newspaper headlines, with the broadcasters and news analysts. But he was not a demagogue in the style of European mob-orators like Hitler and Mussolini; his following came through the medium of the press, radio and television. You could say that he was a subversive in that he made wild charges, flouted normal procedures and incited others to disobey their oaths of loyalty to the government. But these things made good copy, gave others an opportunity to join the debate, sold newspapers and won listening and viewing audiences. The media, in other words, needed McCarthy as much as McCarthy needed the media.

It is in this area that the real significance of McCarthy must be sought. McCarthy appeared in the dawn of the television age. A foretaste had been provided with the televising of proceedings at the United Nations, which turned ambassadors into show-biz stars overnight. In 1951 with the laying of the coaxial cable from coast to coast in the United States all Americans were able to view the same programme simultaneously. The Army–McCarthy hearings were the first programmes of their kind to be carried on television, and they provided sensational nationwide viewing. It is said that McCarthy destroyed himself by such exposure, and a programme by the respected television commentator, Ed Murrow, is often cited as giving the Senator the *coup de grâce*. There is no way of knowing whether this was so. To attribute McCarthy's political demise to a single television programme is giving to the medium a form of power which, if true, raises more questions than it answers. More likely it is that he was finally judged by the headline-writers and media producers to have become a bore. The consensus shifted and needed something new, while mass opinion probably remained much as it had always been. Indeed, on the day of the Senate's censure motion, McCarthy received a message of support signed by over a million people.

Since the days of the Army–McCarthy hearings the growth of television has been inexorable, to the point where in the 1980s it must surely be accounted the dominant characteristic of the Western way of life. Few homes in North America, Western Europe and Japan are now without a television receiver, and most of the occupants of those homes spend far more of their leisure hours watching it than they realise. The majority of Western schoolchildren are educated—in the broadest sense of the word—by sitting in front of a television set rather than in a classroom. It has been calculated that the average citizen in the Western world (Japan included) will spend between one-fifth to one-third of his life watching television. In the Western world, television-viewing has become the third most common activity, after sleep and work.

Many attempts have been made to determine the social effects of this massive amount of television-viewing. According to one study, *Remote Control*, by two American authors, there seems to be a precise correlation between the growth of viewing habits and the decline of interest in political institutions. In 1964, according to surveys, 70 per cent of Americans trusted their leaders. By 1975, the figure had fallen to 30 per cent. In 1980, the poll in the American presidential election was again very low, but there can hardly have been a campaign in which the rival candidates placed greater store on their television appearances, in primaries, in the conventions, and in the main election itself. These studies indicate that television-viewing habits generally induce passivity as far as learning is concerned, while at the same time the figures show that in the 1980s over half of the population of the United States will receive all their information about their country and the world from their television screens.

At the same time, technology and commercial pressures have also profoundly affected the way television programmes are made. In the 1960s came satellites and improved methods of recording material on videotape, and with computers came improved methods of videotape editing. Portable electronic cameras give instant coverage everywhere. These and other technical advantages have vastly increased the programme possibilities open to television producers while at the same time vastly increasing the likelihood of visual falsification and editorial distortion.

At the best of times most viewers are unable to tell what exactly it is they are seeing, whether live or recorded, whether fact or fiction, whether only a part or the whole. So-called drama documentary techniques have further blurred the border-line between reality and fantasy, while the competition for audience ratings has meant that the presentation of news has itself become part of a total entertainment package.

In the light of these developments, we can say that for a majority of people in the Western world news has become a television soap-opera. Events like an assassination, a revolution, an invasion, the taking of hostages and attempts at their release, civil war, public executions, famine, massacres, natural disasters, terrorist attacks, hijackings, the threat of war itself—these events sell news but have no reality beyond the act of viewing them on a television screen. Space shots, summit meetings, papal visits become media events only, the main participants themselves, consciously or unconsciously, playing up to their allotted roles.

To a few specialists, a rocket or a treaty may have political or military significance, to a few devout souls an electronic papal smile may bring solace, but to the mass television audience they are all part of a non-stop entertainment show. In this fantasy world actuality is perceived as a video-game, death is swallowed up in the next episode, poverty is overcome in the next commercial break, and moral anguish turned into a comedy routine. To what reality do pictures of boat-people or earthquake or cholera victims speak once they have passed from the screen? They become media images only, and indistinguishable from other media images whether they purport to be fact or fantasy, real or imagined, actual or dramatised. As they replace each other in an endlessly changing succession of images, all sense of visual memory is lost. Who can remember the troubles in Cyprus when there is a famine in Bangladesh? And who can remember the famine in Bangladesh when there is a revolution in Iraq? And who can remember the revolution in Iraq when Chairman Mao goes for a swim? And so on—no-one recalls yesterday's news; everyone looks forward to new sensations in today's bulletin.

A key date in this process of reducing the cosmos to the dimensions of a television screen was 1960, this being the year of the Nixon–Kennedy debates on television, the first of their kind. Kennedy's victory in the election can thus be claimed as a victory for the skills of his producers in the packaging of a presidential candidate as an advertising product on television. He was also the first President for whom the cultivation of a television image was a conscious part of cold war politics, an answer, if we will, to the new Soviet image created by Khrushchev on his sorties through the Western world.

Even more than his election victory, however, Kennedy's death underlined the way television has affected people's outlook on the world. Ask Americans about Kennedy's assassination and most will reply that they saw it live on television. In fact, no-one did. It was only in 1976 that the general public saw the blurred, amateur film taken by a bystander in Dallas. But the reporting of the event on television made such an impression on viewers that they imagined they had been spectators of the event itself. Even for an experienced journalist like Theodore White television has come to represent the only reality about the event.

> I would slip out of the house to pick for fragments of the story, and then dart back to sit and watch on television to find out what was really happening . . . Sitting with friends in Harriman's parlour and watching the tube was to be in touch with reality, to be part of the national grief. But to slip out, to do one's reportorial duty, to ask questions that must be asked, was a chore.

After Kennedy came the enlargement of the war in Vietnam and 1968, the year of the demonstration. Throughout the Western world, political activists seized on the possibilities inherent in television to enhance the importance of their causes and the numbers of their followers. As it happened during McCarthy's time, what won the attention of the media—which meant, primarily, television—was irrationality, intolerance, defiance of established procedures and the flouting of normal behaviour. The anti-hero who had once been a junior senator from Wisconsin was now as likely as not to be a student leader. Slogans sold commercial products on television and slogans, rather than debate, sold causes. It was enough to chant: 'Ho, Ho, Ho Chi Minh!' or 'Hey, Hey, LBJ, How many kids have you killed today?' or 'de Gaulle to the archives!' or 'Ten years is too much!' or just 'Out! Out! Out!' or alternatively, 'In! In! In!'. Jerry Rubin, a luminary in this counter-culture, put the point clearly in his book, *Do It:*

Television creates myths bigger than reality, Whereas a demo drags on for hours and hours, TV packs all the action into two minutes—a commercial for the revolution. On the television screen news is not so much reported as created. An event happens when it goes on TV and becomes a myth . . . It makes no difference what's said: the pictures are the stories.

While television has been a godsend to political activists of all persuasions, from IRA supporters to nuclear disarmers to women liberationists (sometimes all three combined), the growth of media activity which television has generated has also enormously increased the scope of communist disinformation and Agitprop activities, the consensus being more open to manipulation by these techniques than ever before. As far as the cold war is concerned, a turning-point was the portrayal of the war in Vietnam. It is said that because television screened pictures of the war nightly, the American public eventually became so sickened by them as to make the war's successful prosecution politically impossible. But we must be cautious about accepting this argument at its face value. After all, it was the Republicans, advocates of a tough anti-communist policy, who won the elections in 1968 and 1972—and, despite Reagan's supposed gaffes, in 1980.

It was not that the American people lost the will to fight but that the real issues at stake were obscured by the consensus and by the images of the war which the media chose to present, such as napalmed villages, street-executions and blasted landscapes. There is no doubting that American media coverage of the war was a major factor in determining communist tactics and should provide an important case study in the history of the cold war. Television networks, however, can be relied on to provide re-runs of the footage, with suitable consensus comments, and these, like the enormously popular soap-opera *MASH*, will probably determine the attitudes of each new generation towards national service and the cold war more than anything else governments can do.

In the same way it is more than likely, though impossible to prove, that the hugely successful television series *Roots*, while purveying a typical soap-opera view of its subject, thereby made acceptable to the American public the somewhat absurd figure of Andrew Young as President Carter's roving expert on Africa. Similarly, it is safe to assume that the *réclame* of the television series *Holocaust*, which also came in for the necessary soap-opera treatment, was related to the persistent efforts of the powerful pro-Israeli lobby in the United States, an especially successful lobby when it comes to media operations.

In this respect, we must note a further consequence of the growth of television. To most viewers, it is only those things which are seen which acquire credibility. What, of necessity, cannot be seen does not rate in importance or significance. The result is a world of grotesque disproportion. Television newsreels were unable to provide nightly pictures of Vietcong atrocities because the communists appreciate that to Western minds, conditioned by television, if such pictures are not taken, then the events do not happen. The same disproportion arises over questions of human rights and political freedoms. Television coverage of the Gulag Archipelago is nonexistent. But when a blurred amateur film of one concentration camp at Riga appeared on television screens in the West, it caused consternation among European communists who were momentarily stunned by this visual evidence of what they had always been able to deny ever existed. Despite the considerable body of literary material in existence describing the Gulag, and the personal accounts of survivors and men like Kravchenko, it was only when this tiny piece of visual evidence appeared that some people were at last convinced of the reality of the Soviet system of forced labour. But by the same token, visual material can so easily be faked or exploited. If swastikas are daubed on synagogues in West Germany, most people assume it is the work of neo-Nazis. The consensus will never be persuaded that the communists could think of doing such a thing.

It is not, then, that the West's communications media have been penetrated by communist agents or subversives; but rather that by its very nature these media lend themselves to various forms of exploitation and manipulation by a highly sophisticated apparatus bent on propagating untruths, as Orwell would say.

One simple example may be given of how this manipulation operates. We have seen how Khrushchev came to Paris in 1960 determined to wreck the summit, but choosing a forum which he knew would achieve maximum publicity. His excuse for this propaganda stunt was a harmless act of American espionage—the high-flying U-2 reconnaissance plane. At this very moment, however, the governments of Switzerland and Greece were obliged to ask for the recall of Soviet agents acting under diplomatic cover who were engaged in a far more subversive activity on the actual soil of their countries. Yet these acts of Soviet espionage—the acts of a super-power bullying small nations, one of them a neutral—passed unnoticed by the media, although the threat to the West which they represented was every bit as real as Khrushchev's bluster in Paris.

Although the subversion and terrorism practised by the Soviet Union throughout the world are unrelenting, the West's media do not find it profitable to subject them to the constant glare of cameras, headlines and investigative reporting, as characterised the Vietnam war, say, or fighting in the Lebanon. It is illuminating, therefore, in this context to consider two major Soviet ideological texts. Both were written by Boris Ponomarev, head of the International Department which succeeded Lenin's Comintern after the Second World War. The first appeared in the theoretical journal of the Soviet Communist Party, *Kommunist*, in October 1971 under the inelegant but revealing title: 'Topical Problems in the Theory of the World Revolutionary Process'. The second, clearly a sequel, appeared in June 1974, in the *World Marxist Review*. This organ of the world communist movement is published in Prague in several languages, and is, in a sense, the International Department's magazine. This time, the title was: 'The World Situation and the Revolutionary Process'.

As always, the jargon of Marxism–Leninism needs interpretation. Essentially, the 'world revolutionary process' refers to all events and developments that further the Soviet Union's plans in what we have termed 'this war called peace', and everything that works to the dis-advantage of countries under threat.

If examples are collated from both articles, the term may be said specifically to refer to:

What the communists call the 'general crisis of capitalism'—that is, the sum of economic and financial problems in the advanced countries, including labour troubles, demonstrations against America's war in Vietnam, disorders in Ulster, campaigns for black equality in the United States, and so forth.
The infiltration by Marxist–Leninists into the social democratic parties, especially in Western Europe.
From 1963 on, the new problems of 'capitalism', such as the energy crisis and escalating oil prices, and the combination of unemployment and inflation known as 'stagflation'.
Any conflict between the West and the Third World countries.

Soviet-aided terrorist or guerrillas anywhere, collectively known as the 'national liberation movement'.

The 1971 article contained a strong attack on the miscellaneous Trotskyist, Maoist and other fundamentalist groups known rather misleadingly as the 'New Left'. The interesting point, however, was not his attack on the 'adventurism' and poor organisation of these groups but the fact that he thought they could be useful. As he wrote: 'Their overall anti-imperialist direction is obvious. to neglect this segment of the mass movement would mean to weaken the stress of anti-imperialist struggle and hinder the creation of a united front against monopolistic capitalism.'

There are interesting differences between the 1971 and 1974 articles. When the first appeared, things were going rather well for the Soviet Union in the cold war in Latin America, apart from the failed insurgency in Mexico. In Chile, Allende had recently come to power and the country was moving in a revolutionary direction. In Uruguay, a Marxist terrorist group known as the Tupamaros was defiantly effective. In Peru, the unexpected phenomenon of a left-wing military government, which had made its appearance three years earlier, had stimulated Soviet hopes—marked, in the usual way, by large deliveries of arms and military equipment.

Between 1971 and 1974, however, the Tupamaros had been crushed by the Uruguayan armed forces; and Allende had been overthrown. The collapse of Soviet hopes in Chile was a particularly severe blow, and Ponomarev set out to analyse what had gone wrong. His verdict was that the teachings of Lenin had not been observed: the revolutionaries ought to have consolidated their gains and prepared themselves for any emergencies, especially that of a military *coup*. It was now essential to learn the lessons of Chile and apply them elsewhere. Ponomarev therefore called upon revolutionaries

(1) To make sure they controlled the mass media.
(2) To win the army over to their side.

In the same article, he called on Moscow's people within the social democratic parties to 'neutralise' anti-communists and 'other right-wingers'. He advocated 'joint, practical working-class action' in the form of internationally co-ordinated strikes against the multinational companies. Writing at the height of the Western euphoria about 'détente', he reminded revolutionaries everywhere that '*international détente means extending and carrying deeper the ideological struggle and does not mean "peaceful co-existence" of the two opposed ideologies*'. Not least, he added a warning to non-communist Marxist–Leninists that 'anti-Sovietism' played into the hands of the 'imperialists'.

The message of permanent revolution was clear. To support it, Ponomarev and his colleagues disposed of a vast and sophisticated apparatus, to which we have referred, but which should now be described more precisely.

In the Soviet Union, power flows downward from the top, specifically from the Politburo of the ruling party. Normally, this power is unchallenged, but in an emergency (as Khrushchev showed in 1957), the Politburo can be overruled by the much larger Central Committee. The Secretariat, controlled by the Politburo, is another important body, in effect a shadow government which makes sure the visible government does what it is supposed to do.

During the Brezhnev era, two full members of the Politburo and a candidate member were most closely concerned with subversion in foreign countries. The full members were Yuri Andropov, who was to succeed Brezhnev, and (the late) Mikhail Suslov, generally regarded as the Soviet Union's senior ideologist. The candidate member was, and is, Boris Ponomarev, head of the Central Committee's International Department. Ponomarev continued in his job after Yuri Andropov took over, but in other respects the position was less clear.

The KGB is huge and immensely important. It has armed forces of its own, and is in charge of espionage and counter-espionage. We have mentioned its special 'disinformation' department, charged with fabricating and disseminating false reports. It controls not only spies but 'agents of influence', who deliberately spread facts or falsehoods and arguments that further Soviet interests abroad. The KGB is the dominant element in the USSR's vast spy network (by far the largest in the world), although the GRU (military intelligence) is theoretically responsible to the Minister of Defence.

Moreover, the KGB also controls the security and intelligence services of the satellites, including (as we have seen) Cuba. It often suits the Soviet purpose to sub-contract work to satellite services and those most closely involved in complementary subversive activities are the Czech (STB) and the East German (MFS). It was the

Bulgarian Secret Service (KDS), however, that was involved in the attempted assassination of Pope John-Paul II in May 1981, as revealed later by Italian judicial enquiries.

In recent years, including the years of 'détente', there has been an enormous expansion of Soviet espionage. It is now authoritatively estimated that more than a third of Soviet officials stationed abroad are working for the KGB or GRU. If embassy personnel alone are considered, the proportion is about 75 per cent. In other words, of every four Soviet diplomats (accredited as such) in the NATO countries, three are spies. Between 1962 and 1972, the overall total of Soviet representatives of all kinds (including trade missions and the like) in Western Europe alone rose from 1,485 to 2,146—an increase of about 50 per cent, which meant a proportionate rise in espionage activities. In the first few months of 1983, nine countries expelled more than 70 Soviet spies; France alone accounted for 47 of these.

The biggest Soviet spy centre in the world is undoubtedly the headquarters of the United Nations in New York, where KGB men accredited as international civil servants enjoy the special privilege of being able to travel freely all over the United States. This privilege is not available to their embassy colleagues in Washington, whose travel is restricted in line with the limits placed on American diplomats in Moscow.

The ramifications of the International Department are also very extensive. Inside the Soviet Union it has a special interest in another International Department—that of the party-controlled trade union organisation, the All-Union Central Council of Trade Unions (AUCCTU). The trade union International Department maintains a large research staff which keeps files on foreign trade unions and trade unionists, signalling likely recruits for clandestine work, either through ideological disposition or because their private lives lend themselves to blackmail.

The AUCCTU's International Department also keeps an eye on a major Soviet front organisation, the World Council of Trade Unions (WFTU), with which the international co-ordination of strikes is plotted.

The overt purpose of the Central Committee's International Department (Ponomarev's) is to liaise with communist parties out-side the bloc. But there are many hidden functions as well. One is the general oversight of the international front organisations, of which the most important, apart from the WFTU, is the World Peace Council (WPC). (See Chapter 12.)

An important clandestine function of the International Department is the recruitment and training of foreign terrorists. The candidates come in two distinct streams: those recommended by foreign communist parties, who are sent to the Lenin Institute in Moscow for courses in sabotage, guerrilla war, sharpshooting, assassination, bomb-making and detonating devices: and recruits from 'national liberation' movements, mainly from Third World countries. The 'national liberation' stream candidates are often recruited ostensibly for degree courses in Moscow, where they are processed through the Patrice Lumumba People's Friendship University.

Those selected as future terrorists or guerrillas are then dispersed to various training camps, in Moscow itself, in Odessa, Tashkent, Baku and the Military Academy at Simferopol on the Black Sea.

The most famous, or notorious, terrorist recruited and trained by the Soviets is the man known as 'Carlos' or 'The Jackal', whose real name is Ilich Ramírez Sánchez of Venezuela. His recruiting officer was a KGB man who sent him first to Cuba, then to the Patrice Lumumba University. His biggest exploit was the kidnapping of eleven leaders of the oil-producing States, in Vienna in December 1975, for which the Libyan leader, Colonel Khadaffi, is said to have paid him $2 million.

Khadaffi's own involvement in terrorism is well known, and indeed he himself has often boasted of it. The relevant point in this story, however, is that Libya has become a major client-state of the Soviet Union. A gigantic Soviet arms build-up began in that country in May 1976. The global figure of Soviet arms deliveries to Libya has been estimated at $12 billion, probably the largest deal of its kind ever made. What makes it still more remarkable is that Libya's population hardly exceeds 2¾ million. The quantity of arms delivered or on the way far exceed the capacity of Libya's armed forces. The build-up must therefore be for other purposes, of which the most likely are: the supplying of terrorist forces in different countries; and for use by Soviet or surrogate forces elsewhere in Africa.

Space forbids a comprehensive survey of Soviet involvement in terrorism, but it is of interest to note that it is by no means confined to the Third World. Thus the Irish Republican Army (IRA) and the Baader–Meinhof gang of West Germany were supplied, the former with weapons, the latter with money. Other recipients have included the terrorists of the People's Liberation Army and the various groups of the Palestine Liberation Army (PLO). The PLO involvement is of special importance. For years, the Soviets encouraged certain Arab countries, including Iraq and Syria, to help the PLO terrorists, for instance by arming them with Soviet weapons. This might be termed involvement by proxy.

In August 1974, however, the Soviet took the momentous decision to invite the PLO to open an office in Moscow. It was a similar decision in November 1964, in respect of the Viet Cong, that preceded the Soviet involvement in the Vietnam war. From that time onward, the Soviets have provided training courses for PLO terrorists, usually at the Military Academy in Simferopol.

The monolithic nature of Soviet power, however, is deceptive. Undoubtedly it suits communist propagandists to present an image of the Soviet Union as all-powerful, all-wise, and all-competent. Enough has been said in the pages of this book to demonstrate the fallacy of this image, although it has to be said again that it is the image itself which commands the attention of the West's media, and not the reality that lies behind the image. Power does not flow from the barrel of a gun, because bullets can only kill and wound the body. It is the image of the gun which confers power, because it is the image which corrupts the spirit and produces fear, submission, betrayal and despair.

Ironically during the very period when television has been extending itself throughout the Western world and reinforcing this image of the Soviet Union as the Great Leviathan, a movement has been taking place within the Soviet Union which ultimately must call into question the survival of the regime. This movement owes little, if anything, to the politics of the cold war, but has been an essentially spiritual development which extends throughout the whole Soviet empire and touches every branch of life. We cannot possibly do justice to this subject here, but it is necessary to draw attention to some of its main characteristics, so that readers may be under no illusions that it represents a political force on which the West may count in the cold war.

In November 1961 a manuscript copy of a story about a Soviet labour camp came into the hands of Alexander Tvardovsky, editor of the prestigious Soviet literary journal, *Novy Mir*. Khrushchev's thaw was still in progress in the Soviet Union and Tvardovsky passed the manuscript to Khrushchev, recommending that it be published. The central character in the story was a peasant, and this fact appealed to Khrushchev as it had done to Tvardovsky, both of them being of peasant background. In October 1962, just as the Cuban missile crisis approached its climax, Khrushchev authorised publication of the story, which duly appeared under the title *One Day in the Life of Ivan Denisovich*.

The author was a then-unknown Russian schoolteacher called Alexander Solzhenitsyn, who kept himself very much to himself and appeared uninterested in the official Soviet literary scene. Although 'discovered' by the well-placed Tvardovsky, Solzhenitsyn proved a difficult protégé and in time his fame outgrew Tvardovsky's, outgrew Soviet literary circles, and outgrew, indeed, the Soviet Union itself. In his literary memoirs, *The Oak and the Calf*, which was published in English in 1980, Solzhenitsyn gives an extraordinarily revealing account of the struggle for intellectual freedom which marked his rise to fame. The Soviet authorities applied every kind of pressure to make him conform—attempted bribes, smears, intimidations, false reports, provocations, piracy of his works. Had they realised at the outset what they were letting themselves in for, they would undoubtedly have settled immediately for murder. But Solzhenitsyn's survival, like his appearance in such unlikely circumstances, has been something for which communist ideologues and tacticians were totally unprepared. It turned out that in Lenin's police state a Russian writer was able to shake the Great Leviathan.

Khrushchev's approval for the publication of *One Day in the Life of Ivan Denisovich* came just in time. In March 1963 the Soviet authorities tried to clamp down on the new literary freedom. But the movement grew nonetheless and developed its own methods for circulating literature underground, called *Samizdat*. Religious life was deeply affected and new leaders appeared challenging the official church authorities and their subservience to atheistic laws. In May 1966 five hundred representatives of Evangelical Baptist congregations, drawn from 130 towns and cities all over the Soviet Union, gathered in front of the offices of the Central Committee of the Communist Party in Moscow. It was a peaceful demonstration which had been organised in secret over distances more than 4,000 miles apart. Nothing like it had ever been known before in the Soviet Union, and it drew attention to the fact that despite fifty years of atheism propagated officially by the state, Christianity in the Soviet

Union has grown in strength, if not in numbers. Soviet sources themselves indicate that some 30 to 40 million Orthodox believers
regularly attend church; Baptists account for a further 3 million.
Armenians also 3 million, Lithuanian Catholics 2 million, and
Lutherans over 1 million. Islam, too has many millions of followers.
In the satellite countries of Eastern Europe, the intensity of religious
life has been some compensation for the loss of civic and national
freedom, Poland being a notable example. In Warsaw, a religious
procession has been known to consist of some 400,000 souls, or half
the population of the city. While in the troubles between the labour
unions and the Polish Communist Party in the 1980s, the question of
religious freedom has featured prominently in the workers'
demands.

The invasion of Czechoslovakia in 1968 prompted many scattered
protests, one by a twenty-year-old inhabitant of Leningrad who simply
scrawled up in public 'Brezhnev get out of Czechoslovakia'. He was
at once arrested and given a five-year prison sentence in a severe
regime, later altered to three years in an ordinary regime. But the
most notable protest was made by a group of eight individuals in Red
Square, Moscow, who gathered at the old execution ground and displayed banners with an old Polish slogan 'For your freedom and
ours', indicating that no-one enslaving others can himself be free.
The crowd set upon the group with cries of 'They're all Jews!' and
'Beat up the anti-Soviets!' Victor Feinberg, the most obviously
Jewish of the group, had his teeth knocked in. Natalia
Gorbanevskaya, who had her baby with her, was slapped over the
mouth by a female KGB agent before being bundled off for
interrogation. A rumour was put about that she had tried to strangle
her baby to attract attention. At her psychiatric examination the
notorious Professor Lunts, a KGB colonel in a white coat, signed a
report stating that 'the possibility of low-profile schizophrenia is not
excluded'. The doctors recommended that she should be declared
insane. From her and others similarly treated have come many first-
hand accounts of the way dissidents have been tortured in psychiatric
hospitals with drugs which cause shock and severe physical disorders
and given intravenous injections of sodium amytal to suppress personality, quite apart from the attention they receive from the thugs
and criminals who are enrolled as orderlies and the horror of being
shut up in wards with the genuinely insane.

Solzhenitsyn was now in the front line of a new kind of warfare.

When the KGB seized his archive he found he had been given a new freedom. From then on he conducted his own media campaign, planning strategy like an army commander, throwing into the fight, where most appropriate, books, articles, letters interviews to foreign journalists, as if they were regiments of tanks. In 1970 he was awarded the Nobel Prize for literature, which gave him a new vantage-point for his campaign. Meanwhile, other names were coming into prominence, the most notable being Andrei Sakharov, the Soviet Union's most eminent nuclear physicist. In 1974, Solzhenitsyn was finally expelled from the Soviet Union, but he continued with his own kind of warfare in a series of well-timed speeches and broadcasts, while resolutely refusing to be drawn into the usual media habits of the West.

Indeed, as the force of his arguments began to sink in in the West, so it became apparent that the consensus was gradually turning against him. For Solzhenitsyn was not concerned with the cold war as the Western media portrayed it, but with a life and death struggle for the truth. Inside the Soviet Union, the movement he had played so prominent a part in was a movement for the freedom to believe in the truth even if it meant the loss of material freedom. But the courage and sacrifice which this entailed were unknown in the West, where the pursuit of material happiness, in Solzhenitsyn's eyes, must inevitably lead to a loss of intellectual freedom. 'I put no hopes in the West,' wrote Solzhenitsyn, 'indeed, no Russian ever should.' 'The anti-fascists and the existentialists, the pacifists, the hearts that bleed for Africa, had nothing to say about the destruction of *our* culture, about the destruction of *our* nation . . .'

Because none of this dissident activity can be televised in the manner, say, of the troubles in Northern Ireland or racial clashes in the United States, the reality of it has made no impression on the intellectual consensus in the West, much less on mass opinion. Indeed, if anything, the reality which it proclaims is so unwelcome to Western habits of thought as to be regarded by the consensus with suspicion, and increasingly with active opposition.

No people have suffered more from communism than the Russians. What they have had to endure since Lenin's seizure of power in 1917 is beyond belief, and it is therefore vital for the West's survival that we listen to what those among them who can speak are saying. For the Russian experience of communism has brought men like Solzhenitsyn to realise that it is through suffering that the soul of man finds its true freedom. 'Above all, don't cling to life,' writes Solzhenitsyn. 'Possess nothing, free yourself from everything, even from those nearest to you, because they, too, are your enemies.' It was while he was lying on rotting prison hospital straw that Solzhenitsyn found he was a changed man, so that he could even come to bless the very prison in which he had suffered so much.

For the media in the West, especially television, to communicate this message would be contrary to its essential nature, for it is not a message which can be handled in soap-operas or used to promote high audience ratings. If it were, it would have lost its point. If the message is to be disseminated at all in the West, it will have to be through a Western form of *Samizdat*. There have been signs that some kind of underground culture may exist in the West to which the message would make an appropriate appeal. The mysterious popularity of Mother Teresa of Calcutta is a case in point, as is the longing felt by many young men and women to serve their fellow-men, be they handicapped or destitute or mentally retarded or in some other way placed outside the way of life of television commercials.

In reviewing the course of this war called peace, enough has been said about the role of the media in the West to suggest that Orwell's pessimism as to the behaviour of the consensus which he expressed in *1984* is justified. North America's present obsession with communist China is a case in point. One minute, the images conveyed in countless films and television programmes throughout the West show a China eager to be friends, but a totalitarian power nonetheless of awesome dimensions. The next minute, the smiles are gone; there are frowns and cooler words and mysterious literature suggesting a new 'disinformation' campaign to discredit past leaders. Yesterday, the images were of the screaming hordes of the Cultural Revolution; the day before yesterday, of the human waves which poured down upon MacArthur's army in Korea. What, one wonders, will tomorrow's image be?

Gibbon recounts how, during the declining years of the Roman Empire, the games and circus were in full swing in Carthage, Africa's second Rome, when the Vandals stormed into the city.

In its addiction to television entertainment, is the Western world destined to be overwhelmed by a similar fate?

The West can ensure that it has the military wherewithal to counter Soviet aggression at every point, as we have argued it must do: it can take every step possible to frustrate Soviet terrorism and subversion, as we have argued it must also do. But will the West be able to learn from the Russian people that its only true strength lies in its spiritual resources, those, indeed, on which its civilisation was rebuilt after the Dark Ages which followed the fall of Rome?

Index